Rethinking Black Motherhood and Drug Addictions

Rochelle Brock and Cynthia Dillard
Executive Editors

Vol. 106

The Black Studies and Critical Thinking series
is part of the Peter Lang Education list.
Every volume is peer reviewed and meets
the highest quality standards for content and production.

PETER LANG
New York • Bern • Frankfurt • Berlin
Brussels • Vienna • Oxford • Warsaw

Tierra B. Tivis

Rethinking Black Motherhood and Drug Addictions

Counternarratives of Black Family Resilience

PETER LANG
New York • Bern • Frankfurt • Berlin
Brussels • Vienna • Oxford • Warsaw

Library of Congress Cataloging-in-Publication Data
Names: Tivis, Tierra B., author.
Title: Rethinking black motherhood and drug addictions: counternarratives of
black family resilience / Tierra B. Tivis.
Description: New York: Peter Lang, 2018.
Series: Black studies and critical thinking; vol. 106 | ISSN 1947-5985
Includes bibliographical references and index.
Identifiers: LCCN 2017038559 | ISBN 978-1-4331-3503-3 (pbk.: alk. paper) |
ISBN 978-1-4331-3504-0 (hardback: alk. paper) |
ISBN 978-1-4331-4963-4 (ebook pdf) | ISBN 978-1-4331-4964-1 (epub) |
ISBN 978-1-4331-4965-8 (mobi)
Subjects: LCSH: African American families. | African American mothers. |
African American mothers—Substance use. | Women drug addicts—
Family relationships—United States. | African American women—
Family relationships.
Classification: LCC E185.86.T5135 | DDC 306.85/08996073—dc23
LC record available at https://lccn.loc.gov/2017038559
DOI 10.3726/b11813

Bibliographic information published by **Die Deutsche Nationalbibliothek**.
Die Deutsche Nationalbibliothek lists this publication in the "Deutsche
Nationalbibliografie"; detailed bibliographic data are available
on the Internet at http://dnb.d-nb.de/.

The paper in this book meets the guidelines for permanence and durability
of the Committee on Production Guidelines for Book Longevity
of the Council of Library Resources.

© 2018 Peter Lang Publishing, Inc., New York
29 Broadway, 18th floor, New York, NY 10006
www.peterlang.com

All rights reserved.
Reprint or reproduction, even partially, in all forms such as microfilm,
xerography, microfiche, microcard, and offset strictly prohibited.

Printed in the United States of America

To my parents who taught me to be fair and remain true to myself, sista-friends who supported me along this journey, and my baby girl, Tatiyana. To all Black mothers and babies who were treated like or ever felt like just another junkie, crack ho' or crack baby. May you continue to be resilient and dispel the myth.

CONTENTS

Acknowledgments	ix
Introduction by Laurence J. Parker	xi
Chapter 1. "These People Are Suffering": Help versus Incarceration	1
Chapter 2. Tools for Understanding Drug Addiction and Black Mothers' Standpoint	13
Chapter 3. Origin of the Crack Ho': Mammies, Jezebels, Controlled Images, and Prosecution of Addiction	25
Chapter 4. "From Suga to Shit": The Drug Business and Destruction of Black Communities	45
Chapter 5. More About the Mothers, Research Practice, Black Motherhood and Addiction	67
Chapter 6. "I Had Help": Kinship, Drug Addictions, and Black Family Resilience	95
Chapter 7. "Wasn' No Junkie, I Was a Workin' Addict ... It's a Difference": Self-Definition of Black Mothers' Roles and Responsibilities	115
Chapter 8. Crack Baby Aftermath and Navigating Educational Institutions	139

Chapter 9. "I Was Just Cryin' Out To God": Recovery and
 the Spirituality of Struggle   165

 Discussion: What the Mothers Made Me Think About   187
 Contributor Bio—Dr. Laurence J. Parker   207
 Index   209

ACKNOWLEDGMENTS

This book is truly a village effort with influence and support from many whom I would like to personally thank for their contributions to the completion of this book. First, I would like to thank the mothers who graciously shared their life stories with me. I am truly inspired by their strength, faith, and hope for a better tomorrow. A great deal of gratitude goes to Drs. Eloise Jackson and Ollie Bowman from Hampton University for their guidance and providing the foundation for my academic journey. Thank you also to my Hamptonian sisters and Shawn Baccus Featherstone, Mavis Roberts Lee, Karen Vaughan Palmer, and Beth Freeman Wilson for always having my back. Miles keep us apart but our sisterhood and love for "Our Home By the Sea" always keeps us close at heart. I am also indebted to my circle of sista girlfriends in the academy for steadfast supporting and encouraging me to finish this project. They are: Drs. Carla McCowan, Eboni Zamani-Gallaher, Dawn Hinton, Barbara Jean J. Jones, Dalia Rodriquez, and Thandi Sule. I am so grateful for the sisterhood and continuous love and support from Tatiyana's Aunt Jackies: My homegirl, Dr. Jacque Bowman for her wisdom and guidance; Dr. Jackie Bussey for helping me find my way back home to Michigan; and Jacki Brown and Jackie Brandon for giving me a space to find peace once again at the shore.

I would like to also thank Drs. Robin Jarrett, Lawrence Parker, Arlene Torres, and Assata Zerai for their invaluable knowledge, guidance and support doing work with Black mothers and drug addiction. I also appreciate the mentorship and support of Violet Harris, Arlette Willis, Susan Fowler as well as Susan Noffke, who has transitioned on. Dr. Emery Petchauer's feedback and support has been priceless and I am forever grateful for him encouraging me not to give up on sharing the mothers' stories. I am also extremely thankful for Peter Lang's series editor, Rochelle Brock, her guidance and continued support throughout the completion of this book. Also, Kathryn Harrison, Peter Lang's acquisitions editor's assistance with this book is much appreciated.

A special thank you to Corine Smith, who truly exemplifies fictive kin and embodies what it means to be a "play mother," you are forever treasured in our family. To my "play" aunts Lena T. Fulton, Barbara-Ann Hinksman, Rowena Taylor, and Shirley Viera and godsisters Ann Turpin Williams and Cheryl Sampson Ramsey, your support was invaluable. This book would not have been completed without their love, listening ear, guidance, and encouragement. Special acknowledgement to my parents Bernardine Tivis Carter and Harold Bernard Tivis who have transitioned on but live forever in my heart. Last but not least, thank you to the best daughter in the world, Tatiyana, who has been so patient when I "was always on the computer."

Permissions

Portions of Chapters 1, 2, and 5 are reprinted with permission of Michigan State University Press from *African American Females: Addressing Challenges and Nurturing the Future*, edited by Eboni M. Zamani-Gallaher and Vernon C. Polite (2013).

INTRODUCTION

Tierra Tivis has written a book that I consider the second wave of using theories of race and gender analysis in research methodology, in the form of counter stories and counter narratives from critical race theory. Her work illustrates the depth and complexity of portrait of the lives of young African American women as mothers who have been addicted to heroin or crack cocaine seeking ways to address their addiction and combat negative images of them. In many ways, Tivis has written a book that not only contributes to this methodological analysis but also humanize the portrait of African American women in urban settings.

In the area of critical race studies and intersectionality for example, what I am seeing is what McCall (2005) and Nash (2008) call for in the complexity of intersectionality. These trends speak not only to the centrality of race and racism in CRT, but how in combination for example with gender, disability and other aspects of how persons of color negotiate their identities that are not bound up as fixed and inextricably bound; rather they exemplify an intersectional methodology. I see Tivis' book as an example of a study that moves race and Black feminist research into more areas of methodological complexity.

These can be categorized as anti-categorical complexity: which is based on scholarship calling attention to social processes of categorization and the workings of exclusion and hierarchy that draws and maintains boundaries of race, gender, etc.; intra-categorical complexity in which the research problematizes the exclusionary implications of categorization and then present narratives that represent the multiplicity of persons and who they are and how they represent themselves in ways that demonstrate the problems with defining and interpreting categories such as race, gender, etc.; and inter-categorical complexity which presents a methodological approach grounded in premise there are relationships of oppression among already legally and socially defined groups, and they are not perfect and ever-changing and these relationships are at the center of the analysis. What I think the reader should take away from this book is that Tivis' research exemplifies this particular type of inter-categorical complexity, which can be strategically useful in critical race qualitative research studies that both call the categories themselves into question, but at the same time displays the linkages among the categories of race, gender, etc., and inequality. We can see this in the lives of the women discussed by Tivis in this work. Her book also reminds us of the importance of racial reflexivity as something more than just simple "member checking" of findings, but to deeply question assumptions of why research is being done and for what purpose regarding the researcher as self (Pillow, 2003).

The way that Tierra Tivis intertwines the interview data with the African American women she profiles in her study, juxtaposed with the popular media image that has been portrayed of low-income urban African American women who have used crack or heroin, is an example of what CRT seeks to uncover in terms of the "deep whiteness" that insist that the portrait of whiteness and its projection on to the control of Black female bodies is always right and it can never be contradicted or challenged (Bonilla-Silva, 2015). Tierra's work raises important questions of racial authenticity versus racial sincerity. This book is an example of how as John L. Jackson in his book *Real Black* (2005), pushes readers to explore the differences and tensions methodologically between racial authenticity in research, that often gets constructed into racial sincerity. Tierra Tivis' book is an attempt to address intersecting ends that seek to answer the question as to what, why and how do we do ethnographic research on gender/feminism race, racism and its impact on the lives of African American women.

Laurence J. Parker
University of Utah

References

Bonilla-Silva, E. (2015). More than prejudice: Restatement, reflections, and new directions in critical race theory. *Sociology of Race & Ethnicity, 1*(1), 75–89.

Jackson, J. L., Jr. (2005). *Real black: Adventures in racial sincerity*. Chicago, IL: University of Chicago Press.

McCall, L. (2005). The complexity of intersectionality. *Signs: Journal of Women in Culture and Society, 30*(3), 1771–1800.

Nash, J. C. (2008). Re-thinking intersectionality. *Feminist Review, 89*(1), 1–15.

Pillow, W. S. (2003). Confession, catharsis or cure? Rethinking the use of reflexivity as methodological power in qualitative research. *International Journal of Qualitative Studies in Education, 16*(2), 175–196.

· 1 ·

"THESE PEOPLE ARE SUFFERING"

Help versus Incarceration

These people are addicted ... are suffering ... these pill mill clinic owners ... these doctors, they're just preying on that suffering, for ... cash ... profit.
—Mark Trouville, Special Agent

Opioid and heroin addictions as well as over dose deaths have sky rocketed in white urban and rural communities. Discussion of this drug "crisis" even seeped into the 2016 National Presidential Campaign. Back in 2011, I am watching television and hear "CNN Presents: Addicted At Birth. The new face of America's new pill epidemic, innocent infants." I see a White mother cuddling her infant daughter as the news reporter asks "If you know you are pregnant ... you know it's harming the baby, why don't you just quit using the pills?" The mother sadly replies "it's just not that easy, you feel like you're gonna die." Later, an image briefly appears of a brown curly headed baby crying uncontrollably in a neonatal intensive care unit (NICU) crib. The narrator says, "new generation of addicts is being born" as the tiny brown foot emerged from the NICU crib appears on the screen.

I immediately thought of similar television images during the 1980's War on Drugs. Media warned America of financial burdens caused by this brown skinned crack baby with birth defects, mental retardation, and brain damage. The viewers learned about life long special education and medical needs depleting government funds. Videotaped tiny brown babies continuously crying in NICU cribs were the backdrop of these warnings. This brown infant foot looked horribly reminiscent of the infamous crack baby plastered all over televisions during the 1980s crack scare. The crack baby image is so powerful that anyone remembering these news stories will probably provide the same description, an underweight brown baby's body jerking and crying, inconsolably while hooked up to several tubes and monitors. There lies the birth of the crack baby forever linked to prenatal crack exposure. These images could have depicted any premature infant requiring medical intervention but this racialized image became the face of the crack baby.

As I watched the brown infant foot, I expected to hear stories from Black mothers. Contrarily, except for a glimpse of a brown skin mother in the back of a room, the program was all White. A brown baby's image introduces the story but the voice of Black mothers and people remained absent. The news reporter, mothers, infants, grandmothers and other characters are all White in this program about motherhood and Oxycodone addiction. Yet after more than 20 years, the brown crack baby image continues to signify prenatal drug exposure to illegal drugs even when the mothers are White.

The viewer meets Jessica, a white mother as she cuddles her infant daughter, Casey throughout the entire interview. The interview takes place in their brightly colored clean room in the rehabilitation center as Jessica refers to Casey as a princess. Jessica inundated her body with Oxycodone during pregnancy but was weaned off of the drug before her delivery. She enjoyed the privilege of detox with medical supervision and without fear of incarceration or losing custody of Casey. Jessica expressed concerns that her drug use is probably responsible for Casey's frequent respiratory infections on national television. Yet, she is not incarcerated for child neglect or endangerment. Instead, Jessica presents an image of her expressing sorrow and regret for drug use during pregnancy.

As a prenatal drug user, Jessica is portrayed as caring, concerned, and deeply remorseful for exposing her infant to Oxycodone. Images are presented of Jessica and Casey engaging in healthy and positive infant-mother interactions as she continues with her drug recovery. Juxtapose this to the 1980's Black mother demonized by the press and our society, branded a crack mother whom many referred to as a "crack ho." You seldom saw media presentations of Black mothers after detox or during abstinence from crack telling their story. Instead, news report images from the 1980s presented mostly Black mothers as crack users (Ortiz & Briggs, 2003) supporting the crack ho' image. The crack ho' can be described as a Black woman (not always a mother) addicted to crack caring more about feeding her addiction than of mothering her child. Unsubstantiated claims were even made suggesting chemical properties of crack eradicated the mother's biological drive to care for her children. The media also presented society with images and information inferring maternal drug use would only be found in the Black community (Roberts, 2002; Zerai & Banks, 2002). These images persisted throughout the 1990's and even in Hollywood with Halle Barry's characters Vivian in *Jungle Fever* (1991) and Khaila in *Losing Isaiah* (1995).

Women using crack cocaine typically experience a high level of trauma due to events prior to initial crack use and during crack use (e.g., being raped, children taken away). They also experience stigma trauma such as being regarded as a crack ho' or an unfit mother (Fullilove, Lown, & Fullilove, 1992). Crack is sometimes used to ease the pain of depression resulting from rape, death of a loved one, and/or their children being removed from them. Post Traumatic Stress Disorder further complicates the mother's addiction and recovery and they may engage in sexual bartering for crack, continuing the cycle of pain and shame. Yet, their behavior is more complex than a simple moral decision that willingly involves a bad choice of sex and drugs. Fullilove et al. (1992) explain:

> Women crack users suffer shame and grief as a result of the loss of culturally defined gender roles ... shame parallels that of torture victims who are forced to betray friends or loved ones (Alloudi, 1991), or of rape victims who believe "I brought it on myself." ... compelled by circumstances ... beyond human control to commit acts that are otherwise unthinkable. The "act" has been committed, but ... the victim (a ... addict) was not the responsible "actor." ... horror and shame associated with the act must be balanced by the recognition that coercion (or addiction) can overcome human will. (1992, p. 285)

The common belief is that all female crack users barter sex for drugs but this is a myth as they do not all engage in prostitution for crack. Female crack users, who were single, homeless, and 25 years old and younger were more likely to barter sex for drugs (Sterk, Elifson, & German, 2000). Rather than dehumanizing Black mothers, reducing them to simply crack ho's, understanding the complexities of gendered crack cocaine addiction experiences provides a more comprehensive look at their family resilience. Just like Jessica, mentioned earlier, Black mothers using crack are also in need of compassion and comprehensive, humanized and culturally relevant services.

Understanding prenatal drug use in Black families requires reassessment of images associated with poor Black "crack mothers" and white professional women seeking treatment for cocaine addiction. Once racism, sexism, drug phobia, and elitism is exposed, it becomes obvious that these are different women but addicted to the same drug. Unfortunately, controlled images support the narrative of White women being inherently good and better mothers than Black mothers with the criminal behavior of drug abuse (Zerai & Banks, 2002). White women with advantages are privileged, while at the same time resources for poor Black women are eliminated. These two diverse images of motherhood and cocaine addiction help justify providing middle class White women and not poor Black women access to treatment, prenatal care, and other resources (Zerai & Banks, 2002).

During the media frenzy of the crack ho and her baby, Black mothers' voices are totally silenced as no one bothered to interview them and seek out their perspectives on the horrors of drug addiction and resilience. The stereotypical image of the crack ho' and her crack baby informed public opinion and policy. Media coverage of the crack-addicted mother promoted negative images of poor Black mothers without resources, backing the master narrative of unworthiness of motherhood, sympathy, support and better off incarcerated.

This 2011 CNN Presents episode illustrates an example of grossly different representations of Black and White motherhood and illegal drug addiction. The problems of Pain Clinics in South Florida as well as the "victims" of prescription pill mills are addressed. I noticed White community members are considered victims of the illegal drug industry, while Black families in impoverished neighborhoods were considered the cause of the crack problem. They were not warranted the same sympathy. Community members and parents of those who have died from the prescribed Oxycodone Opiodes (nicknamed "heroin in a pill") voiced their outrage, concerns, and pleas for help. During this program, the County Sheriff even points out difficulties addressing the drug problem because doctors hide behind the protection of their medical licenses. A White nurse whose daughter is addicted to Oxycodone is interviewed and allowed to explain why she is unable to stop her daughter from becoming a drug addict. To the contrary, during the 1980s' crack epidemic, Black mothers were not allowed to speak truth of their daily-lived experiences during the crack cocaine epidemic. Instead, harsh negative representations of Black families and communities within the context of the crack business and addiction persisted and were rarely viewed in a positive manner. Following such representation, legislators passed some of the toughest criminal laws related to drug addiction in our country's history.

Representations of prenatal drug exposure are vastly different among White and Black mothers battling powerful illegal street drugs. While Oxycodone is a prescription drug, it is still obtained illegally by White mothers who are not criminalized as a group. This is a privilege not afforded to poor Black mothers addicted to crack during trending media coverage of the crack epidemic in the 1980s. This CNN segment ends with the reporter saying, "… These are the faces of that suffering. One mother who has already lost her child, another mother who is hoping her past hasn't ruined her child's future." This sentiment advances an image of a white mother/daughter dyad being victims of and not criminals in the illegal prescription drug industry. At the same time, conceptualizations of Black motherhood and crack addiction infer she is an inept mother unworthy of motherhood and part of the industry. These ideas of poor Black families emerge from assumptions that Black mothers' pathology is generational but with no critical examination of external social structures.

The prenatal drug user of Oxycodone is presented as a good mother simply recovering from a health problem but equipped with effective parenting skills. Juxtapose Jessica's image of a drug abusing mother to that of a poor Black mother in the 1980s addicted to crack, the pill mills versus crack houses, crack dealers versus medical doctors, and White families versus Black families. Images of drug dealers selling crack on the street and in crack houses is often associated with violent images of the mean Black man and immoral drug addicted Black mothers. One cannot deny the dangers and violence associated with the crack businesses in impoverished Black neighborhoods or the extent to which someone addicted to drugs would go to acquire the drugs. However, those images are rarely viewed within the context of political, social, and economic structures of those communities. Those images also fail to acknowledge or include the caring hard working citizens not involved in the crack industry or have been victims of the illegal crack business. The images from CNN Presents humanized White mothers and drug dealers as decent and caring people. The mother loves, cares about, and is concerned about her infant. Jessica's image becomes a humanized conception of a poor mother victimized from the exploitation of the medical doctors' greed in need of and worthy of government sympathy and assistance.

As a prenatal drug user, Jessica did not have to negotiate a stereotype like the crack ho' making a crack baby as she sought out and accessed available services for her family. Similarly, her White community was viewed positively unlike those images of drug infested impoverished Black neighborhoods. These are the same Black neighborhoods abandoned and isolated from full participation of the American dream before crack came on the scene. This

South Florida Community was depicted as a place where decent people lived but were victims of the illegal prescription drug business. Empowered community members felt entitled to their human rights and demanded they be respected as humans spoke out on camera. Likewise, these White community members gained the sympathy and support from local government officials and law enforcement. This is in stark contrast to the majoritarian images and realities of poor Black families residing in crack-infested neighborhoods where they are typically blamed for the crack problem. A glaring example of difference is how an entire industrial prison industry was developed and flourishes as a result of the crack epidemic. This is contrary to the Government's more humane response to the publicized rise in heroin addiction among White middle class families.

Race clearly influences representations of prenatal drug users, their families, and communities when comparing images of crack and Oxycodone addictions. The humaneness of drug distributers (South Florida medical doctors), drug dealers, and prenatal drug users depends on representation and narratives advanced based on the particular drug. Crack is typically considered a Black drug (Agar, 2003). Unlike the Black mother addicted to crack, her White counterpart addicted to Oxycodone has opportunity to contextualize her drug addiction and motherhood when in the media.

There were no images presented of Jessica's behaviors during active addiction, prior to rehabilitation or of Casey when she was first born during drug withdrawals. On national television, this White prenatal drug user displays positive parent-infant interactions and motherhood images humanizing her as a loving and caring mother with remorse for her prenatal drug exposure. These images leave the viewer with a sense of compassion and sympathy for mothers like Jessica. There were no media clips of Jessica getting high while she was pregnant or of her neglecting her daughter due to her addiction.

Although Jessica's prenatal drug use is the same behavior as many Black mothers, controlled images of motherhood are more influenced by the actual drug, community, and mothers' race. The state of Florida happens to be where the first prosecution of a Black mother for prenatal crack exposure occurred. In the same state as Jessica, Jennifer Johnson, a 23-year-old Black mother was arrested in 1989 for delivering a controlled substance to a minor when her newborn infant tested positive for prenatal crack exposure (Roberts, 1997). Jennifer's interactions with the law were quite different than Jessica's experience in Broward County, Florida. Unfortunately, Jennifer was not considered by the local DEA as an individual suffering because of her addiction and exploitation by the drug dealers or distributers. Instead, Jennifer, also addicted to drugs was considered a criminal deserving incarceration and her baby placed in foster care because of maternal neglect. Unlike Jessica, the crack ho' was deemed a criminal and unworthy of motherhood and support for overcoming her drug addiction.

In 1985 media reports of Middle class women's addiction to powder cocaine was explained away, while poor women's addiction to crack were emphasized in the media (Zerai & Banks, 2002). The dichotomous relationship of race and the drug user and seller (e.g. medical doctor vs. notorious drug kingpin, exploited mother vs. crack ho) is clearly indicated in this response to crack and Oxycodone and heroin addiction. Thus, the contexts from which mothers are judged are representative of the same racial discrimination that impact institutional racism from the social, educational and legal systems.

Rethinking Black Motherhood and Drug Addictions: Counternarratives of Black Family Resilience seeks to unsilence Black mothers and illegal drug addictions. My wish is that the mothers in this book serve as agents of change that disrupt the negative discourse on Black mothers. This especially holds true for Black mothers with young children impacted by crack, powdered cocaine, crank, and heroin addictions. It is my hope this book allows Bethena, Barbara, Desirea, Ladonna, and Sharonda's survival texts (Etter-Lewis, 1996) to speak truth to their lives (Collins, 2013) about their drug recovery and family resilience.

Bethena, Barbara, Desirea, Ladonna, and Sharonda's wanted their stories to be a blessing to other mothers struggling with addictions and to give hope for a better day. My desire is that the mothers' stories add to a collective sense of positive self-perceptions resisting and replacing controlled images of the crack ho with self-defined knowledge (Collins, 2000) about drug addiction and Black family resilience. The credibility and intentions of the power behind those who have previously defined Black mothers addicted to crack and other street drugs will be questioned when the mothers themselves self define daily lived experiences. There will no longer be an assumption that others have the authority to interpret their reality (Collins, 2000). Importance was placed on the mothers' opportunity to share their resources of knowledge within a safe, informant-defined space that was empowering and allowed them to systematically process their experiences (Few, Stephens, & Rouse-Arnett, 2003) with parenting, drug addiction, and recovery. *Rethinking Black Motherhood and Drug Addictions: Counternarratives of Black Family Resilience* allows Bethena, Barbara, Desirea, Ladonna and Sharonda to teach us about addictions, parenting, recovery and hope.

Overview of Chapters

The purpose of this book is not to glorify parenting and drug addiction as an optimal environment for child safety and development. Instead, I offer an understanding of Black family resilience and recovery from illegal street drug addiction from the Black mother's perspective. An important goal was to provide a platform for the mothers to self-define their lived experiences as drug addicts and mothers in opposition to the master narrative of Black mothers, crack ho's and crack babies. In the following chapter, *Tools for Understanding Drug Addiction and Black Mothers' Standpoint*, I contend that existing frameworks of illegal drug use in educational research is limited. Common frameworks include colorblind perspectives with few implications for practice supporting Black families in culturally responsive ways. I introduce Black Feminist Thought, Critical Race Feminism, and resiliency as more appropriate theoretical lenses to understand drug addiction and survival among Black mothers. Giving an overview of these frameworks related to this book, I illustrate how they result in Black mothers' powerful self-definitions of lived experiences with drugs.

Chapter Three: Origin of the Crack Ho': Mammies, Jezebels, Controlled Images, and Prosecution of Addiction provides the historical context and descriptions of negative controlled images applied to the identity of Black women and mothers. I unpack origins of Mammy, Jezebel, Black Matriarch, Welfare Queen, and the infamous Crack Ho that so powerfully shape popular thinking about Black womanhood and motherhood. I explore how these images and stereotypes directly impact common sense perceptions of Black women as mothers justifying ineffective policy decisions. I also argue negative controlled images of Black mothers and addictions have contributed to the trend to criminalize them instead of providing opportunities for treatment and support. In *Chapter Four: "From Suga to Shit:" The Drug Business and Destruction of Black Communities* I include historical, sociopolitical, and economic contexts of illegal drug business in Black communities. I pay particular attention to Detroit, MI and Atlantic City, NJ, as these were the hometowns of most mothers in this book. The exception is one mother who grew up in a New York Bourough but moved to Atlantic City during her recovery. I highlight intense devastation these communities endured during the crack and illegal drug industries, arguing knowledge of this larger context helps us better understand choices the women made and their journeys. The mothers are introduced here with discussions of their drug introductions and neighborhood context of their addictions.

I also draw from how the real events and figures (e.g., local drug bosses) in the mother's communities have been represented in popular movies and media. This chapter unpacks how crack and powder cocaine and heroin addictions have been and continue to be an American problem. Yet, typically poor Black residents are those forced to live in communities overwhelmed by easy access to these highly addictive illegal drugs and danger due to the industry.

In *Chapter Five: More about the Mothers, Research Practice, Black Motherhood and Addiction*, I further introduce the women whose stories are at the center of this book with more detail about their background. I briefly address the tensions that exist within conducting research practice with Black women who have experienced addiction and trauma. These tensions include researcher-participant relationships and nuances unique to interacting with Black mothers recovering from drug. I also include the dilemmas of self-reflection as I considered positionality, accountability, and the use of language during the research process. In *Chapter Six: "I Had Help": Kinship, Drug Addictions, and Black Family Resilience*, I explore the essential role of kinships among the mothers that were key to their survival. The mothers' narratives explain how grandmothers and others inside and outside of the families were important resources as they navigated their addictions.

In the next three chapters, I use the mothers' "survival texts" (Etter-Lewis, 1996 p. 17) to broaden my understanding of drug addiction, Black motherhood, and recovery as discussed from their perspectives. In *Chapter Seven: "Wasn' No Junkie, I Was A Workin' Addict ... It's A Difference:" Self-Definition of Black Mothers' Roles and Responsibilities*, I illuminate the mothers' self-definitions of their lives through narratives as multifaceted women who were parents and drug addicts. Existing paradigms of parent-child interactions among Black mothers and drug addictions force us to see them as simple flat characters by ignoring the complexity of their lives. The mothers' narratives in Chapter Seven provide a snapshot of their parenting styles and family values and beliefs from their own perspectives. New insights are explored about their family's resilience through self-definitions of parenting, parent-child interactions, and discipline. Their narratives highlight parental roles as active and recovered drug addicts across their children's life spans. In *Chapter Eight: Crack Baby Aftermath and Navigating Educational Institutions*, the mothers' narratives dispel the myth that Black families do not engage in efforts to support children's academic achievement. This chapter illustrates the mothers' intentional efforts to change the academic trajectory for their children due to their strong desire for them to be effective and successful students. Stories about encouraging and supporting academic achievement, perceptions of their children as students, and problems encountered at school are presented. I also give attention to the mothers' values regarding education and home/school partnerships.

Black family resilience is often achieved through religious beliefs (Hill, 2003). Narratives in this book come from Black Christian mothers with strong religious values and beliefs. Thus in Chapter Nine: "I Was Just Cryin' Out to God:" Recovery and the Spirituality of Struggle, I address Christian spiritual values and beliefs as the foundation of their lives as they attend church regularly. I share how the mothers self-defined their recovery directly related to their faith in God. Two mothers heavily critique drug rehabilitation programs and other social services aimed at supporting those with drug addictions. Thus, they relied on their relationship with God instead of inadequate rehabilitation programs for sobriety. Their narratives illustrate strength in their belief that God's love and power is responsible for their recovery and overall safety. The mothers' stories illustrate their experience with God's protection, intervention during life-threatening moments, and voice during their drug addiction.

The book ends with the Discussion: What the Mothers Made Me Think About, which provides a summary of my most salient lessons and implications for a variety of fields and professions. For human service professions, I discuss how an asset-based perspective may promote meaningful interactions with families impacted by illegal drug addictions. A focus on resilience is suggested for educators working in Black communities vulnerable to addiction. Resisting and understanding the strength of stereotypes and the superficial war on drugs are also important aspects of understanding their resiliency and community. Lastly, I include a section on What They Taught Me. Here, critical thoughts and ideas to consider are shared as I move forward in understanding the full economic and sociopolitical destruction of crank, powder and crack cocaine, and heroin on Black families and neighborhoods throughout generations and their resilience.

References

Agar, M. (2003). The story of crack: Towards a theory of illicit drug trends. Addiction Research & Theory, 11(1), 3–29.

Alloudi, F. A. (1991). Assessment and treatment of torture victims: A critical review. Journal of Nervous and Mental Disorders, 179(1), 4–11.

CNN Presents. (Aired 2011, July 31). Florida's Drug Addicted Babies reporting by Amber Lyon.
Collins, P. H. (2000). *Black feminist thought* (2nd ed.). New York: Routledge.
Collins, P. H. (2013). *On intellectual activism*. Philadelphia, PA: Temple University Press.
Etter-Lewis, G. (1996). From the inside out: Survival and continuity in African American women's oral narratives. In G. Etter-Lewis & M. Foster (Eds.), *Unrelated kin: Race and gender in women's personal narratives* (pp. 169–179). New York, NY: Routlege.
Few, A. L., Stephens, D. P., & Rouse-Arnett, M. (2003). Sister-to-sister talk: Transcending boundaries and challenges in qualitative research with Black women. *Family Relations*, 52(3), 205–215.
Foner, N., & Koch, H. (Producers), Gyllenhaal, S. (Director). (1995). *Losing Isaiah*. United States: Paramount Pictures.
Fullilove, M. T., Lown, E. A., & Fullilove, R. E. (1992). Crack 'hos and skeezers: Traumatic experiences of women crack users. *The Journal of Sex Research*, 29(2), 275–287.
Hill, R. B. (2003). *The strengths of Black families*. Lanham, MD: University Press of America.
Lee, S. (Producer & Director). (1991). *Jungle Fever* [Motion Picture]. United States: 40 Acres & A Mule Filmworks.
Ortiz, A. T., & Briggs, L. (2003). Crack, abortion, the culture of poverty, and welfare cheats: The making of the 'Healthy White Baby Crisis.' *Social Text* 75, 39–57.
Roberts, D. E. (1997). *Killing the Black body: Race, reproduction, and the meaning of liberty*. New York, NY: Pantheon Books, a Division of Random House.
Roberts, D. E. (2002). *Shattered bonds: The color of child welfare*. New York, NY: Basic Civitas Books.
Sterk, C., Elifson, K., & German, D. (2000). Female crack users and their sexual relationships: The role of sex-for-crack exchanges. *Journal of Sex Research*, 37(4), 354–360.
Zerai, A., & Banks, R. (2002). *Dehumanizing discourse, anti-drug law, and policy in America: A "crack mother's" nightmare*. Burlington, VT: Ashgate Publishing.

· 2 ·

TOOLS FOR UNDERSTANDING DRUG ADDICTION AND BLACK MOTHERS' STANDPOINT

Much of the educational research (Bolzani Dinehart, Dice, Dobbins, Claussen, & Bono, 2006; Carta et al., 1997; Kraus et al., 2000;) about drug addiction among mothers is often conceptualized from a positivist paradim and ignores race, class, and gender oppressions. Although unintentional, by excluding the mothers' voice, research results in value-laden knowledge claims about Black mothers' daily experiences often steeped in biased assumptions about drug addictions in Black families and ignores their resilience. Challenging scholarship advancing existing Black mother stereotypes require theoretical frameworks that engage research practices focused on hearing from Black mothers. My intentions for this book is to provide a fresh lens through which to consider and understand Black mothers addicted to heroin, crack, powdered cocaine, and crank.

This chapter has three major objectives: (a) establish a discursive environment to discuss Black motherhood and heroin and crack cocaine addictions; (b) engage in a community in which drug addiction and recovery among Black mothers is situated; and (c) provide practitioners, researchers, participants, and the general public frameworks to understand Black families impacted by drug addiction in ways that resist pathological conceptions and acknowledges their resilience. Next, I present a glossary of concepts that are key to my analysis of the mothers' narratives in this book. They include:

(1) Racism: "(a) One group deems itself superior to all others, (b) the group that is superior has the power to carry out the racist behaviors, and (c) racism benefits the superior group while negatively affecting the other racial and/or ethnic groups" (Solórzano & Yosso, 2009, p. 132).
(2) Systematic Racism: "Refers to the European American oppression of African Americans since the 1600s … (Feagin, 2006, p. xiii) … Encompasses a broad range of white-racist dimensions: the racist ideology, attitudes, emotions, habits, actions, and institutions of whites in this society. Thus, systematic racism is far more than a matter of racial prejudice and individual bigotry. It is a material, social, and ideological reality that is well-embedded in major U.S. institutions" (p. 2). "Systematic racism includes a diverse assortment of practices; the unjustly gained economic and political power of whites; the continuing resource inequalities; and the white-racist ideologies, attitudes, and institutions created to preserve white advantages and power" (Feagin, 2000, p. 16).
(3) Oppression: "Any situation in which 'A' objectively exploits 'B' or hinders his or her pursuit of self-affirmation as a responsible person is one of oppression … it interferes with the individual's ontological and historical vocation to become more fully human …" (Freire, 2007, p. 55). An unjust or cruel exercise of authority or power (Merriam-Webster, n.d.). Oppression can occur based on race, social status, class, gender, sexuality, and other identities.
(4) Critical Race Theory (CRT): Originated in legal studies and is a: "Radical legal movement that seeks to transform the relationship among race, racism, and power" (Delgado & Stefancic 2012, p. 159). CRT is transdisciplinary and includes: (a) belief that racism is systemic and embedded in the fabric of our society, (b) valuing of storytelling, and (c) Derrick Bell's (1995) *Interest Convergence Theory* (Delgado & Stefancic).
(5) Black Feminist Thought (BFT): A comprehensive theoretical stance for the empowerment of Black women in the United States that is often associated with the work of Patricia Hill Collins. Important features of BFT include (a) an analysis of daily-lived experiences of race, class, and gender oppressions among Black women in the United States, (b) internalization of positive self-definitions that repudiates negative stereotypes types and controlled images; (c) Black women's Standpoint; (d) social justice orientation; and (e) Black Feminist Epistemology (Collins, 2000).
(6) Critical Race Methodology (CRM): Critical race theorist, Solórzano and Yosso (2009) define CRM as: "A theoretically grounding approach to research that foregrounds race and racism in all aspects of the research process …" (p. 131) and includes: (a) The intercentricity of race and racism, (b) The challenge to dominant ideology, (c) The commitment to social justice, (d) The centrality of experiential knowledge, and (e) The transdisciplinary perspective. (pp. 132–134).
(7) Narrative: "Etymologically, narrative has two meanings: 'to tell' *(narrare)* and 'to know' *(gnārus)*. (Kim, 2016, p. 303) Riessman (2008) argues that "narratives are composed for particular audiences at moments in history, and they draw on taken-for-granted discourses and values circulating in a particular culture" (p. 3).

(8) Counter-storytelling: "Writing that aims to cast doubt on the validity of accepted premises and myths, especially ones held by the majority" (Delgado & Stefancic, 2012, p. 159). " ... a method of telling the stories' of those people whose experiences are not often told (i.e. those on the margins of society). The counter-story is also a tool for exposing, analyzing, and challenging the majoritarian stories of racial privilege" (Solórzano & Yosso, 2009, p. 138). The following are three types of counter-storytelling: personal stories or narratives, other people's stories or narratives, and composite stories or narratives (Solórzano & Yosso, 2009).

(9) Master-narrative: A master narrative reflects knowledge claims and interpretations of history from the dominant culture without critique. Barone (2006) states that they are "... meta-stories that aim to bring final meaning to cultural phenomena ... the words and images drive and illuminate the story, free to operate within the political spectacle, to pervade public awareness" (p. 215). Solórzano and Yosso (2009) contend "that the ideology of racism creates, maintains, and justifies the use of a 'master narrative' in storytelling" (p. 134). Master narratives "... generates a biased set of knowledge or framework for which the system functions. This knowledge not only influences the functionality of a society, it influences, the economic, political, religious, and educational function of a society as well. When presented in this fashion, the point of view of the majority overpowers the point of view of many minority, oppressed, and underclass community" (Easton-Brooks, 2012, p. 34).

(10) At-Risk Factors: Characteristics of children and families considered by most institutions charged to support them as problems interfering with their well-being and overall functioning. Poverty, female-headed households, racial and linguistic diversity, crime, medical problems, poor neighborhoods are often considered to be risk factors for children.

(11) Cultural Deficit: Cultural deficit theories of education are used to explain the differences between poor and students of color in development and academic achievement. Based on the idea that "... poor students shared a 'culture of poverty' that was considered to be antithetical to school achievement. Poor and minority students were viewed with a lens of deficiencies, substandard in their socialization practices, language practices, and orientation toward scholastic achievement" (González 2005, p. 34). This framework was also used for conceptualizing, conducting and interpreting research about Black families.

(12) Moral Deficit: Inability to conform to a standard of what is agreed upon by the dominant culture as appropriate behavior. Commonly held belief that single Black mothers in poverty were immoral which sustained the negative controlled images of the lazy welfare mom and jezebel.

(13) Discourse: "Is a discursive language, spoken or written, in which the social, cultural, and political perspectives of the people involved in it are embedded" (Kim 2016, p. 66).

(14) Asset Approach to Understanding and Working with Families: Refers to theoretical frameworks and philosophies that focus and build upon family strengths

rejecting deficit models. Seeks opportunities for children and families to demonstrate their competence and resiliency.
(15) Resilience: The ability to endure and recover from life's adversity and is considered a dynamic process centering on adapting to adversity (Luthar, Cicchetti, & Becker, 2002).
(16) Family Adaptation: Family's outcome obtained by their resilience after recovering from stressors. Racial and ethnic family's adaptation is an active and proactive process. During this process these families are able to maintain, affirm, and assert their ethnic heritage and identity. They adapt to their conditions simultaneously as change agents challenging society to become more supportive and respectful to those who are marginalized (McCubbin, H., Futrell, J., Thompson, E., & Thompson, A., 1998).

During 1998, which was the tail-end of the crack scare, Americans as a whole were experiencing demographic changes across ethnic and class lines. Traditional family structures were being replaced with more births occurring outside of marriage with an increase of divorce and blended and stepfamilies. Economic stress with parental unemployment, senseless violence and the flow of drugs in rural, urban and suburban areas impacted all societal groups. However, the negative consequences of these social problems were more pronounced in Black families (McAdoo, 1998). While Black families are not monolithic and include diverse economic and social experiences, barriers to social and financial resources still remain. The "free-flow of drugs into the black community" (McAdoo, p. 19), AIDS, other health issues, and gang-like behavior in youth, are negative factors that were plaguing many Black families during the era of crack cocaine. These factors added to the burden of negotiating poverty in Black families. Nonetheless, McAdoo (1998) argued practitioners and researchers could learn from Black families by focusing on resilience and not solely on their problems. Exposing the origins of barriers placed on family environments is key to avoid holding Black families responsible for hostile environments in many communities.

Different Way of Seeing Things

The narratives of five Black mothers and drug addiction are explored in this book through the lens of frameworks that allow us to highlight their family resilience in spite of negative structural forces. Discussing drug addiction among Black mothers through the lenses of Black Feminist Thought (BFT), Critical Race Feminism (CRF), and resilience provides a counternarrative that resists the dominant narrative of their families.

Black feminist thought

Black Feminist Thought is a comprehensive stance for the empowerment of Black women that acknowledges the complexities of race, class, and gender oppressions on daily-lived experiences (Collins, 2000; Cooper, 1886; hooks, 1989, 2000; Johnson, 2000). Although not referred to as such, BFT emerged as a means of legitimizing the concerns of Black women as early as the nineteenth century. Waters (2000) points out Black women writers in the 1800s provided a voice for Black women challenging misrepresentations that maintained their silence and supported their fight against oppression. In the 1800's, as a pioneer, Maria Stewart set the stage for other Black women to speak about race, class, and gender oppressions as she addressed issues of equal employment and discrimination of Black girls (Waters, 2000). Other Black women like Anna Julia Cooper and Nannie Helen Burrough also contributed significantly to BFT as they advocated for human and civil rights of Black women during the nineteenth century. Through civic and political activism, Cooper and Burroughs engaged in resistance toward racial oppression, gender subordination, and economic exploitation. They founded the National Association of Colored Women and the Women's Conference to help achieve group survival and institutional transformation (Johnson, 2000).

BFT allows for a Black feminist epistemology (BFE) as an alternative for knowledge validation based on Black mothers' subjectivity as the basis of analysis of their daily-lived experiences and taken-for-granted knowledge (Collins, 2000). BFE values narrative and reveals the link between social conditions and Black women's viewpoint, while also acknowledging them as important agents of knowledge (Collins, 2000). An *ethic of accountability* and *caring* are key features of a BFE approach to research. An *ethic of accountability* is essential to assessing knowledge claims made about Black women by closely examining the character, values, and ethics of individuals making claims. The *ethic of caring* places an emphasis on individual uniqueness, acknowledges the appropriateness of emotions in dialogues, and develops the capacity for empathy (Collins, 2000).

Critical race feminism (CRF)

Critical Race Feminism embraces the major tenants of CRT but with a focus on the concerns of women of color (Delgado & Stefanic, 2012). CRF scholars recognize components of CRT such as: (a) belief that systematic racism exists, (b) valuing of storytelling, and (c) Derrick Bell's (1995) Interest Convergence

Theory. Interest Conversion Theory originated from Bell arguing that the majority group simply tolerates progress in racial justice only when in its best interest. For example, "... civil rights gains for communities of color coincide with the dictates of white self-interest. Little happens out of altruism alone" (Delgado & Stefanic, 2012, p. 22).

Leading CRF scholar Adrien Wing (1997, 2002) pointed out that CRF emerged because existing legal paradigms (e.g critical legal studies, CRT) do not adequately address the needs of women of color. Women of color are not "simply white women plus some ineffable and secondary characteristic, such as skin tone, added on" (Wing, 1997, p. 3). Thus identity is multiplicative and not additive (Wing, 1997). CRF utilizes feminism by accepting their focus on gender oppression within a male dominated society. However with CRF, the varied experiences of women of color are no longer examined only within the context of the experience of white middle-class women. The major role of white supremacy in the subordination of women of color by both white men and women is closely examined (Wing, 1997, 2002). CRF scrutinizes the oppression of women of color and how White supremacy is manifested in the justice system and maintains their subordination (Bell, 1995; Crenshaw, Gotanda, Peller, & Thomas, 1995; Solorzano & Yosso, 2009; Wing, 1997, 2002).

CRF examines the knowledge making process and embraces a multidisciplinary research approach challenging traditional research interest by including the roles of people of color by utilizing Critical race methodology (CRM) (Delgado, 1989; Solorzano & Yosso, 2009). CRM acknowledges the contradictions and multiple layers of oppression and goes beyond the boundaries of traditional research interest (Solorzano & Yosso, 2001, 2009). CRM calls for the use of counter-storytelling, oral traditions, historiographies, poetry, and films to challenge existing biological and cultural deficit stories (Delgado, 1989; Solorzano & Yosso, 2001, 2009). CRM captures the voice of those typically oppressed through research processes and exposes racist injustices. Empowerment for people of color occurs when those oppressed realize that they are not alone, understand how arguments against them are developed, and most importantly learn to establish their own arguments in their defense (Solorzano & Yosso, 2009).

Similar to CRT, CRF is based on the assumption that from the beginning, racism has been a fundamental component of the American legal system as opposed to being some rare abnormality. Thus, many CRF scholars (Roberts, 1997, 2002; Wing, 2002) do not believe in a color-blind legal system and unapologetically accept color-consciousness and identity politics as a method of offsetting the current inherit racist nature of the American legal system. CRF acknowledge the role of class but also that more people of color live in poverty and are treated different than their white counterparts (Wing, 2002).

BFT and CRF values the collective personal experiences of Black women as having legitimate meaning. For example, Collins (2000) argues that Black women collectively in the United States are challenged with living in a society that has routinely and historically denigrated and exploited them. BFT does not assume all Black women will have the same experiences or always agree on issues affecting them. Nonetheless, the diverse responses to these experiences help frame Black women's group knowledge or standpoint and their collective personal experiences as having legitimate meaning (Collins, 2000). I have collected stories from five Black mothers who survived drug addiction to crack and powder cocaine, crank, and heroin. These dual frameworks challenge traditional knowledge claims, exposes injustices and values the Black mothers' voice (Delgaldo, 1989; Collins 2000; Solorzano & Yosso, 2009). Their experiential knowledge is embraced as legitimate empirical data and an analytical tool for understanding parenting, drug addiction & recovery within the context of their triple oppressions (Collins 2000; Delgaldo, 1989; Solorzano & Yosso, 2009).

Educational policies and practices render themselves ineffective when simply targeting children prenatally exposed to drugs while ignoring the social and cultural context of the family. It is problematic when research methodologies imply a colorblind perspective and discount intersecting oppressions. This silences the Black mothers' voice resulting in continued use of negative controlled images of her family. Thus, making it difficult for them to move beyond the horrors of drug addiction. Educational practices and policies are often based on findings from educational research and rarely addresses family resilience or the socio cultural context of children prenatally exposed to drugs. Thus, qualitative inquiry with theoretical lens that challenges existing stereotypes and values the Black mothers' voice (Alicea & Friedman, 1999; Roberts, 1997a; Roberts, 1997b; Baker & Carson, 1999; Zeari & Banks, 2002) adds important dimensions to the discourse of prenatal drug use, parenting, and child development.

Black family resilience

Family resilience is seldom included in early childhood and educational practice and research especially within the context of prenatal drug exposure and drug addiction in Black families. Exploring the resilience of Black families provides important insights about their abilities to negotiate drug addiction and parenting. This asset approach acknowledges existing coping abilities often expressed by family members themselves, in the case of this book, the mothers surviving drug addictions.

Resilience is (a) the capability of enduring life's adversity, (b) the capability of recovering from life's adversity, (c) considered a dynamic process, (d) centers on adapting to adversity, (e) focuses on outcomes for those facing adversity, and (e) varies across individuals (Luthar et al., 2002). There is variation across families in their adaptation to life's adversity, and Walsh (2002) has discussed three key processes in family resilience. The first process is through family belief systems that (a) make meaning of adversity, (b) have a positive outlook, and (c) employ transcendence and spirituality. The second process uses organizational patterns that include (a) flexibility, (b) connectedness, and (c) social and economic resources. The third are communication processes that (a) establishes clarity, (b) includes open emotional sharing, and (c) collaborative problem solving (Walsh, 2002).

Black families embrace unique characteristics of resilience that offer an alternative view of families in distress (Hill, 2003, Luthar et al., 2002; McCubbin et al., 1998; Walsh, 2002). Black family resilience has been essential to their survival in the United States. Historically, strong kinship bonds, strong work orientation, adaptability of family roles, strong achievement orientation, and strong religious orientation are key characteristics of strong Black families (Hill, 2003). These qualities are not unique to just Black families but do manifest themselves differently due to historical racism and tools required to survive and advance in a hostile environment (Hill, 2003). Ignoring these strengths and resilience in Black families impedes our knowledge of their families' positive attributes. Thus, understanding Black family resilience requires frameworks specific to families of color.

The notion that adaptation requires engaging in the majority culture while compromising your ethnic identity and worth challenges the well-being of many families of color. Family adaptation to adversity should not be a passive process determined by a powerful mainstream culture (McCubbin et al., 1998). Much of the problem with understanding Black mothers and drug addiction is the majority of educational research on this topic ignores intersecting race, class, and gender oppressions (Claussen, Scott, Mundy & Katz, 2004; Bolzani Dinehart et al., 2006; Cross, Fletcher & Neumeister, 2011). Family problems are often framed as a result of deficient cultural and moral resources in their oppressed communities and families. When helping these families, there is an assumption of a level playing field when implementing support programs that replace these scarce resources via participating in government programs designed and run by the dominant culture (Sleeter, 1995).

Black feminist thought, critical race feminism, and Black family resilience are presented in this chapter as theoretical frameworks for discussing Black motherhood impacted by heroin and crack cocaine additions. The combination of CRF and BFT as theoretical lenses allows for interpretations that disrupt the master narrative of drug addiction and parenting for Black families and values the Black mother's voice and the use of oral narrative research. Drug addiction and parenting among Black mothers through the lenses of BFT, CRF, and Black family resilience provides practitioners, researchers, participants and the general public with tools to better understand their problems.

In this book, drug addiction, recovery and parenting is situated within the context of acknowledging the intersection of race, class, and gender oppressions. Using these frameworks, the mothers' counternarratives challenge existing biological and cultural deficit stories of prenatal drug exposure, drug addiction and Black motherhood. Here, the mothers have an opportunity to self-define their lived experiences and construct and tell their own realities (Collins, 2000) of drug addiction, parenting, and recovery. The mothers self-define their daily-lived experiences with their children as they navigated crack, crank, and heroin addictions and recovery. The next chapter explores the origins of negative stereotypes of Black motherhood, implications for criminalization with specific attention given to the crack ho.

References

Alicea, M., & Friedman, J. (1999). Millie's story: Motherhood, heroin, and methadone. In M. Romero & A. J. Stewart (Eds.), *Women's untold stories: Breaking silence, talking back, voicing complexity* (pp. 159–173). New York, NY: Routledge.

Baker, P., & Carson, A. (1999). I take care of my kids: Mothering practices of substance-abusing women. *Gender and Society, 13*(3), 347–363.

Barone, T. (2006). Making educational history: Qualitative inquiry, artistry, and the public interest. In G. Ladson-Billings & W. F. Tate (Eds.), *Education research in the public interest: Social justice, action, and policy* (pp. 213–230). New York, NY: Teachers College Press, Columbia University.

Bell, D. A. (1995). *Brown v. Board of Education* and the interest convergence dilemma. In K. Crenshaw, N. Gotanda, G. Peller, & K. Thomas (Eds.), *Critical race theory: The key writings that formed the movement* (pp. 20–29). New York, NY: New Press.

Bolzani Dinehart, L. H., Dice, J. L., Dobbins, D. R., Claussen, A. H., & Bono, K. E. (2006). Proximal variables in families of children prenatally exposed to cocaine and enrolled in a center-or home-based intervention. *Journal of Early Intervention, 29*, 32–47.

Carta, J. J., McConnell, S. R., McEvoy, M. A., Greenwood, C. R., Atwater, J. B., Baggett, K., & Williams, R. (1997). Developmental outcomes associated with in utero exposure to alcohol and other drugs. In M. R. Haack (Ed.), *Drug-dependent mothers and their children: Issues in public policy and public health* (pp. 64–90). New York, NY: Springer Publishing.

Claussen, A. H., Scott, K. G., Mundy, P. C., & Katz, L. F. (2004). Effects of three levels of early intervention services on children prenatally exposed to cocaine. *Journal of Early Intervention, 26*, 204–220.

Collins, P. H. (2000). *Black feminist thought: Knowledge, consciousness, and the politics of empowerment* (2nd ed.). New York, NY: Routledge.

Cooper, A. J. (1986). Womanhood: A vital element in the regeneration and progress of a race. In C. Lemert & E. Bhan (Eds.), *The voice of Anna Julia Cooper: Including "A Voice from the South" and other important essays, papers, and letters* (pp. 53–71). New York, NY: Rowman & Littlefield.

Crenshaw, K., Gotanda, N., Peller, G., & Thomas, K. (1995). Introduction. In K. Crenshaw, N. Gotanda, G. Peller, & K. Thomas (Eds.), *Critical race theory: The key writings that formed the movement* (pp. xiii–xxxii). New York, NY: New Press.

Cross, J. R., Fletcher, K. L., & Speirs Neumeister, K. L. (2011). Social and emotional components of book reading between caregivers and their toddlers in a high-risk sample. *Journal of Early Childhood Literacy, 11*, 25–46.

Delgado, R. (1989). Storytelling for oppositionists and others: A plea for narrative. *Michigan Law Review, 87*, 2411–2441.

Delgado, R., & Stefancic, J. (2012). *Critcal race theory: An introduction* (2nd ed.). New York, NY: New York University Press.

Easton-Brooks, D. (2012). The conceptual context of knowledge. In S. R. Steinberg & G. S. Cannella (Eds.), *Critical qualitative research reader* (33–42). New York, NY: Peter Lang.

Feagin, J. R. (2000). *Racist America:Roots, current realities,and future reparation*. New York, NY: Routledge.

Feagin, J. R. (2006). *Systemic Racism: A theory of oppression*. New York, NY: Routledge.

Freire, P. (2007). *Pedagogy of the oppressed* (30th Anniversary ed.). New York: Continuum.

González, N. (2005). Beyond culture: The hybridity of funds of knowledge. In N. González, L. C. Moll, & C. Amanti (Eds.), *Funds of knowledge: Theorizing practices in households, communities, and classrooms* (29–46). New York: Routledge-Taylor & Frances Group.

Hill, R. B. (2003). *The strengths of Black families*. Lanham, MD: University Press of America.

hooks, b. (1989). *Talking back: Thinking feminist thinking Black*. Boston, MA: South End Press.

hooks, b. (2000). Black women: Shaping feminist theory. In J. James & T. Denean Sharpley-Whiting (Eds.), *The Black feminist reader* (131–145). Malden, MA: Blackwell

Johnson, K. A. (2000). *Uplifting the women and the race: The educational philosophies and social activism of Anna Julia Cooper and Nannie Helen Burroughs*. New York, NY: Routledge Publishing, Inc.

Kim, J. H. (2016). *Understanding narrative inquiry*. Los Angeles, CA: Sage Publications.

Krauss, R. B., Thurman, S. K., Brodsky, N., Betancourt, L., Giannetta, J. & Hurt, H. (2002). Caregiver interaction behavior with prenatally cocaine-exposed and nonexposed preschoolers. *Journal of Early Intervention, 23*(1), 62–73.

Luthar, S., Cicchetti, D., & Becker, B. (2000). The construct of resilience: A critical evaluation and guidelines for future work. *Child Development, 71*(3), 543–562.

McCubbin, H., Futrell, J., Thompson, E., & Thompson, A. (1998). Resilient families in an ethnic and cultural context. In H. I. McCubbin, E. A. Thompson, A. I. Thompson, & J. A. Futrell (Eds.), *Resiliency in African American families* (pp. 329–351). Thousand Oaks, CA; Sage Publications.

McAdoo, H. (1998). African American families: Strengths and realities. In H. I. McCubbin, E. A. Thompson, A. I. Thompson, & J. A. Futrell (Eds.), *Resiliency in African American families* (pp. 17–30). Thousand Oaks, CA; Sage Publications.

"Oppression." Merriam-Webster.com. Merriam-Webster, n.d. Wed. 28 Mar. 2017.

Riessman, C. K. (2008). *Narrative methods for the human sciences.* Los Angeles, CA: Sage Publications.

Roberts, D. E. (1997). *Killing the Black body: Race, reproduction, and the meaning of liberty.* New York: Pantheon Books, a Division of Random House.

Roberts, D. E. (2002). *Shattered bonds: The color of child welfare.* New York, NY: Basic Civitas Books.

Sleeter, C. E. (1995). Forward. In B. B. Swadener & S. Lubeck (Eds.), *Children and families "at promise": Deconstructing the discourse of risk* (pp. ix–x). Albany, NY: State University of New York Press.

Solórzano, D. G., & Yosso, T. J. (2001). Critical race and LatCrit theory and method: counterstorytelling. *Qualitative Studies in Education, 14*(4), 471–495.

Solórzano, D. and Yosso, T. (2009). Critical race methodology: Counter-storytelling as an analytical framework for education research. In E. Taylor, D. Gillborn, & G. Ladson-Billings (Eds.), *Foundations of critical race theory in education* (pp. 131–147). New York, NY: Routledge.

Walsh, F. (2002). A family resilience framework: Innovative practice applications. *Family Relations, 51*(2), 130–137.

Waters, K. (Ed.). (2000). *Women and men political theorists: Enlightened conversations.* Malden, MA: Blackwell.

Wing, A. K. (1997). Brief reflections toward a multiplicative theory and praxis of being. In A. K. Wing (Ed.), *Critical race feminism: A reader* (pp. 27–34). New York, NY: New York University Press.

Wing, A. 2002. Critical race feminism: Legal reform for the twenty-first century. In D. T. Goldberg & J. Solomos (Eds.), *A companion to racial and ethnic studies* (pp. 160–169). Malden, MA: Blackwell.

Zerai, A., & Banks, R. (2002). *Dehumanizing discourse, anti-drug law, and policy in America: A "crack mother's" nightmare.* Burlington, VT: Ashgate Publishing.

· 3 ·

ORIGIN OF THE CRACK HO'

Mammies, Jezebels, Controlled Images, and Prosecution of Addiction

Reflecting on the origins of the crack ho,' I am reminded that motherhood for descendants of enslaved African females has never been honored or respected in our country. Negative controlled images of Black women advanced since her arrival on the shores of the United States illustrate lengths used to devalue her motherhood. This chapter traces the roots of the crack ho by first illustrating how throughout our country's history, these images served to maintain the subordinate status of Black women. Second, research's role in the construction and maintenance of pathological frameworks of Black motherhood are also addressed. Third, I unpack the role of negative controlled images in the criminalization of Black mothers and provide alternatives to a focus on punishment.

Images like mammy and jezebel reinforce the notion Black women are inept at mothering their children resulting in society's social problems thus, giving reason to criminalize her maternal behavior.

Research and Controlled Images

Only within the past 30 years, have methodological issues and biases in research related to Black families been acknowledged and challenged by scholars. Historically, research practice with Black mothers in general has been problematic. The concern was so pronounced that Black psychological researchers collaborated to eliminate biased research practices in their discipline. For example, Harriet Pipes McAdoo and John Lewis McAdoo (1985) described the significance of the *Empirical Conference of Black Psychology* in the preface of the book *Black Children Social, Educational, and Parental Environments* (1985). The need for such a conference illustrates the extent of the problems in research methods at the time as these scholars attempt to address these challenges.

Devaluation of Black motherhood

Negative controlled images function as a means of dehumanizing Black women supporting their unworthiness of motherhood. Devaluation of Black motherhood dates back to her enslavement in America where she was first denied her reproductive freedom (Brent, 1861; Collins, 2000; Roberts, 1997, 2002; Washington, 2005). White male plantation owners were allowed to rape and actually breed enslaved females with no legal recourse for her protections. Her human and reproductive rights were so violated that even naming her children's father was a criminal offense (Brent, 1861). During slavery, enslaved African women were dehumanized and considered only useful for working, plantation owner's sexual pleasures, and childbearing.

The act of childbearing was valued more than the actual life of the enslaved pregnant women as suggested by their punishment. For example, enslaved women were usually punished using a system designed to physically protect the unborn fetus but not her overall wellbeing. The enslaved pregnant woman was required to lay face down in a hole in the ground to protect her unborn fetus as her back is being lashed with a whip (Roberts, 1997). Clearly, the unborn fetus (considered property too) was valued more than the life of the mother herself. Also, unethical, cruel and inhumane medical experimentation on enslaved female's reproduction systems were indeed legal and set the foundation for the medical specialization of gynecology (Roberts, 1997; Washington, 2005). During that era enslaved women had no legal claims to their children. Often, their masters controlled childbearing and separated them from their infants after birth for purposes of being sold to other slaveholders (Roberts, 2002; Washington, 2005). Even after the institution of slavery became illegal, Black women continued to endure such sexual abuse with no legal recourse as domestic workers in the homes of white families (Roberts, 2002).

Black motherhood's value was also compromised by the practice of disproportionately removing Black children from their homes by our country's child welfare agencies (Roberts, 2002). Similar to their experiences during slavery, poor Black mothers continue to struggle to maintain legal claims to their children. Black mothers living in poverty are more likely to rely on governmental agencies for support (Roberts, 1997; Zerai & Banks, 2002), allowing for ample opportunity for the government to intervene in their lives (Roberts, 1997). These family interventions are supposedly designed to protect Black children but are based on strategies and ideals of white middle-class family structures. When poor Black families do not fit these models of family function, Black mothers are considered to be abusive and deficient therefore in need of government intervention. Thus, while Black motherhood is being devalued, the integrity of the white, middle-class family functioning is upheld (Roberts, 1997).

The coerced sterilization as a means of controlling reproduction has also disproportionately impacted Black and Puerto Rican women. These efforts at population control, illustrates yet another example of how the dominant society regards Black women as unworthy of motherhood. Historically, some doctors only agreed to deliver babies or perform abortions on Black mothers if they consented to sterilization. Federal and state regulations have since then deemed this practice illegal. However, government-funding policy supported the encouragement of sterilization instead of the use of contraceptives (Roberts, 1997). As late as the 1970's, poor Black teen-aged girls were research participants to examine what is now known as the long-acting contraceptive Depo-Provera that unknowingly resulted in their sterilization (Roberts, 1997).

Historically, controlled images of Black mothers have negatively impacted public opinion, policies, and laws. These policies and laws are often framed with intentions of assisting Black families. Yet, because they are based on stereotypical negative controlled images of Black women, their implementation do nothing less than continue marginalization and maintenance of their subordinate status (Collins, 2013; Geiger, 1995; Roberts,1997; Zerai & Banks, 2002). A complete discussion of the reproduction of negative stereotypes through controlled images and stereotypes of Black women and mothers is beyond the scope of this chapter. My intention is to explore how controlled images result in labels serving no productive purpose and only further marginalizes Black families impacted by illegal drug addiction. These images function as sense-making tools for educational and human services personnel and policy makers when considering the needs of cocaine and heroin addicted Black mothers. Black mothers' worthiness of empathy is often filtered through negative controlled images shaping decisions made to blame them for their current condition rather than help.

From 1967 to 1995, much of the research on Black families was restricted to methodologies laden with limitations (Johnson, 1995). Yet, findings from these studies informed policy makers' decisions about critical issues impacting the quality of Black mothers' lives. Research findings about Black mothers from traditional research practice was typically based on racist assumptions often highlighting only negative aspects of family life, disregarded Black families' resilience, and relied on meaningless comparative analysis with White families.

Pathological conceptual frameworks

Theoretical frameworks such as cultural deviant, cultural equivalent, and cultural variant, were traditionally used when conducting research on Black mothers living in poverty (Dickerson, 1995). These frameworks reinforced negative myths and stereotypes about Black families. The cultural deviant model, based on Eurocentric perspectives compared poor Black family life experiences with values, beliefs, and experiences of middle-class Euro-American families. Differences observed between the two groups are interpreted as deviant behavior in the Black family. Their "deviant behavior" is often considered the cause of social problems prevalent in Black families (Dickerson, 1995). Even worse, these so-called deviant behaviors are thought to be generational and perpetuated forever within families. A major premise of the deviant model is based on the assumption that slavery destroyed the Black family and eliminated the father from the family system (Dickerson, 1995).

The cultural equivalent theory is also a popular framework in research practice. This theory is based on the assumption Black families would become "normal" once they assimilated to and adopted values, beliefs, and practices of European American culture (Dickerson, 1995). Hence, Black families are to deny their cultural values, beliefs, and customs. While Black family characteristics are not directly viewed negatively, European values, beliefs and customs are promoted as superior (Dickerson, 1995).

Research based on the cultural deviant and cultural equivalent frameworks support the continued negative portrayal of Black mothers. Instead of positive self-definitions, research findings produce self-fulfilling prophecies that do not enlighten values, strengths, and variations in female-headed Black families. Knowledge claims include no analysis of external structural forces impacting their daily-lived experiences (Dickerson, 1995). In response to these limitations, the cultural variant theory emerged as a model valuing strengths and diversity in Black families. Differences are perceived in Black families as strengths and coping mechanisms for survival in an oppressive society (Dickerson, 1995). The cultural variant theory is a move toward valuing the Black mother and her children as a legitimate family structure. On the other hand, the construct "at risk" can easily be construed as a modern reproduction of previous frameworks that pathologized families of color and who are poor (Swadener, 1995). Black families disproportionally live in poverty and little research addresses their diverse economic backgrounds. Existing educational research relying on the at-risk construct and cultural deviant frameworks, result in knowledge claims failing to provide a comprehensive view of Black family resilience.

The crack ho' and her crack baby is another pathological framework resulting from the research practices and politics that suggest poor Black women are largely accountable for social problems. Many of the studies with findings challenging existing views of crack mothers embraced by the elite group of scholars and dispute that crack cocaine is related to permanent damage were undermined. Studies first published about prenatal drug use typically supported an attack on crack mothers (Zerai & Banks, 2002). Gatekeeping policies of many professional organizations only accepted presentations with claiming adverse effects of cocaine on infant development and health. These proposals were accepted five times more than research that found no adverse effects (Zerai & Banks, 2002). This has significant implications for early childhood and early childhood special education because qualitative research acknowledging intersecting oppressions are seldom accepted for publication in their top tier journals. Thus, race, class and gender oppressions experienced by Black substance abusing mothers are seldom addressed through the research process. The conceptualization, implementation and dissemination of research allow for the crack ho' and her crack baby to live on in the minds of public and professionals tasked to serve them. These research findings also promote the mythical ideas of, crack babies' futures and their at risk status of being huge social and economic burdens.

Future research on prenatal drug exposure with Black mothers should consider the social and economic context of illegal drug industries. There is a call to move beyond simply defining distorted images, manipulated public opinions, the environment as the mother's lifestyle, and ideologically based research demands (Zerai & Banks, 2002). Research becomes more meaningful when it reflects the reality and expose structural variables contributing to pregnant women's substance abuse and direct consequences for healthy development of the unborn fetus (Zerai & Banks, 2002). Embracing theoretical lens and methodological approaches acknowledging race, class, and gender oppressions will also disrupt these pathological frameworks. Research practice can defy the image of the crack ho and her crack baby when poor Black mothers' are able to self-define their experiences of drug addiction and recovery.

Our knowledge of drug addiction in Black families becomes incomplete through these narrow perspectives. Instead, exploring family functioning and child competence within the social context of their daily lives allows for a more comprehensive view of Black families. Many quantitative studies about Black families in poverty fail to provide a comprehensive lens of the neighborhood effects on child development. Additionally, family and parenting strategies that offset tribulations of living in poor neighborhoods are better illustrated in qualitative studies (Jarrett, 1997). Qualitative research about neighborhood effects on child development have potential to highlight important positive aspects of the families' daily-lived experiences. Not all Black families are adversely impacted by negative features of poor neighborhoods or the lack of basic resources (Jarrett, 1997). Instead, many families implement critical strategies to facilitate positive child development outcomes. Family practices such as family protection strategies, child-monitoring strategies, parental resource-seeking strategies, and in-home learning strategies are examples of what families living in poor neighborhoods do to remain resilient (Jarrett, 1997). Other qualitative studies suggest that poor Black women are very capable, loving and involved parents who on a daily basis successfully survived huge social and economic barriers (Cook & Fine, 1995). These works reject pathological constructs of Black families living in poverty and disrupt the master narrative offering a more informed picture of the realities of Black families.

Costs of Controlled Images of Black Motherhood

White supremacy in American institutions has set a historical pattern of stripping Black mothers of their human rights through the use of negative controlled images. More specifically, their reproduction rights have been compromised since their life on southern plantations and remained under attack across historical timelines. The slavery experience, disproportionate removal of Black children from their homes, and the sterilization of women of color illustrate the devaluation of Black motherhood. These events illustrate the institutionalized and systematic means of denying Black mothers' reproductive freedom across timelines within the context of American society (Roberts, 1997).

Controlled images of Black mothers

The mammy, breeder, jezebel, matriarch, welfare mother, welfare queen, and crack ho are common negative controlled images of Black women. Institutions advance these images through media, research practice, and policy as they misrepresent their roles and abilities as mothers depicting them as being inept at caring for and parenting their children. The first image of Black mothers was the mammy who was "loved" and garnered some authority within her so-called White family. Yet she remained in an obedient and servitude role accepting her subordination by staying in her place. Her job as a mother is to transfer her skills of Black accommodation to her next generation (Collins 2000). The mammy image was also asexual with the ability and desire to work assiduously for White people even at the expense of her own family (Collins 2013). Even after the emancipation, Black mothers continued to work outside their home doing long hours of domestic and agricultural labor for White people. This type of work was thought to compromise Black women's maternal roles, rendering her unable to manage her own home. The controlled image of the ideal mother who works inside the home with no wage labor was never a reality for Black women, leaving them to be portrayed as aberrant and negligent (Roberts, 2002).

The next image is that of the matriarch who is the bad Black mother ignoring traditional duties as a woman in the home and thus responsible for social ills in her community. Collins describes the Black matriarch as:

> Spending too much time away from home, these working mothers ostensibly could not properly supervise their children and thus were a major contributing factor to their children's failure at school. As overly aggressive, unfeminine women, Black matriarchs allegedly emasculated their lovers and husbands. These men understandably, either deserted their partners or refused to marry the mothers of their children. From the dominant group's perspective, the matriarch represented a failed mammy, a negative stigma to be applied to African American women who dared reject the image of the submissive, hardworking servant. (Collins 2000, pp. 75)

Thus, the Black mother is "damned if she does and damned if she don't," and either way she is that "bad" mother. She is considered lazy if she does not work and stays home to care for her children but irresponsible if she spends time away from them while working.

The matriarch and breeder images are the foundation of the stereotyped welfare mother whose image of Black motherhood is also to blame for the demise of the Black family structure. She was considered "bad" when motherhood for her did not match the same values and beliefs of her White counterpart (Collins, 2000). Unlike the working mother matriarch or the enslaved breeder (who was not compensated financially for having babies), the welfare mother is unemployed and is content with having babies and collecting government paychecks (Collins, 2000; Geiger, 1995; Roberts, 1997; Zerai & Banks, 2002).

Controlled images, public opinion and policy

Public opinion about poor Black mothers is often based on these stereotypes and common myths of Black women living in poverty. The idea that most poor people are on welfare and mothers have more babies to collect more benefits are common myths connected to images of welfare recipients (Geiger, 1995). The myth of the lazy Black welfare mother unable to model a work ethic for her children is powerful and has maintained longevity. For example, the then 2012 Republican party's presidential candidate and former House Speaker, Newt Gingrich in a speech on his campaign trail in December 2011 said:

> … Really poor children, in really poor neighborhoods have no habits of working. And have nobody around them who works. So they literally, they have no habit of showing up on Monday. They have no habit of staying all day, they have no habit of I do this and you give me cash, unless it's illegal. … (CNN Politics, 2011, December 5)

In an attempt to clarify his statements in response to the backlash of his comments, his comments remained with racially coded language:

> … Some people … suggest that the working poor by definition, know how to work. Which is true that is why they are called the working poor. I was talking about people who come out of … neighborhoods where they may not have that experience … (Huisenda, CBS News, 2011, December 5)

Gingrich later references that the unemployment rate for Black teenagers is 43 percent and says:

> It would be great if inner city schools and poor neighborhood schools actually hired the children to do things … What if they cleaned out the bathrooms? … what if they mopped the floors? … What if the summer they painted the school? … they were

actually learning to work, learning to earn money, they had money on their own, they didn't have to become a pimp or a prostitute or a drug dealer. If they had money on their own, they had the dignity to work and learned how to be around adults who actually wanted to mentor them ... (Tapper, ABC News, 2011 December 2)

In these segments, Newt Gingrich cleverly omitted the word Black, yet used code words (e.g. inner-city, pimps, drug dealers) signaling to many, he is obviously referring to Black children. During the Republican Presidential Debate 2012 for Fox News, Juan Williams asked Newt Gingrich "You recently said Black Americans should demand jobs and not food stamps. You also said poor kids lack a strong work ethic and propose having them work as janitors in their schools. Can't you see that this is viewed at a minimum, as insulting to all Americans, but particularly to Black Americans?" He responded "no", while the audience cheered. The crowd continuously booed Juan Williams during this presidential debate as he presented questions challenging other racially insensitive comments by Newt Gingrich (Ward, Huffington Post, 2012, January 17). Newt Gingrich as well as audience members clearly embraced the Black welfare queen and her children as their reality and truth. Thus, it remains crucial we continue to resist and expose the power and racism behind negative controlled images of Black mothers and their children.

Newt Gingrich's comments illustrate how public opinion about Black mothers is often based on stereotypes and false truths of Black women living in poverty. Another common assumption of this stereotype is the national treasury is exhausted by the welfare system and Blacks depend on welfare across several generations. Other myths include most single mothers and welfare recipients are Black, and that there is a high incidence of fraud among welfare recipients (Geiger, 1995). This resulted in the emergence of the welfare queen stereotype. Yet, Black single mothers are more likely to be negatively impacted by public policies regarding child support, child care, health care, pay equity, welfare reform, social services, affordable housing, and family-workplace issues such as maternity leave and parental leave (Geiger, 1995).

Black mothers bore the brunt of welfare policy changes from 1980 to 1984 and more likely experienced barriers and delays in receiving benefits due to these changes and bureaucratic red tape (Geiger, 1995). Although the poverty rate among female-headed households has decreased between 1967 and 1987, the prevalence of poverty among Black female-headed households remains higher than other groups in America (Geiger, 1995). Black mothers remain in poverty and in need of services more than other mothers. Yet, they are burdened with navigating social service agencies as they resist the welfare queen stereotype. The facts about welfare are inconsistent with Black mother stereotypes but are continuously advanced as factual (Collins, 2000; Geiger, 1995; Roberts, 2002; Zerai & Banks, 2002) and have even found their way into presidential campaign debates.

The stereotyped welfare mother and queen depicts Black mothers as lacking the ability to pass on a work ethic to the next generation, resulting in all Black people being racially stereotyped as lazy. This perceived laziness potentially justifies limiting assistance when indeed the problem is that support programs for poor Black female-headed households have become expensive (Collins, 2000; Geiger, 1995; Roberts, 1997; Zerai & Banks, 2002). The perceived Black mothers' laziness becomes politicized as she becomes a reasonable excuse for not providing support instead of the cost. The link between the welfare queen and the poor Black mothers' identity often serves as a rationale for welfare reform (Hancock, 2003). Thus, by controlling the welfare mother image and blaming her as the core reason for her and her community's poverty, the victim is blamed with no attention placed on the structural sources of poverty (Collins, 2000).

In the 1980's, many of Regan's administration's budget choices were justified based on negative controlled images of Black Mothers and presented them with devastating challenges (Collins, 2000; Geiger, 1995; Roberts, 2002; Zerai & Banks, 2002). During this era, the welfare queen emerged as a welfare dependent Black mother who is a domineering, manless, working-class, and highly materialistic Black woman. These images situated Black mothers as symbols of failures in American society as well as failed social policies that deplete the government's resources (Collins, 2000). The stereotypes also fall right into the hands of President Clinton and his welfare reform and drug laws that were devastating to many Black families during this era.

The focus on the welfare queen stereotype distracted us from the real consequences government program cuts for the poor and building basic infrastructures for poor communities had on Black mothers in poverty (Collins, 2000). Interestingly, these governmental policy changes occurred the same time of the infiltration of crack cocaine into many poor Black communities (Collins, 2000; Geiger, 1995; Roberts, 2002; Zerai & Banks, 2002). Simultaneously, a "War on Drugs" is waged and attacks the Black family with unfair cocaine sentences, resulting in many Black males being incarcerated for nonviolent crime such as drug possession (Alexander, 2012). Thus, limited opportunities for drug rehabilitation, inadequate medical care, lack of employment, housing, and education were detrimental to already burdened pregnant Black women overcoming drug addiction (Geiger, 1995).

Dehumanizing Black motherhood not only contributed to policies working against Black families, it also justified America's tendency to ignore Black mothers' fertility rights. Historically, Black women have seldom shared the same rights governing their fertility as their White counterparts. As far back as on southern plantations when slave masters relying on enslaved African females for breeding, stripped them of their fertility rights. Stereotyped breeder and welfare mother images benefit policies aimed at controlling Black mothers' fertility (Collins, 2000; Roberts, 1997; Zerai & Banks, 2002). Navigating these stereotypes becomes a barrier for Black women experiencing motherhood at similar levels as her White counterparts. These stereotypes reflect controlled images suggesting their fertility is not only nonessential but also possibly dangerous to the values of our country. The image of lazy welfare mothers breeding children at the taxpayers expense are widely accepted as justification for governmental policy and health care practices that negatively impact poor Black women (Roberts, 1997). These images also function as rationales for limiting Black mothers' fertility based on the dominant group's perception that they continue to have too many children who are economically unproductive (Collins, 2000). This has important implications for Black pregnant women who were drug users seeking rehabilitation. These myths attached to the breeder and welfare queen stereotypes also support the government's choice to criminalize Black mothers with punishment instead of assisting them.

Criminalization of Black Women

Public policies and laws based on negative controlled images of Black mothers predispose them to more involvement with agencies identifying them as crack mothers with crack babies as this family defies that of the ideal. Because of negative controlled images of the crack mother and poor Black women they become scapegoats for the government's failure to establish policies providing adequate support and infrastructures aimed at remedying race, class, and gender oppressions (Roberts, 2002; Zerai & Banks, 2002). This racist exclusionism in turn supports the movement to criminalize Black mothers and prosecute Black pregnant women who are crack addicted. Criminalization efforts targeted at Black prenatal drug users only exposes the hypocrisy behind the policies, practices, and laws intended to protect the fetus and child. As illustrated by the consequences of criminalization, these policies, practices and laws have very little to do with the best interest of Black children prenatally exposed to drugs (Roberts, 1997; 2002; Zerai & Banks, 2002).

The mothers in this book were selected because of their resilience and noninvolvement with social services or the law. They avoided prosecution related to their prenatal drug use even though their home states New Jersey and Michigan have prosecuted mothers for drug use during pregnancy. However, as the popularity of drugs change from crack to methamphetamine and prescription drugs so do the drug laws from the 1980's to now. In 2013, New Jersey's high court ruled doing drugs while pregnant cannot be prosecuted under child abuse laws and a positive drug test alone could not be grounds for neglect. In 2014 the same court ruled prenatal use of methadone is not abuse. In 1991, Michigan Court of Appeals decided that drug laws did not apply to pregnant drug users (Miranda, Dixon, & Reyes, 2015). Only two of the mothers, Barbara and Ladonna reported encounters with the law because of circumstances indirectly related to their drug use. Both had been arrested for shoplifting but none of the mothers in this book were arrested for using drugs while pregnant. Maybe their resilience and kinship networks shielded them from victimization of the criminalization movement of the 1980 and 1990's crack scare. However, a discussion about the criminalization of Black women as prenatal drug users is fitting because during this era at least two hundred women in thirty states were charged with maternal drug use (Roberts, 2002). Not all Black mothers addicted to heroin and crack were as fortunate as the mothers highlighted in this book.

The criminalization of Black mothers has a long history. Black motherhood has been criminalized as far back as life on the plantation when it was illegal for her to identify the father of her children (Brent, 1861). Black men were not the only causalities of the war on drugs during the crack era. Many pregnant Black mothers did not receive the same privileges as mothers like Jessica described at the beginning of the book (Roberts 2002; Zerai & Banks, 2002;). Rather, they negotiated criminal prosecution and incarceration while experiencing childbirth, motherhood and detox of drugs. Thus, Black mothers were also the victims of the prison complex industry, yet often left out of the narrative of mass incarceration. Current events of police brutality and Black women dying in police custody suggest even now, she is more likely to be treated as a criminal underserving of human rights when encountering the police. This continuously occurs throughout our country's history and is noteworthy to the discussion of Black motherhood, drug addiction and resilience. Thus, it is important to problematize the criminalization and prosecution of Black mothers as we understand their drug use during and after pregnancy as parents.

Prosecution of pregnant women

The catalyst for treating fetal abuse as a crime began with the "Roe v. Wade" (1973) court case ruling women had a right to reproductive privacy. The fetus was not considered a person but the court decision encouraged momentum for antiabortion movement. However, during the 1980's crack scare the fetus became an innocent victim of crack addiction exposed to addictive and toxic substances prenatally. The mother's crack addiction positioned her as a criminal who abuses her unborn infant giving reason for child abuse incarceration.

Criminal prosecution of prenatal drug users has not been effective socially or economically (Roberts, 2002; Washington, 2005; Zerai & Banks, 2002;). Effective treatment requires programming that meets the needs of women's drug addictions. Pregnant women who use drugs and their children benefit more from services instead of purely punitive consequences (Roberts, 2002; Washington, 2005; Zerai & Banks, 2002). Lawmakers claiming concern for the child's welfare should be challenged to closely examine the legal and social implications associated with fetal abuse legislation. Only then will the contradiction of these laws rarely serving in the best interest of children be exposed (Washington, 2005; Zerai & Banks, 2002). Criminalization of Black mothers tend to focus more on control and surveillance instead of the fetus and child's well being. The effectiveness and fairness of criminalization of fetal abuse has been questioned with no evidence suggesting these policies are effective on an economic or social level. Yet, many states continued to pursue criminal punishment for pregnant women addicted to crack. These punitive legal practices pitted the State's interest of the fetus against the mother's human, reproductive, and privacy rights (Roberts, 1997) and overwhelmingly effect poor Black mothers (Roberts, 2002; Washington, 2005; Zerai & Banks, 2002).

Criminalization of prenatal drug use

Crack cocaine drug addiction is proportionately more of a problem for poor Black mothers than powdered cocaine use. Powdered cocaine addictions are typically associated with individuals who are White and more affluent (Roberts, 2002; Zerai & Banks, 2002). Crack is a rock like substance that is smoked instead of snorted resulting in an instantaneous high and much cheaper than powdered cocaine (Roberts, 1997). Although in different forms, it is the same illegal substance.

Many pregnant Black mothers exercise caution when accessing prenatal care or decide not to because of government monitoring and intrusion in their lives. Black mothers living in poverty are more likely to be surveilled by the government (Roberts, 2002; Zerai & Banks, 2002) because their families do not match the standard of the ideal family (e.g. mother, father, two and half children). Poor Black mothers are typically discovered and targeted more because of frequent use of government agencies and racist attitudes of many health professionals that result in being reported more frequently than their White counterparts (Roberts, 2002). Subsuming to pathological frameworks' tenets of families, professionals working with Black mothers often deem their family functioning as "wrong" and in need of agency intervention and oversight.

Yet, some media outlets have attempted to correct the wrongs of their field. For example, on July 17, 2014, the headlines of an online article from the *New Republic* reads *Pregnancy: The Terrible War on Pregnant Drug Users*. Deborah L. Rhode goes on to say:

> "When Regina McNight, a young African American woman, suffered an unexpected stillbirth, she was convicted of homicide by child abuse. … used cocaine during her pregnancy … was sentenced to twelve years in prison. In 2008, the South Carolina Supreme Court overturned her conviction based on ineffective counsel at trial … McNight pleaded guilty to manslaughter … sentenced to the eight years … already served … The case exemplifies a broader trend to punish pregnant women for drug and alcohol use, particularly low-income women of color.

Earlier that same year on March 18, 2014, another article from online *ProPublica: Journalism in the Public Interest*, written by Nina Martin, March 18, 2014 says:

> Rennie Gibbs' daughter, Samiya, was a month premature when she simultaneously entered the world and left it, never taking a breath … the stillborn infant's most likely cause of death was also the most obvious: the umbilical cord wrapped around her neck. But within days of Samiya's delivery in November 2006, Steven Hayne, Mississippi's de facto medical examiner … came to a different conclusion.

The autopsy revealed traces of a cocaine byproduct in Samiya's blood and the medical examiner identified her death as a homicide due to "cocaine toxicity." This resulted in a grand jury indicting this 16-year-old Black teen for "depraved heart murder" because of crack use during pregnancy. Thus, Ms. Gibbs "unlawfully, willfully, and feloniously" killed her baby which carries a maximum prison sentence of life in prison.

Rennie Gibbs' case was later overturned in April, 2014, yet prosecutors vowed to re-indict her during summer 2014 (Martin, 2014). These two cases illustrate the problems with criminalization of young Black mothers because of their crack addictions. In this same article, lawyer Lynn Paltrov, executive director and founder of the National Advocates For Pregnant Women, points out why Ms Gibbs' case warrants attention. Mississippi's laws allow sentencing pregnant mothers as murderers, yet also holds the worst record for maternal and infant health in the United States. She further explains that "The biggest threats to life, born and unborn, do not come from mommies but rather from poverty, barriers to health care, persistent racism, environmental hazards, and prosecutions like these" (Martin, 2014).

Acceptance of stereotypes of the crack ho' and crack baby justified the criminalization and prosecution of Black mothers using illegal substances which gained momentum during the mid 1980's. These controlled images are directly linked to ineffective policies and laws for prenatal drug users, usually Black women (Frank & Zuckerman, 1993; Gomez, 1997; Paltrow & Flavin, 2013; Roberts, 1997; Swadener, 1995; Zerai & Banks, 2002). The prosecution of pregnant Black mothers addicted to crack highlight issues of equality and rights of privacy. This legal action is situated in a political and historical context that restricts reproductive choice for Black women who live in poverty. Black mothers addicted to crack are prosecuted for deciding to have a baby but would not be for having an abortion (Roberts, 1997).

Race, class, and gender oppressions are manifested in legal practices of punishing and not assisting Black pregnant drug users (Roberts, 1997, 2002; Washington, 2005; Zera & Banks, 2002;). This also accounts for the inhumane treatment of pregnant Black women addicted to drugs. Many of these women deliver babies under harsh conditions like being handcuffed to beds and or taken directly to a jail cell after delivery sometimes without even a sanitary napkin (Roberts, 1997, 2002). Similar to child-birthing experiences on the plantation, Black mothers give birth under horrendous conditions with no dignity as their newborn is removed from them immediately (Roberts, 1997, 2002). These same mothers are also simultaneously burdened with the physical, psychological and medical aspects of detoxing from their chemical addiction with no assistance living in a jail cell.

The criminalization of prenatal crack use began in 1989 in Florida when a 23-year-old Black mother was the first to be prosecuted. After both of her children tested positive for cocaine sixty seconds after birth, Ms. Johnson was charged with delivering a controlled substance to a minor (Roberts, 1995).

Prosecutions of pregnant Black mothers using crack reached its peak during the same time crack businesses overflowed in many poor Black communities. Thus, Black mothers were granted instant access to crack while drug rehabilitation was only an option to mostly White affluent mothers. Poor Black mothers might have had easier access to purchasing crack than a healthy meal for her family.

Criminalizing prenatal crack using mothers disproportionately impacts Black mothers. If the true intention of prosecution is to protect the unborn from harm, the focus would not be solely on crack cocaine (Roberts, 1997). There is evidence that alcohol, tobacco, and nicotine do far more harm to the unborn fetus (Roberts, 1997; Zerai & Banks, 2002) than crack cocaine and heroin. Drinking during pregnancy has the potential to cause Fetal Alcohol Sydrome often associated with birth defects and intellectual disabilities. Smoking cigarettes while pregnant is linked to spontaneous abortions and Sudden Infant Death Sydrome (SIDS). During the crack scare, there were more babies born with prenatal exposure to alcohol and cigarettes than crack (Roberts, 1997). Therefore, focusing on crack use cannot be justified based solely on the harm crack does to the fetus or number of women addicted to crack compared to alcohol and nicotine. Also, prosecutors typically base their claims on the delivery of crack to the fetus by the mother, not prenatal drug exposure to the infant (Robert, 1997). The delivery of crack is the criminal offense keeping the focus on the Black mother who has already been deemed unworthy of motherhood.

Had the focus of prosecution been on alcohol or prescription medication instead of crack, the trend to criminalize pregnant women would have been short lived during the 1980's. Pregnant mothers ingesting these substances would include more White mothers representing the model image of motherhood. This is illustrated by the current rise in heroin use in White communities and society's more humanizing response focused on treatment not criminalization, like with Jessica. Keeping the crack ho' as the dominant image to shape prenatal drug law and policy, maintains the focus on the crack-addicted mother and not on other important issues related to illegal drug businesses. Thus, no real war on drugs occurs and poverty, racism, and ineffective health care policies resulting in high infant mortality rate among poor Black mothers remain unanalyzed. The compelling image of the crack ho is used to disable analysis of related social causes to prenatal drug use among Black mothers.

Although, the devaluation of Black women as mothers has roots in slavery, it persisted by punishing poor Black women's reproductive choices and dehumanizing them as mothers. Calling attention to the historical and political context of criminalizing Black mothers exposes the contradictory and racist nature of governmental policies and practices. The government's response to prenatal use of crack should be to value the personhood of Black mothers and award her the same rights as their White counterparts. Thus, providing opportunities for medical services, drug rehabilitation and treatment for both the Black mother and her unborn infant with care and compassion would be called for in a humane society.

The legal practice of prosecuting Black pregnant women using crack appears to more likely maintain their oppression instead of actually assisting their children. The horrible conditions of American prisons, like access to street drugs among many other factors compromises a healthy prenatal environment. Pregnant Black mothers who use illegal substances such as crack, heroin and marijuana can be provided comprehensive interventions like Jessica and Casey discussed at the beginning of the book. Such a response requires systems to value the pregnant Black woman as a legitimate mother the same as her White counterpart addicted to heroin and prescription drugs. If the responses were equitable, Black pregnant mothers would be warranted the same protections from illegal substances allowing them to heal as a family, moving forward like Jessica and Casey. The intent here is not to ignore the well being of the drug exposed infant or prioritize the mother's personhood over the needs of her child. Instead, my goal is to examine how the movement to criminalize Black mothers addicted to drugs is historical, steeped in racial prejudice and further marginalizes her entire family. This criminalization movement ignores Black family resilience and does not provide opportunities for Black mothers using drugs to recover and shift her family towards a path of progress and hope.

Rethinking prosecution and prenatal drug use

Resisting the power of the crack ho' and her crack baby, requires us to question the democracy claimed to be imbedded in our country, especially within our legal system. In order to change the systemic response mechanism of criminalization to prosecute Black mothers addicted to drugs, it is essential that we understand the heuristics that guide and justify this. It is easier for society to embrace the crack ho' and baby image advanced as the face of drug addiction among Black mothers, than to expose and understand the underlying inequities of the system. Negative controlled images of Black motherhood block our ability to see how poor Black mothers are treated in comparison to their middle-class White counterparts. For example, there is a discrepancy in how mothers experience United States health care systems and employment policies that demonstrate White middle-class lives are privileged and valued more than those of poor Black women (Zerai & Banks, 2002).

Challenging the unjust laws supporting the inhumane treatment of pregnant Black women and shifting to a more humanizing process requires a focus on treatment that is fair, caring and compassion. One approach may include multidisciplinary collaboration among practitioners such as doctors, nurses, school aged educators, early childhood education, as well as the legal system to prioritize compassion over harsh punishment (Lee & Zerai, 2010). This multidisciplinary approach should seek to demarginalize Black mothers with addictions by deconstructing the myth of the crack ho' and her crack baby. Demarginalization, mutually trusting relationships, quality of life and social functions are important program components for successful treatments. However, criteria from program success should be reconceptualized to include participants' voice as they articulate their own experiences and processes for successful drug treatment (Lee & Zerai, 2010).

As we noticed with Jessica in the beginning of the book, the legal, medical, and media response to her maternal addictions were met with compassion. Her recovery process was not burdened by challenging the stigma like that of a crack ho.' Instead, she received comprehensive assistance that focused on her empowerment and access to treatment as well as her total well-being. Jessica was able to initiate help for treatment without the dreadful fear of Casey being removed from her custody or going to jail. Instead of criminalizing Black mothers who struggle with drug use, they should be afforded the same response as Jessica to her battle with addiction. Exposing the unfair implications and race, class, and gender oppressions of the prenatal exposure legal practices for Black mothers provides critical information for social change. Particular attention should also be made to a critical analysis of the political, sociocultural and economic context of illegal crack and heroin industries in Black communities.

The next chapter examines the historical, sociopolitical and economic context of the mothers' experiences with drug addictions in Atlantic City, Detroit and New York City. We will also learn more about Barbara, Ladonna, Desirea, Bethena and Sharonda as I discuss their introduction to drug use.

References

Alexander, M. (2012). *The new Jim Crow: Mass incarceration in the age of colorblindness*. New York, NY: New Press.
Brent, L. (1861). *Incidents in the life of a slave girl*. Boston: Published For The Author.
Collins, P. H. (2000). *Black feminist thought* (2nd ed.). New York: Routledge.
Collins, P. H. (2013). *On intellectual activism*. Philadelphia, PA: Temple University Press.
Cook, D. A., & Fine, M. (1995). "Motherwit": Childrearing lessons from African American mothers of low income. In B. B. Swadener & S. Lubeck (Eds.), *Children and families "at promise": Deconstructing the discourse of risk* (pp. 118–142). Albany, NY: State University of New York Press.
CNN Politics. (Aired 2011, December 5). Gingrich: Poor kids have no work habits. Retrieved from http://www.cnn.com.
Dickerson, B. (1995). Centering studies of African American single mothers and their families. In B. Dickerson (Ed.), *African American single mothers: Understanding their lives and families* (pp. 1–20). Thousand Oaks, CA: Sage Publications.
Frank, D. A., & Zuckerman, B. S. (1993). Children exposed to cocaine prenatally: Pieces of the puzzle. *Neurotoxicology and Teratology, 15*, 298–300.
Geiger, S. M. (1995). African American single mothers: Public perceptions and public policies. In K. M. Vaz (Ed.), *Black women in America* (pp. 244–257). Thousand Oaks, CA: Sage Publications.
Gomez, L. A. (1997). *Misconceiving mothers: Legislators, prosecutors, and the politics of prenatal drug exposure*. Philadelphia, PA: Temple University Press.
Hancock, A. (2003). Contemporary welfare reform and the public identity of the "welfare queen." *Race, Gender and Class, 10*, 31–59.
Huisenda, S. (2011, December 5). *Gingrich seeks to clarify statements on poor children and work*. Retrieved from http://www.cbsnews.com.
Jarrett, R. (1997). Bringing families back in: Neighborhood effects on child development. In J. Brooks-Gunn, G. J. Duncan, J. L. Aber (Eds.), *Neighborhood poverty, Vol. II: Policy implications in studying neighborhoods* (pp. 48–64). New York: Russell Sage Foundation.
Johnson, L. (1995). Three decades of black family empirical research: Challenges for the 21st century. In H. McAdoo (Ed.), *Black Families* (3rd. ed., pp. 167–182). Thousand Oaks, CA: Sage Publications.
Lee, H. S., & Zerai, A. (2010). "Everyone deserves services no matter what:" Defining success in harm-reduction-based substance user treatment. *Substance Use & Misuse, 45*(14), 2411–2427.
Martin, N. (2014, March 18). A stillborn child, a charge of murder and the disputed case law on 'fetal harm. *ProPublica: Journalism in the Public Interest*. Retrieved from http://www.propublica.org.
McAdoo, H. (1998). African-American families: Strengths and realities. In H. I. McCubbin, E. A. Thompson, A. I. Thompson, & J. A. Futrell (Eds.), *Resiliency in African-American families* (pp. 17–30). Thousand Oaks, CA; Sage Publications.

McAdoo, H. & McAdoo, J. (1985). Preface. In H. P. McAdoo & J. L. McAdoo (Eds.), *Black children: social, educational, and parental environments* (preface). Thousand Oaks, California: Sage Publications.

Miranda, L., Dixon, V., & Reyes, C. (2015). How states handle drug use during pregnancy. *ProPublica: Journalism in the Public Interest*. Retrieved from http://www.propublica.org.

Paltrow, L. M., & Flavin, J. (2013). The policy and politics of reproductive health arrests of and forced interventions on pregnant women in the United States, 1973–2005: Implications for women's legal status and public health. *Journal of Health Politics, Policy and Law*, 38(2), 299–343.

Roberts, D. E. (1997). *Killing the Black body: Race, reproduction, and the meaning of liberty*. New York, NY: Pantheon Books a Division of Random House.

Roberts, D. E. (2002). *Shattered bonds: The color of child welfare*. New York, NY: Basic Civitas Books.

Roe v. Wade. (1973). 410 U.S. 113.

Rhode, D. L. (2014, July 17). Pregnancy: The terrible war on pregnant drug users. *New Republic*. Retrieved from http://www.newrepublic.com.

Swadener, B. B. (1995). Children and families "at promise": Deconstructing the discourse of risk. In B. B. Swadener & S. Lubeck (Eds.), *Children and families "at promise": Deconstructing the discourse of risk* (pp. 17–49). Albany, NY: State University of New York Press.

Tapper, J. (2011, December 2). Gingrich says Obama must have cognitive-dissonance about plight of African-American community. *ABC News*. Retrieved from http://abcnews.go.com.

Ward, J. (2012 January 17). Newt Gingrich seeks South Carolina boost from racially charged exchange with Juan Williams. Retrieved from http://www.huffingtonpost.com.

Washington, D. A. (2005). "Every shut eye, ain't sleep": Exploring the impact of crack cocaine sentencing and the illusion of reproductive rights for Black women from a critical race feminist perspective. *Journal of Gender, Social Policy and the Law*, 13, 123–137.

Zerai, A., & Banks, R. (2002). *Dehumanizng discourse, anti-drug law, and policy in America: A "crack mother's" nightmare*. Burlington, VT: Ashgate Publishing.

· 4 ·

"FROM SUGA TO SHIT"

The Drug Business and Destruction of Black Communities

Historically, Black communities have been disfranchised by the larger society baring the burden of criminal enterprises. Government data suggest that heroin and crack cocaine addiction remains an American problem (NIDA, 2015, September 10). Yet, it is typically Black residents who are forced to live in dangerous communities overwhelmed by the illegal drug industries. Seldom do drug addicts frequent suburban White neighborhoods looking for places to purchase and use crack and heroin. The political and economic landscape of illegal drug industries is significant to the discussion of prenatal drug exposure among Black mothers. Survival texts from the mothers in this book emerged from daily-lived experiences in communities where historically, Black people were able to maintain a middle and upper class lifestyle economically and socially. Political and economic downfalls in these cities were the backdrop for the mothers' stories of their own unique experiences with crack and heroin businesses. This chapter discusses the history of crack and heroin as well as the political and economic context of Black communities laying the foundation for these successful businesses. The mothers in this book are also introduced as the drug industries in their perspective cities Detroit, Atlantic City, and New York are discussed.

Perfect Space for Heroin and Crack Industries

Understanding the historical context of the abundance of heroin and crack in Black communities provides important insights into the nuances of the crack and heroin industries. The beginnings of illegal drug businesses shed light as to why it appears to be an endless stream of crack and heroin into Black communities. Why were poor Black neighborhoods ideal environments for the crack business? In the spirit of an "imagined global reality" (Wilson, 2007, p. 147), Black communities have suffered at the hands of public policy and planning that supported the demise of impoverished Black neighborhoods and their residents. This places many poor Black neighborhoods in a position to be easily exploited financially. Wilson describes this ruin in the following excerpt about public policy and the economic and educational context:

> ... desperately poor and dispirited people now struggle to make lives within new institutional and economic circumstances: trapping Workfare programs, low-wage dead-end jobs, church rooted assistance centers, acres of disinvested blocks, predatory retail configurations, weakened health-care providers, and punitive police and court systems. ... public schools have deteriorated ... with eviscerated funds and depleted staffs, increasingly operate as institutions of confinement that less educate than hold and contain. Schools struggle to teach this youth within punishing, segregative neoliberal times. (Wilson, p. 147)

The political landscape and realities of poor Black communities described by Wilson (2007) above provided the milieu for Black youth to make a reasonable career choice (Adler, 1995) in a booming crack business. These communities became prime locations for setting up shop for the crack cocaine industry. Considering, extreme social and economic decline, one could surmise that crack was a great rare business opportunity (Adler, 1995). Major changes in the political landscape during the 1980's help set the stage for the explosion of the crack business. Declined manufacturing industries and increase in services occurred while both manufacturing and services relocated to the suburbs and President Reagan reduced social support services. Typically poor urban residents relied on these manufacturing jobs to lift them out of poverty. Also, opportunities to relocate and train for new jobs and receive family support while still living in poverty were key to survival (Agar, 2003).

Crack distribution provided employment opportunities (Agar, 2003) and ironically some individuals addicted were able to work in the industry in order to supply their habit (Williams, 1992). While results of governmental policies set the stage for a prosperous crack business, unfair laws and policies further devastated those in the Black community who became addicted. Yet, this acknowledgement should never negate the responsibility individuals involved in the crack business bare for their role in the demise of their own neighborhoods.

Historically, the United States government has used "drug scares" (Reinarman & Levine 1997, p. 1) irrespective of actual increased drug use to advance political agendas. These scares provided a platform to advance a narrative suggesting social problems were the result of a particular chemical. However, this chemical substance would be used as a scapegoat typically linked to subordinate groups such as working-class immigrants, racial or ethnic minorities, and rebellious youth (Reinarman & Levine, 1997). However, the most severe drug scare of the twentieth century occurred from 1986 to 1992 (Reinarman & Levine, 1997) resulting in flawed social policy due to the so-called war on drugs.

Government data suggested prior to the arrival of crack, heroin addiction was already prevalent in many impoverished minority urban communities (Agar, 2003). While heroin addiction was an existing problem, the production and sale of cocaine was also on the increase in these same impoverished communities prior to crack. Prior to the onset of crack, both cocaine and heroin use had increased with heroin being even more prevalent for a brief time period (Agar, 2003). The government had knowledge of existing cocaine and heroin drug addictions in impoverished Black communities but where was the media hype then? Black drug use did not become a media craze until it served political purposes. Although crack was a new form of cocaine, crack was not the Black resident's introduction to dangerous street drugs. Yet, this was the master narrative advanced about crack resulting in the emergence of public policy and laws negatively impacting Black people generations later.

Historical Context Heroin and Crack

Heroin

The illegal drug industry has called Black communities home for decades. While heroin and crack addictions continue, their historical roots and introduction to the Black communities are quite different. Understanding the historical processes is key to enhancing our knowledge about drug use trends among specific groups of people (Agar & Reisinger, 2002). Ethnographic work on the political and economic context of the heroin epidemic among Blacks in Baltimore in the 1960's suggests two major culprits. One contributing factor was the change in the distribution and supply of heroin. The second reason was related to the mixed feelings of hope and dispair from the early civil rights movement (Agar & Reisinger, 2002).

Prior to World War ll, heroin addiction was only prevalent in major cities and the addicts were typically White males. In the late 1950's heroin trafficking was mainly linked from France to the Mafia wholesalers in the United States (Agar & Reisinger, 2002). Prior to the 1960's, heroin use among Blacks and Hispanics was confined to the music industry and used among those on the bebop jazz scene. This changed in the 1960's when Fidel Castro attempted to remove the American Mafia from Cuba modifying their functions in the United States. This change and Kennedy's anti-organized crime efforts resulted in American Mafia's financial incentives to provide Blacks and Hispanics opportunities for heroin distribution. Black and Hispanic heroin distribution coupled with turmoil of struggling for equality contributed to the rapid increase in heroin addictions among the Blacks in Baltimore during the 1960's (Agar & Reisinger, 2002). While Baltimore is quite different than New York City and Atlantic City, each are well known cities on the east coast within relative close proximity to each other.

Crack

Heroin has been on the scene in Black communities prior to 1960's and continues to remain a problem. However in the 1980's, crack cocaine advanced as the main drug destroying Black communities. Crack's "entre" into the Black community was intense but has a unique history often absent from the discourse of crack addiction. After the 1960's, cocaine was widely accepted as a safe nonaddictive drug used simply as a party drug (Agar, 2003). Smoking cocaine was popular during the mid 1970s, when freebasing was reserved mainly for Hollywood jetsetters, pro-athletes, musicians, and stockbrokers (Reinarman & Levine, 2004). During this time cocaine was a status symbol for those considered to be successful (Agar, 2003).

While cocaine use for some did spiral out of control with life changing experiences, others were able to engage in the pleasurable experiences of cocaine with no life altering effects (Agar, 2003). It was not until the 1980's when the problems of powder cocaine were beginning to surface as a response to media stories about celebrity deaths and near death encounters (e.g. John Belushi's death, Richard Pryor's near death). In the 1980's, Arnold Washton, an established clinical psychologist in East Harlem, New York who ran a heroin treatment center began to see an emergence of patients for cocaine addictions. His clientele was 20 to 30 years old, White, middle-to-upper class and employed without a history of drug or psychiatric problems. It typically took these patients five years to seek out treatment for their addictions and came to Washton after seeking help from others who insisted cocaine was not an addictive drug (Agar, 2003).

For decades, the government has always been informed of this country's drug use trends but responds to the problem according to needs of politicians. However, Congress responded to the cocaine problem in the early 1980's in a manner supportive of the wellbeing of those addicted. During this time, Congress responded to this drug trend among wealthy drug abusers with laws requiring health insurance to cover drug rehabilitation (Agar, 2003). Thus, emerged the treatment industry with increasing number of available beds. During the next decade, smoking cocaine in the form of crack emerged in impoverished Black and Latino communities. Congress then replaced treatment center beds with jail cells. Congress passed laws to extend criminal sentences for crack offenses, hence the prison industry with increased numbers of available cells requiring new residents (Agar, 2003).

The discourses of policy-makers, legislators, and law enforcement promoted by the negative controlled images of Black motherhood shaped public policy and opinions about Black motherhood and addiction. Likewise, myths and negatively controlled images of crack made it a Black drug linking it to the master narrative of crack addiction. Five myths contribute to many of the inhumane public policies addressing the problem of crack cocaine (Reinarman & Levine, 2004). These myths resulted in racist representations and negative controlled images of crack cocaine users.

One major myth is crack is a different drug than cocaine and is instantly and inevitably addicting. Other myths suggest that crack spreads to all sectors of society, causes crime and violence, and crack use during pregnancy causes crack babies (Reinarman & Levine, 2004). These myths along with visible drug markets, economic problems and racist images contributed to crack becoming a "Black drug" (Agar, 2003) and the crack scare (Reinarman & Levine, 2004). Both cause an unprecedented disproportionate imprisonment of poor Black and Latino people in the United States. Instead of unfair harsh punishments, the more humane, "American" and effective response would have been implementing a national plan to address the housing, school, and employment crisis. This response may have given inner city residents realistic hopes for a better future (Reinarman & Levine, 2004). Instead, families and communities generations later are still coping with the devastating consequences of the drug business, laws and policies from the crack era.

I carefully considered whether or not to identify the mothers' cities or keep them anonymous. Given the historical, economic and sociocultural context of both cities and their significance to the cocaine and heroin industries, I decided to name each site. This also holds true for New York City where Desirea remained active in her heroin addiction but was interviewed in Atlantic City. Although vastly different cities, both Detroit and Atlantic City were impacted by heroin dealing but were completely devastated by the crack industry. Detroit, Atlantic City, and New York City's illegal drug industries were so rampant that the major drug kingpins inspired major motion pictures or television documentaries about their businesses.

Mothers and Detroit's Crack Business

Sharonda

Sharonda and Bethena were both addicted to crack cocaine and lived in Detroit, Michigan. Sharonda was a 44-year-old mother with 10 children and was a new bride at the time of our conversations. She used crack regularly for 17 years since she was 27 years old with three years of sobriety.

Sharonda was a well-groomed woman who looked much younger than a forty-four year old and held various jobs since she was a young girl until her drug addiction. Until she left high school, she worked through a student coop program with Detroit Public Schools and as a sales clerk at Hudson's Department Store Downtown. At that time, Hudson's was a famous Michigan store being the tallest department store in the world and was only second in size to Macy's Department Store in New York City. As with the automobile industry, Hudson's declined over the years and the store was demolished in 1998 (Austin, n.d.).

After high school, Sharonda worked her way up to manager at Dairy Queen for five years and later in 1997 worked in the operations division at Detroit City Airport. In 2003, she became office manager for a mortgage company, eventually becoming a loan officer and remained on this job until a conflict with a coworker. During this time most of the jobs and services were now located in Detroit suburbs, where Sharonda later worked also as a loan officer. Unfortunately, she terminated her employment there because she did not have transportation to get from the city to her job located in the suburb. At the time of our conversations, she was working at one of her daughter's middle school as a cafeteria and classroom assistant.

Bethena

Except for during their active crack addictions, Sharonda and Bethena both maintained employment while living in Detroit. Bethena is originally from a southern rural town but had relatives in Detroit employed by automobile factories. A year after high school graduation, she migrated to Detroit and shortly afterwards became employed with a major automobile company. In 1976, Bethena gained access to employment providing a middle-class lifestyle in a matter of days after she put in an application. These job opportunities are basically nonexistent now in Detroit because several automobile plants are completely closed. Her job allowed her financial independence as a single mother. With her salary, she was able to purchase a car and home in a middle class neighborhood and remain employed until 1987, when she was introduced to crack cocaine.

Detroit's Crack Business

Unfortunately, like many impoverished Black communities during the 1980's, Detroit was a prime location for the crack business. Wilson's (2007) earlier descriptions of the political and economic landscape of most poor Black communities during the 1980's mirrored the plight of Detroit at that time. By this time, the booming automobile industry was over and Detroit had already began to experience a recession in the late 1970's with many plants closing. With Hudson Department Store and several plant closures and loss of jobs, the city's capital as well as middle and working class residents left for the suburbs. When Black residents with financial means moved from the inner city, community infrastructures such as recreation centers, small businesses, and schools began to diminish (Adler, 1995). Thus, by the 1980's even entry-level dead end jobs were nonexistent and the "the inner-city economy was driven largely underground and entrepreneurial, and among the leading entrepreneurs, the community's new role models, were the Chambers brothers" (Adler, p. 9). The Chambers Brothers are the 1980's infamous crack cocaine dealers of Detroit who inspired the movie *New Jack City* (1991).

It was during the 1980's when Bethena was introduced to crack through her relationship with a male coworker. This was around the same time the Chambers Brothers family's migration from Arkansas to Detroit led them to becoming one of the wealthiest residents of the city through their crack business (Adler, 1995). Billy Chambers began selling marijuana out of his party store in Detroit.

He subsequently lost his liquor license and began to sell crack from his house in 1984. That same year during a Fourth of July holiday, Billy Chambers made $10,000 in one day from selling crack having more customers than he had product. Thus, began The Chambers Brothers' crack business and by 1986, their business was the major industry on Detroit's east side (Adler, 1995).

The American Dream was virtually an unobtainable goal for many who left the Southern plantation fields to come to inner city ghettos. However, the automobile industry allowed those escaping the horrors of Jim Crow and southern racism to participate in the American Dream. The disappearance of the automobile plants by 1980, left little or no hope for many seeking this Dream in Detroit. The Chambers Brothers were intelligent and ambitious young Black men seeking the wealth, power, and respect of the great American Dream. They viewed crack as a profitable enterprise and opportunity for upward mobility. Thus, in the 1980's they became two of Detroit's most successful entrepreneurs (Adler, 1995). That is of course until their arrests in 1988.

The devastation on the daily lives of residents in poor Black Detroit neighborhoods and on those crack addicted grew rapidly in a short period. Bethena reported that life for her started to go downhill rather quickly after she started smoking crack. She would eventually lose her daughter, her home, and her job. Here Billy Chambers explains this destruction upon his return to Detroit after being away for only one year:

> When Billy returned, crack was everywhere: on every block of the east side neighborhoods he frequented, in party stores ... fast-food restaurants ... street corners, in houses, and apartment buildings. The change was startling: 'Peoples I never thought would be hooked was ripping and running the streets wild,' he says 'And peoples I never thought would be selling crack were selling it. Everything was just different, everybody acting different.' (Adler, 1995, p. 117)

Prior to the arrival of crack in 1983, only 100 patients were in Detroit's treatment clinics for cocaine use. Yet, during the peak of the Chambers brothers' business in 1987 there were approximately 4,500 patients. There was also an increase in emergency-room visits from 450 (in 1983) to 3,811 (in 1987) related to cocaine (Adler, 1995).

Not all automobile plants were closed in the 1980's and a segment of autoworkers remained gainfully employed but did not escape the wrath of crack addiction. Bethena and select coworkers from her job were introduced to crack during this time frame. She shared stories about how the majority of, if not all of her coworkers' salary went directly to the dope man as she would collect their checks for crack payments. Bethena says

> ... like I say money wasn't a problem, he was working at (automobile company), I was workin at (automobile company) and we had a couple more friends working at (automobile company). And we getting all this beaucoup money and everybody putting they money together, and it wasn't a problem cause everybody had money and we smoking, smoking. ...

The devastation and consequences of crack addiction was swift and intense. Bethena developed a serious relationship with a male coworker whom she later realized was addicted to crack. This same guy turned some of her cousins, friends and herself on to smoking crack. It did not take long, she says "... every damn body that ... with us and our family was on crack. One little guy, got everybody ... smoking this here crack ..." Bethena shared how she just wanted to try it because everybody else was doing it "... but God knows that I didn't have no idea that the drug was that detrimental. That the drug was that potent, that it could just, just the craving of it was so strong ..."

Bethena illustrates the financial cost of her crack addiction here when she says

> ... Like I said, I live on northwest side, all of them live on the east side. So I had a house and ... workin at (Company's name) ... a two car garage and everything. Doing fine me and my daughter (oldest).

She could not understand why her male friend making the same salary became homeless and lost his vehicle. Bethena shared:

> "... but I didn't realize what it meant until later, years later ... that the crack wouldn't let you have any thang. And I let him move in and it went from suga ta shit in six months in a year. ... like I said, working at (automobile company), had so much money ... Chile, before I knew it I was smoking shit, got hooked, crack said leave your job at (automobile company). Walked away ... It just turned my world upside down honey.

Bethena's story is consistent with Billy Chambers' (Adler, 1995) account of the rapid destruction caused by crack addiction in Detroit during such a short time frame. I want to point out that Bethena's economic status was not a buffer from the demise of crack addiction. The economic consequences though are startling, as we consider the lost annual salaries and generational wealth from Bethena's, her friends and family's contribution to the crack industry. Although, Bethena lived in a nice home with a two-car garage on one side of town, she spent quite a bit of time on Detroit's east side with family and friends, where Billy Chambers mentioned earlier, crack reigned king.

Through Bethena's employment at the automobile plant, she established the American Dream, moving beyond self-proclaimed poverty that she left in her rural southern hometown. Her place of employment, a house in a nice neighborhood, two-car garage, and a new model car became symbols of the American Dream for many Blacks who migrated to Detroit. Unfortunately, the introduction of crack rapidly changed Bethena's class status "from suga ta shit in six months in a year" as crack depleted her financial resources and ruined her career at the automobile plant. The fluid boundaries between the Black middle-class and the criminal element in lower –class Black neighborhoods allowed Bethena easy access to crack and other criminal elements (Patillo-McCoy, 1999). This access to crack during the reign of The Chambers Brothers' crack empire spiraled into an addiction that quickly derailed her life from any sense of humanness. During her active crack addiction, she was just treated "any o kinda way" just because she was a female and addicted to crack. Bethena smoked cracked consistently until her youngest daughter was two years old. This daughter was a senior in high school at the time of our interviews.

Desirea and New York's Heroin Business

Desirea was interviewed in Atlantic City but was raised in a New York Borough and lived there during her active addiction to heroin. At the time of our interviews, Desirea was in her mid-fifties and misused heroin from her teenage years throughout most of her adulthood. She has one adult daughter and five grandchildren. Desirea received prenatal care and her daughter was born full-term with no complications.

As a teen-ager, Desirea worked at a dry cleaners, restaurant, American International Press and World Counsel of Churches. She also worked for a real estate company and referred to herself as a street peddler. Although Desirea was not HIV positive, she received money to participate in a research project about HIV while she was enrolled in a methadone clinic in New York. She was able to maintain employment throughout her addiction. She distinguishes herself between a street addict and working addict when she says "Late 80's early 90's … worked real estate too for a time period. Sometimes … work two jobs, along with that, I was also still active … was one of those working addicts. I wasn't no street addict."

As a young adult, Desirea sang in a small band spending quite a bit of time hanging out with musicians during her years of addiction. As mentioned earlier, heroin use was initially associated with musicians yet, she distinctly recalls being fully engaged in her heroin addiction by high school. This time period also happens to be the peak of infamous Frank Lucas' heroin business. Frank Lucas is the drug lord whose life inspired the motion picture *American Gangster* (2007). According to Lucas' interview for BET's documentary *American Gangster Series* (2007), he made at least one million dollars a day proclaiming "I want to be rich. I want to be Donald Trump rich. And ... I made it."

Frank Lucas moved to Harlem in late 1940s from a small farming town in North Carolina where his parents were sharecroppers. At a very young age, Lucas witnessed the brutal murder of his young cousin by the Ku Klux Klan. As a result of racism and this life-changing event, he moved to Harlem and became immediately impressed, wanting to join the life style of affluent Blacks in Harlem. By 1959, sixty percent of the heroin traffickers were Black and by the mid 1970s, New York City was considered *Smack Central*, with smack being the nickname for heroin. Lucas initially went to jail in 1976 and was released in 1981. Three years later, he went back to jail and has been out of prison since 1991 (*BET American Gangster*, 2007).

The late 1960's and throughout the 1970's, Frank Lucas' drug empire reigned supreme by the time Desirea was in the tenth grade and thoroughly drenched in her heroin addiction. Black neighborhoods in Harlem were completely devastated by the open-air heroin market during Lucas' million dollar a day business (*BET American Gangster*, 2007). Harlem was not the only neighborhood impacted by the explosion of heroin addiction. Desirea describes this devastation:

> It was snowballing ... we was at a hookey party ... snuck in the building. That would be the very first time that I was introduced ... You know this is crazy, cause when I think about it we could have killed ourselves. So many had overdosed ... This was about 68 or 69 ... in the newspaper that day ... a 12-year-old was found on the rooftop down in Harlem, with a needle in his arm. 12 years old. Dead from a drug overdose. A Heroin overdose. And I didn't never connect the thing that I had sniffed that day ... tried to be with the crowd. ... That was some place I had no business being ... you didn't know how to get out of this thing.

Desirea was first introduced to heroin during the day when she should have been in school. Instead, she skipped school and tried heroin under peer pressure. She reportedly began hanging with this group because they would bully her fiercely daily until she finally joined them. Initially, she tried not to skip what she referred to as "important" classes because of her continued interest in learning. Eventually, her academic interests were overpowered by the call of her heroin addiction. Desirea and her associates would also skip class returning to school high. Unfortunately, during her early years of addiction and Lucas' heroin business it was not unusual to see students under the influence at her high school.

> ... But the teachers were aware ... police department doing the same thing. ... And they take it out their (police) pockets and put it back out there and say it was stolen. You got rogue cops just like you got rogue teachers ... this thing with drugs in school was just like a fire. Man, it was exploding. It look like everybody was on drugs (heroin) all of a sudden. Not too many kids had missed that one. We went heroin mixin. ... We was gettin stuff that you know, (laughing), we didn't have to pal around whatever to get it ... was in our neighborhood and at school. We had opium ... heroin ... cocaine ... all the liquor and beer you could get. ... An adult would gladly go in there for you and get it.

When Desirea refers to "rogue" teachers she indicts important school personnel for turning a blind eye to and benefitting from students' drug addiction. She recalls being in class visibly under the influence of heroin, singled out and sent to the office to speak with two female guidance counselors.

> ... I can't say on a regular basis. But I know that day what I seen. (using her fingers to tap on the table) ... we was called from the classroom ... We was all sitting there we were stoned to the hills. And was all sitting like this in the class OK (she imitates nodding) and the teacher all had us removed. ... And nobody ... ain't call no parents ... sent us to these 2 counselors ...

The guidance counselors, in possession of heroin asked Desirea's friend about its street value and threatened to call his parents if he did not respond.

> ... And he told him cause, they told him ... we was gone get suspended and they was gone tell his mother ... So he told the street value. And he put it back in his (the student) hands. And we was suppose to turn it over that night. ... I'm very serious. They put it back in his hand and made us turn it over. So that made me feel like the school know ...

School should be a place of learning for Desirea. Instead, her experiences with schoolmates led to her heroin addiction in the late 1960's when Frank Lucas' heroin business flooded Black New York neighborhoods. Her heroin addiction haunted her from that time until her recovery in 1996.

Mothers and Atlantic City's Drug Business

Ladonna

Ladonna was 44 years old when we met living in Atlantic City with her husband and youngest daughter. She is the mother of two girls who during our conversation were 24 and 13 years old. Ladonna received prenatal care for both of her girls and they were each full-term pregnancies. She smoked cigarettes and used powder cocaine all day throughout her pregnancies with both daughters reporting that she used cocaine for seven months with her oldest daughter and nine months with her youngest. Ladonna also used crank (methamphetamine) all day on a daily basis with her oldest daughter until her seventh month. Both of Ladonna's daughters had some medical difficulties during birth. Her first daughter went through drug withdrawals and the youngest daughter had a prolonged hospital stay after Ladonna was discharged.

At the time of our conversations, Ladonna had been clean 8 years, 10 months and 24 days. Unlike the other mothers in this book, her drug of choice was crank, an illegal substance also known as methamphetamine that she injected and powder cocaine not heroin or crack. In junior high school, Ladonna played hooky from school and hung with older guys. Like Desirea, playing hooky from school would be the catalyst for drug use. It would be in this environment where Ladonna first encountered the street drug crank with a man much older than her. As a teenage girl attracted to guys much older than her, she found herself in a position where she could be influenced to try drugs for the first time. Ladonna tells the story of her introduction to crank resulting from being what might be interpreted as coercion to use crank.

> Before I turned 16 years old, … I started smoking … marijuana … I remember a day I was over a girlfriend's house and I had started doing that crank … I remember this guy said to me he was like, cause I told you I was hangin with the older dudes, and they all was drug dealers and users, heroin and stuff. You know, I wasn't attracted to the heroin or none of that stuff. I didn't even think about that at that time … kept saying to me … 'Why you don't want to get high with me?' … So he talked like for a couple of hours. And I finally said, I said alright, and I let him shoot me up with some crank. And I liked the way it felt. You know and a little bit a time went by and he said well you want some more. And I said yeah …

As with most of the mothers in this book, there was easy access to drugs as they did not have to look too far to purchase or obtain drugs. Similar to Desirea, Ladonna was introduced to drug use as a teenager in the presence of older adult men during the day when she should have been attending school.

Throughout Ladonna's addiction, she was able to maintain jobs for short periods of time when she was not an active drug user. Prior to her current job, she was employed at a local casino in environmental services sweeping the floor of the casino and lobby. Ladonna also worked at a fast food restaurant at another Casino and a local laundry that has since been demolished. During our meeting, Ladonna was working for what used to be a high rise apartment called the Sea Surfer (pseudonym) in the bay area overlooking the ocean but now is a timeshare with their main office located on a nearby island and really enjoyed her job. Ladona indicated regardless of her addiction history, she was respected by her coworkers and boss. She was really proud of being employed by the Sea Surfer and it gave her a sense of accomplishment and hope in spite of her many years of addiction. Ladonna had really turned her life around and being gainfully employed was significant to her. Below, Ladonna talks about her coworkers.

> Yeah they know, but it's like, you know-we don't believe you. (laughing) you know what I'm saying. And Yeah they know … and it's like the people in my office you know, we talk and stuff. Like my supervisor, um she comes to me for advice. She comes to me like when she got to make decisions about stuff in the office. You know what I'm saying um. That's a wonderful feeling in me … we just did our reviews, and I was reading mine, and I was like, wow, this is what you think of me. She said no, that's not what I think of you. That's the truth. You know. Because you know, I have became the person that I am suppose to be.

Barbara

At the time of our conversations, Barbara was in her sixties and the oldest mother in the book and has since passed away. She had five adult children (four girls and one boy) reporting that except for her son who had a minor operation at three months old, all of her children developed without major problems. Barbara met her second husband over thirty years ago while out dancing and socializing with her friends. She was already addicted to heroin before she met him and like Desirea and Ladonna, her addiction to drugs began as a teenager. Barbara did not share much about how she became addicted to heroin but only that she was around fifteen or sixteen when she was introduced to the drug. She also reported that she smoked a pack of cigarettes daily and used crack cocaine for about two years before she went into drug treatment. Barbara's poly drug use also included marijuana, cough syrup, CIBs, Tumeralls, red devils, yellow jackets and Zanax.

Barbara maintained employment throughout her active heroin addiction. Her first major job was at the employment office that included filling job positions for the new casinos being built along the boardwalk in the 1970's. Barbara also obtained a Number 2 Casino Gaming License allowing her several jobs involving counting money. She maintained employment while she was an active drug addict until she was fired from one casino job because of child-care problems. Barbara was employed at a local casino for five years but was fired when she was forced to change from night shift to day shift. She reports

> I stayed at da (Casino) for 5 years ... the only reason I left. It hurt me to my heart. That child up there [points to a picture of her daughter] the one that's out getting high now. Was going out the window, messing around with a simple boy. I dared them to go with any fellas in Shore Homes. Cause ain't none of them worth nothing. ... I take him (husband) (to work) during the day. You know he go to sleep (in evening) and she sneak out. You know ... he was aware of it ... whipped the devil off his conscience and he wanted me to come home. So what I had to do is switch from night shift to day shift. And I had did it for so many years till my body (was used) ... to staying up at night ... And when it was time for vice a versa and it was time for to shake that money, I be nodded and sleep. And I lost my job. I had never been fired in my life. I was so hurt.

Barbara adjusted her work schedule in order to supervise her teenaged daughter and her body did not adjust to the shift change making it difficult to maintain her job responsibilities. Although Barbara was fired from her job, her Casino Gaming license and job access allowed her to become employed as a cashier, counting money in another casino.

Barbara's narratives of working at the casino spoke to the complexity of parenting, working and heroin addiction. She was remarkable as she spoke so matter of factly about working, yet she was a hardcore heroin addict. She jokingly reported that she was not able to work unless she was high. As a drug addict, Barbara worked around millions of dollars, indicating there was no way she would have ever considered stealing money from the casino. Although, she admitted to shoplifting professionally, she was never tempted by the amount of money she came in daily contact with at work because she understood the risk and consequences. Barbara and her husband were heroin addicts and worked for years within the casino industry requiring some type of casino license from the Casino Control Commission. In spite of their addictions they were able to maintain consistent employment without the help of public assistance. Jobs in Atlantic City during the time of Ladonna and Barbara's addictions were available for those who did not have a college education. Although Atlantic City experienced a decline in tourism during the mid 1970's, the casino industry provided some opportunities for employment starting in 1978. However, Atlantic City is once again experiencing an economic decline as many casinos have closed.

Atlantic City's Drug Business

Atlantic City's Black neighborhoods varies in location across the small peninsula. However, Kentucky Avenue was the Mecca for entertainment and nightlife for Blacks in Atlantic City from the late 1930's to 1970's. The infamous Club Harlem located on Kentucky Avenue is where famous Black entertainers from all over traveled to perform. Even Black entertainers fortunate enough to perform at major Atlantic City venues (pre casinos), would frequent Club Harlem. Here, Barbara provides a description of nightlife on Kentucky Avenue during the 1960's and 1970's. She talks about her experiences on Kentucky Avenue with so much fondness and happiness. This was demonstrated by her facial expressions with passion and excitement in her voice.

> Blacks would be down in here … you looking for anything or into anything or anybody. Kentucky Avenue was the place … I'll start on Kentucky and Baltic. That's where the Village was where people lived. The Lincoln Motel … wanted to spend the night, … Club that was on the corner. Next to that was the Elks home … downstairs, they let us have Elks Home dances. … We had a seafood place. Proud owned by Blacks, Bar B Q place, … had a camera shop … and you got Club Harlem, Grace's Belmont …

Barbara made it a point to emphasize that although there were "… pimps, whores, the drug addicts, the drug dealers …" She bragged about a certain level of sophistication required to belong to this scene. "… But I mean they got class now. Just no anybody off the street can't get up in there. They ain't gone allow that. They be dressed. (verbally emphasized) couldn't tell em they wasn't sharp …"

Barbara's eyes lit up and smiled as she recalled

> Club Harlem … That was the club that all Black entertainers came down to. And that picture there (picture hanging on the wall with her husband and relatives) was Gladys Knight and the Pips we went to see. And Aretha Franklin was in audience there to visit Gladys. Ahhh. I had a good time. Had my drugs in my pocket book. (Laughter)

Barbara's account of the happenings on Kentucky Avenue illustrated that along with the excitement of the entertainment world and nightlife came the vices of street life. Heroin has been historically connected to the music industry (Agar & Resinger, 2002) and the entertainment scene in Atlantic City was no exception. Robert "Midget" Molley, the renowned drug kingpin also talks about Kentucky Avenue with the same fondness and nostalgia as Barbara (American Gangster, 2008). They both spoke about the drug culture and the heroin and crack businesses along Kentucky Avenue.

During our time together reminiscing about the old Atlantic City prior to casinos, Barbara would often speak about the "good ole days" and the strong Black community prior to integration and the casinos. She spoke with so much passion as she discussed Black businesses that had closed along Kentucky Avenue and how you now have to go "off shore" (out of Atlantic City) to purchase quality things that you need most. Barbara also highlighted once Black entertainers had the option to perform at venues in the casinos and on the boardwalk, they stopped coming to Club Harlem. Here she offers her comments

> ... These same entertainers I'm talking about now. They go on the boardwalk now. At these different casinos. Used to go right to (hits the table) Club Harlem ... Whitie knew what he was doing ... When them casinos made them change. Things started fallen. Atlantic City started fallin'. That's only because Whitie knew what he was getting ready to do. They knew what they was gonna do ... They had it all planned. Had it all planned.

Barbara's interpretation of Atlantic City's political and socio cultural landscape as "... Things started fallin' ..." is precisely what many of Atlantic City's Black residents believed. Her commentary of the city's plight was heartfelt and real to her and her community. We never discussed what she meant by "... had it all planned ..." but she clearly believed that Atlantic City's Black community suffered after integration and casinos. Her passionate voice when speaking on this topic let you know for certain that she believed when the state government agreed to casinos in Atlantic City, it did not consider the Black community's best interest.

Both Barbara and Robert "Midget" Molley talked about the changes in the Black community and Kentucky Avenue since the casinos. The casinos made a positive impact on parts of the city, however, those in impoverished Black neighborhoods have not seen the wealth put back into their community. Both also spoke about the prevalence and availability of drugs along the famed Kentucky Avenue. However, it is important to emphasize here that Kentucky

Avenue represented more to the city's Black residents than simply a space for drug use and other illegal activity. This strip embodied pride and a cultural space Black residents called their own at a time when they were excluded from the larger community. We should not ignore the fact that Kentucky Avenue was also a major hub for Black tourists during their summer excursions to the South Jersey Shore. Out-of-town travelers came from all over to enjoy bathing at Chicken Bone Beach and a show at Club Harlem on Kentucky Avenue.

Barbara's heroin addiction spanned from the 1960's to the 1990's. While her drug of choice was heroin, she also began to use crack during the 1980's. It was during the 1970's that drug kingpin Robert "Midget" Molley began to sell Heroin in Atlantic City at 17 years old and within three years had a lucrative heroin business. In 1980, he was convicted of aggravated assault and sentenced to six years in jail (American Gangster, 2007). He emphasized "in heroin, out crack," explaining that when he went to jail in 1980, heroin was the popular drug. Yet in 1986 when released as mentioned earlier, crack was everywhere. Not long after his first release, he later acquired a successful crack business and deemed himself the "king" of Atlantic City by actually purchasing and wearing a gold crown. Barbara's addictions to heroin and crack were supported through both eras of Midget Molley's drug businesses. Similar to the Chambers Brothers' drug empire, the business reeked havoc on the community as open-air drug markets appeared and drug violence increased. His crack empire was allegedly making 1 million dollars per month. He eventually got arrested for what is considered to be the largest drug operation in the history of Atlantic City on February 14, 1989 and was released from prison June 14, 2006 (American Gangster, 2007).

Continued Drug Use Trends

Government data indicates, cocaine and heroin addictions continue to plague many residents of Detroit, Atlantic City, and New York City. New Jersey's Division of Addiction Services (2009) provides annual data on drug trends. According to a 2015 report, in Atlantic County (a smaller county in New Jersey) 2304 people were admitted into residential treatment for heroin and 176 for cocaine. Forty eight percent of admissions into treatment centers in Atlantic County were for heroin and opiate addictions. This same 2009 report indicates that of all of the municipalities of Atlantic County, Atlantic City had the highest admissions into treatment centers for cocaine (83 people, 92% of total county's admissions) and heroin (527 people, 58%

of total county's admissions). Thus, governmental research data clearly indicate the need to support effective drug treatment opportunities for its citizens impacted by illegal drug addictions.

In 2003, Detroit's drug related statistics ranks 10 among twenty American cities for crack cocaine related crimes and treatment admissions (NIDA, 2003) and in 1997, Wayne County was designated as a high intensity drug trafficking area (ONDP, 2007). In the first half of 2013, cocaine still ranks second and heroin third in police reports as items seized and analyzed for Wayne County and the State of Michigan. Admissions to Detroit publicly funded treatment programs for cocaine as primary drug was 15.7% of total admissions, which is higher than the rest of Michigan. Ninety-one percent of these cocaine admissions were for crack, which of 36% were females and 92% were Black. In 2013, 33% of admissions to drug treatment was for heroin, 35% were female and 82% were Black (indicating a slight increase from 2011) (Arfken, 2014 February).

No information was reported in Rainone & Marel's (2014) report on racial and gender demographics. Nonetheless, based on treatment admissions and police reports, cocaine and heroin continue to be drugs of choice in New York City. Primary cocaine treatment admissions have declined but clients have reported primary, secondary, or tertiary problems with cocaine than with any other drug (Rainone & Marel, 2014), suggesting cocaine continues to be readily available in New York City. Heroin is recurrently a significant problem for New York City as it is considered the major heroin market and distribution center in the United States and accounts for one-quarter of all treatment admissions (Rainone & Marel, 2014). Crack and heroin addictions are still a problem in the poor impoverished neighborhoods.

Government data indicates that people in Atlantic County, New Jersey, Detroit and New York City continue to be plagued by powder and crack cocaine and heroin addictions. Bethena, Sharonda, Desirea, Ladonna, and Barbara were addicted to dangerous street drugs readily available to them since they were young teenagers until adulthood. School and adults outside the family (usually adult males) made no effort to shield many of the mothers from the dangers of heroin and crank addiction. The peak of the mothers' drug addictions occurred during the empires of notorious drug kingpins in their cities. The mothers, some more than others, were able to maintain employment throughout active addiction. While Desirea and Barbara were able to maintain consistent employment during their addictions to heroin, Ladonna's crank addiction prevented her from working. Bethena was the only mother considered to have enjoyed the markers of a middle-class lifestyle prior to her addiction but lost her job because of crack addiction. The mothers' employment and drug use provide only a snippet of their lives as Black women, mothers and drug addicts. Chapter four will explore more of the mothers' family, neighborhood, and educational backgrounds as well as research practice with the mothers.

References

Adler, W. M. (1995). *Land of opportunity: One family's quest for the American dream in the age of crack*. New York, NY: Atlantic Monthly Press.

Agar, M. (2003). The story of crack: Towards a theory of illicit drug trends. *Addiction Research and Theory, 11*(1), 3–29.

Agar, M., & Reisinger, H. S. (2002). A heroin epidemic at the intersection of histories: The 1960s epidemic among African Americans in Baltimore. *Medical Anthropology, 21*(2), 115–156.

Arfken, C. L. (2014). Drug abuse patterns and trends in Detroit, Wayne County and Michigan-Update: January 2014. *National Institute on Drug Abuse*. Retrieved from https://www.drugabuse.gov.

Austin, D. (n.d.). Hudson's department store. Retrieved from http://www.historicdetroit.org.

Division of Mental Health & Addiction Services & Office of Planning, Research, Evaluation and Prevention. (2016). New Jersey Drug and Alcohol Abuse Treatment Substance Abuse Overview 2015 Atlantic County. Trenton, NJ: Limei Zhu. Retrieved from http://www.nj.gov/humanservices/dmhas/publications/statistical/Substance%20Abuse%20Overview/2015/Atl.pdf.

Jackson, G., & McHenry, D. (Producers), & Van Peebles, M. (Director). (1991). *New Jack City* [Motion Picture]. United States: Warner Brothers.

National Institute on Drug Abuse (NIDA). (2003). *Epidemiologic trends in drug abuse, volume ll, Proceedings of the community epidemiology work group*. Retrieved July 9, 2008, from http://www.drugabuse.gov.

National Institute on Drug Abuse (NIDA). (2015, September 10). *Results from 2014 national survey on drug use and health: Detailed tables*. Retrieved from http://www.samhsa.gov.

Office of National Drug Control Policy (ONDP). (2007). *State of Michigan, profiles of drug indicators*. Retrieved May 22, 2008 from http://www.whitehouse/drugspolicy.

Pattillo-McCoy, M. (1999). *Black picket fences: Privilege and peril among the Black middle class*. Chicago, IL: The University of Chicago Press.

Rainone, G., & Marel, R. (2014). Drug abuse patterns and trends in New York City-update: January 2014. National Institute of Drug Abuse. Retrieved from https://www.drugabuse.gov.

Reinarman, C., & Levine, H. G. (1997). Crack in context: America's latest demon drug. In C. Reinarman & H. G. Levine (Eds.), *Crack in America: Demon drugs and social justice* (pp. 1–17), Los Angeles: University of California Press.

Reinarman, C., & Levine, H. G. (2004). Crack in the rearview mirror: Deconstructing drug war mythology. *Social Justice, 31*(1/2), 182–199.

Unknown. (2007). Frank Lucas and the coffin connection (Season 2, Episode 5). In N. George & J. Koch (Producers), *BET American gangster.* United States: A. Smith & Co. Productions.

Unknown. (2008). Robert "Midget" Molley: The king of the boardwalk. (Season 3, Episode 3). In Unknown, *BET American gangster.* United States: A. Smith & Co. Productions.

Whitaker, J., & Zallian, S. (Producers), & Scott, R. (Director). (2007). *American Gangster* [Motion Picture]. United States: Universal Studios.

Williams, T. (1992). *Crackhouse: Notes from the end of the line.* New York, NY: Addison-Wesley Publishing.

Wilson, D. (2007). *Cities and race.* New York, NY: Routledge.

· 5 ·

MORE ABOUT THE MOTHERS, RESEARCH PRACTICE, BLACK MOTHERHOOD AND ADDICTION

Little is known about pre and postnatal crack, powder cocaine, heroin and crank exposure, recovery, and parenting from Black mothers' perspectives. My intentions are for this book to encourage us to rethink the master narrative of Black mothers who have drug addictions and their children. This chapter provides a short overview of research methods and tensions in research practice with Black mothers experiencing trauma and illegal drug addiction. I briefly discuss dilemmas of self-reflection as I considered positionality, accountability, and use of language during the research process. Background information is presented about the mothers' family, school and neighborhood serving as a backdrop for their narratives.

This book emerged from qualitative research exploring drug addiction, parenting and recovery with five Black mothers addressing the following research questions: What are the perceptions of five Black mothers who were prenatal drug addicts regarding their: (a) drug addiction and recovery, (b) parent-child interactions, and (c) their children's academic achievement. I sought to obtain counternarratives about drug addiction, recovery and parenting while highlighting their resilience. The mothers served as important agents of knowledge and educated me about motherhood, addiction and recovery from a standpoint of authority.

The stories are from in-depth interviews (Seidman, 2013) with Black women living in Detroit, Michigan, and Atlantic City, New Jersey who were formally very active in crank, crack cocaine and/or heroin addictions. However, during my interactions with the mothers, they were abstinent from their drug of choice. The constant comparative approach (Glaser & Strauss, 1967 as cited by Bogdan & Biklen, 2007) was used to identify themes directly from the interview data. Codes were developed and refined as I continuously developed concepts by simultaneously coding and analyzing the data. Concepts were refined when I repeatedly compared specific incidents from the data, identified their properties, and explored their relationships between one another (Bogdan & Biklen, 2007). Direct quotes are also used to support descriptions of predominant themes as the mothers' voices define the phenomena related to the topics discussed. Black Feminist Thought (Collins, 2000) and Critical Race Feminism (Solórzano & Yosso, 2009) were conceptual frameworks for methodology to examine. Thus, I was able to approach the research process with intentions of challenging hegemonic understandings of Black mothers and drug addictions. My goal was for the mothers to disrupt existing ideologies of Black mothers who were crack and powder cocaine and heroin users. My objective was to privilege their self-definitions of daily-lived experiences as a means of resistance and exchanging negative controlled images with positive self-perceptions (Collins, 2000).

Sista-Girl Conversations

Bethena, Sharonda, Ladonna, Barbara and Desirea were referred to me by personal contacts familiar with the research project in each location whose relationship they valued and trusted. Personal contacts served as gatekeepers from Baptist Churches and identified members with past drug addictions based on common knowledge among church members. The gatekeepers were well respected and trusted by Bethena, Sharonda, Ladonna, Barbara and Desirea. Although they initiated contact with me, the gatekeepers had vouched for my credibility making it easier for me to gain insider status, which helped with them speaking freely to me about their personal lives.

As Black women, the mothers and I shared an understanding of our existence and language that brought us together in conversation. Yet, I wanted to convey to the mothers that it was an honor to be welcomed into their space and be privy to their private lives gaining the privilege of listening to personal stories of pain, trauma and resilience. When I expressed this sentiment though, they all responded with gratitude for opportunities to share their stories and voiced that nobody had ever asked them about their life and drug addictions. The mothers also strongly believed that others would be blessed by their stories.

Objectivity is typically an expectation for research methods but becomes problematic when the researcher and participants share the same race, culture, values and struggles. Likewise, Ladonna, Barbara, Desirea and I shared knowledge of community context and I had close relationships with those with addictions living in Atlantic City, which added to the ease of the interviewing process. Our shared identities also provided a cultural frame of reference required to understand and respond to the subtle nonverbal communication cues during the interviews (Dunbar, Rodriguez, & Parker, 2002). This was most obvious when I attempted to ask some of my scripted interview questions such as "What games did you play with your child when they were young?" or "How did you demonstrate responsiveness to your child?" Every mother responded to me with that "girl please?" facial expression. Bethena even responded with a frown on her face, "girl, what kind a question is dat? I don't know." Most, if not all of the questions in my formal interview protocol had to be reworded and I relied on my broad questions that allowed them to simply tell their story. I also used a language style that was a good fit for my interactions with the mothers. Our conversations were not objective or neutral. Our mutual identities provided a cultural context for conversations with the mothers that did not support an atmosphere of neutrality and objectivity (Dunbar, et al., 2002).

I could not share stories about drug addiction but we did exchange personal stories about being Black women and mothers. Sharing personal experiences in my life assisted with establishing personal relationships with the mothers. As Black women, we shared a collective experience (Collins, 2000) and conversations occurred smoothly because there were unspoken understandings and culture specific phrases that required no interpretation. This "sista-ta-sista" talk also included ongoing discussions often comprised of nonverbalized answers with culture-specific hand gestures and facial expressions (Johnson-Bailey, 1999). Our shared language style contributed to the smooth flow of my conversations with them as we utilized verbal and nonverbal communication functions unique to two Black women using African American Language.

It was important to me that I honored the mothers' voices by allowing them to tell their story in their own way. They did so and often in a manner illustrating their authority and expertise on certain topics, taking pride in explaining information I was learning for the first time. This was especially true when discussing specific details about their drug use, recovery and their spiritual life. During my interactions with the more senior mothers, Barbara and Desirea would often provide parenting tips or mention information that I needed to include in my "write up" in their motherly or big sister manner. For example, on several occasions, Barbara and I enjoyed time together traveling along the shore area running errands for her to the drug store, shoe repair shop, and our favorite discount department store. As we drove around, she pointed out places included in some of her stories about her addictions. Once, we ended our time together with a dining excursion at one of my favorite restaurants.

Her love for children was evident in her interactions with her grandchildren and my own daughter. Barbara would often make comments in an authoritarian/motherly way about her observations of my interactions with my daughter. She would refer to me as "baby" in that older Black motherly tone and demeanor. Barbara always wanted to meet at her home and most of our conversations took place there at her dining room table in her highrise apartment building for senior citizens. We sat at her dining room table and talked for what seemed like hours. I always wanted to treat her to dinner but except for one time, each visit she insisted on preparing a meal for me. This setting provided a very comfortable and relaxed "at the kitchen table" atmosphere.

As an insider I do share many spaces of identity with the mothers. However, my insider position sometimes became painfully suspect as my interactions with Barbara, Desirea, and Ladonna forced me to confront my personal bias related to class. Issues of class sometimes offset the bonds formed with the women based on race and gender. Researchers have found that during conversations among Black women researchers and participants, distinctions between class statuses may sometimes present barriers to the research process (Johnson-Bailey, 1999). Sometimes I secretly struggled with thinking that I was "being fake" with the mothers in Atlantic City because I never revealed my original connection to the city. They knew I previously lived there and worked for the school district. However, I never shared my family vacationed and owned summer properties there for three generations. This is where perceptions of neighborhood safety initially took me out of my comfort zone as I interviewed Ladonna and Barbara in their own homes. From the perspective of those in my social circles, not only were their neighborhoods considered extremely dangerous, so were the people that lived there. Part of my professional duties while working at the school district required home visits. However, I was visiting them in their home and had it not been for this study, I probably would have never stepped foot in their housing areas to socialize. A close family member even judgingly inquired: "You have to go over there? And you're taking (my daughter)" when I told her that I would be hanging out with my new friend and I would be ok. I trusted the mothers and eventually felt safe traveling to their homes. I was enough of an insider to establish a close rapport adequate for the mothers to share their personal life with me about their addictions. I questioned was I "faking" this insider position? My insider status helped to facilitate the "sista-ta-sista" talks but I obviously was not an insider in their neighborhood or as a drug addict. Yet, the mothers welcomed me into their space and spoke freely.

The mothers and I shared a language style but language posed a problem with hiring a transcriber because of the use African American language during our conversations. It took a total of working with four different experienced transcribers (two Black females and two White females) until finally a fellow doctoral student's Black wife from Alabama was able to transcribe the tapes accurately. It was important to me that the transcriptions reflected the mothers' authentic language and this transcriber understood both African American Language and Standard English.

Part of my member checking process included sharing interview transcripts with the mothers. I did not anticipate Desirea's response to the member checking process when she read her interview transcripts. She passionately expressed disappointment in her bad English skills and talked about how she needed to go back to school. Desirea's narratives provided important sophisticated and analytical critique of U.S. institutions and comments on the oppression of the illegal drug industry and Black people. She presented a level of passion and desire for revolutionary change in the status of our people that was absent from conversations with others. Yet, she believe that her voice from the interview was bad or less than.

It bothered me that Desirea thought her voice was somehow less than because she did not use the dominant language. My words failed me as I attempted to explain to her my "academic knowledge" about the value of an individual's first language and why it should be honored, and considered just as legitimate as those who speak the dominant language. After all, I was able to code switch with access to the privileges that come with the skill of reading, writing and speaking Standard English. She did not possess the same skillset and no words were able to change her mind or feelings toward her bad and inadequate English. I wish that I had more time with her so that we could devise a plan (e.g. writing partners, local writing or poetry class) to facilitate a more positive perception of her voice. I am still troubled by not using this as an opportunity to support her concerns about her writing skills.

This tension between the mothers' authentic voice and Standard English emerged again as colleagues reviewed initial versions of this text. The direct quotes that were included with the mothers' authentic language were difficult for them to understand and took away from allowing the manuscript to read smoothly. I eventually just translated all of the direct quotes from the mothers to Standard English so that all of the readers would have access to their stories, narratives and voice. At the same time, there is still a piece of my heart that questions if I compromised their voice at the expense of gaining favor with my academic audience. However, I am certain that Bethena, Barbara, Desirea, Sharonda and Ladonna's narratives still provide oppositional knowledge. Their stories give new meanings to Black motherhood while navigating drugs addictions and expose the "crack ho' and baby" and their origins for what they really are, a myth.

Our shared language style allowed us to laugh and sometimes cry together. Yet, there were still times when it would also take me a minute to "get" what they were saying due to their strong regional accents and sayings. My identities as a middle class Black woman, mother, graduate student and qualitative researcher also presented interesting dynamics to my interactions with the mothers. As a Black female qualitative researcher, my time spent with Bethena, Sharonda, Ladonna, Barbara and Desirea was life changing as our relationships developed and they shared their life stories. Throughout the research process, I developed an ethic of caring and accountability (Collins, 2000) for the mothers that guided my actions throughout the research process.

Bethena, Desirea, Barbara, Ladonna and Sharonda spoke candidly about some of the darkest moments of their addiction. It was during these conversations I struggled the most, unprepared for my emotional reactions to their narratives of danger that I would only see in the movies. These reactions would often not surface until after interviewing and I was listening to or reading the interview transcripts. Nonetheless, Bethena, Sharonda, Ladonna, Barbara and Desirea spoke truth about the life of Black mothers negotiating parenting and drug addictions. Together we brought truth, enlightment and healing as we spent time sharing our lives through conversation (Hambrick, 1997). These moments changed my life as I listened to the mothers relive their experiences with drug addiction and I felt connected to them as a fellow Black mother. However, I was clearly an outsider to drug addiction. Yet they trusted me and made it a point to teach me what I did not know. Their stories were full of pain, passion and their lived truths and I had grown to care about them and their families.

More about the Mothers

The mothers or their families in Atlantic City and Detroit migrated to these cities for economic reasons in an effort to obtain the American Dream. Sharonda, Bethena, Barbara, Ladonna, and Desirea came from diverse family backgrounds with working parents that focused on religious morals and where many valued education. Drug use during and after pregnancy among the mothers varied across families.

Sharonda

Sharonda has ten children, six girls ages 12, 14, 15, 18, 24, and four boys ages 4, 7, 16, and 22. All of Sharonda's children were born full-term babies except for her 24-year-old daughter, who was born prematurely but prior to her crack cocaine addiction. She used crack cocaine, drank alcohol, and smoked cigarettes at some point during most of her other pregnancies but did so on a daily basis with her 12-, 14-, and 15-year-old daughters. Sharonda recalled smoking crack more consistently, two to three times daily with her 16-year-old son but only once weekly with her youngest two children.

Sharonda's family migrated to Detroit from a New England state when she was three years old but her father eventually moved back. She believed he showed favoritism toward her older sister and "did not like her" because he would send for her siblings to visit but not her. This sister eventually moved back to New England to live full time with her father. Growing up in Detroit, Sharonda's home included her stay at home mother, stepfather, one sister, and three brothers. She shared a special father-daughter relationship with her stepfather who worked for an automobile company. He played a positive role in Sharonda's childhood and even walked her down the isle during her recent wedding.

Sharonda described her early years with fondness and describes herself as being a "little spoiled rotten kid." However, her relationship with her mother was strained during her teenage years and stressed with strict rules and regulations. As a teenager, Sharonda's mother burdened her with total responsibility of keeping the house tidy, laundry, and caring for foster children in their home. Sharonda believed her mother treated her unfairly because "just the little things that she did that you just [she gasps] 'you're my mother' and I know you didn't do that." Yet, when she paid rent to live in a house next door owned by her mother, Sharonda admits that it was nice living so close to her mother.

As a child, Sharonda's family celebrated typical American holidays and traditions with biological paternal aunt hosting huge family get-togethers, "up north" at her cabin. These events included relatives traveling from their New England hometown. Christmas celebrations were a special time for her because it was the only time she recalls her mother demonstrating love to her. She believed that Christmas time was "her way of showing love cause she gave us extremely good Christmases ..." During elementary school, Sharonda described herself as "real quiet" and "good kid in school." However, junior high school became challenging as she began to rebel against her mothers' structure and dominance. Sharonda's mother expected her to adhere to a very demanding schedule during high school with the expectation that she would be responsible for most household duties.

> That's why I quit in the twelfth grade ... I was too young to be tired ... quit both jobs and school ... we'd wake up at six, eat my breakfast, ... bus stop at seven, ... school at eight. Leave the school like twelve thirty-ish, ... be at work at one, get off a one job, go to another one till midnight. Come home ... my mother would have the dishes there for me ... my older siblings were gone by that time ... I had dishes to wash and clothes to dry and fold ... by the time I went to bed it was like four o'clock ... I had to get up at six ... did that for years, so I was just tired.

Sharonda did not believe that her mother supported or encouraged her academically. Yet, she described herself as an all A and B student throughout high school until her senior year. By then, she preferred being with friends instead of adhering to her mother's strict protocol. While hanging out with her peers was important, Sharonda emphasized the main reason she left school was because she was too tired and unable to handle the demanding responsibilities of home and school.

Bethena

My first interview with Bethena took place early one morning during an extremely cold November in Detroit. We had previously been introduced prior to the scheduled interview but greeted each other with hugs as if we were old friends. The atmosphere during our first interviews was consistent throughout our subsequent sista-ta-sista talks except she shared more about her life. Bethena was so proud to be off of crack and was eager to talk about her days of addiction in the event that it would help others understand about being addicted to crack.

Bethena was born and raised in a rural southern town, where she lived with her parents, an older and younger brother and two younger sisters. She had two older siblings 9–10 years her senior raised by her grandmother in the same neighborhood. Her father worked in a sawmill and her mother worked in a factory making light switches. Bethena reports her father liked to drink but "my momma was the backbone of the family, you know how some women just have to take over … she was the head of the household." As a young child, Bethena lived in a small house with an outdoor bathroom until her family built a three-bedroom house once she got older. Growing up, Bethena spent the majority of her social time with her cousins listening to records and playing cards. They were the same cousins she came to be with in Detroit. Although they had a newly built house, she self-defined her family as poor but remembered receiving a brand new coat and shoes every one or two years during the George Washington Birthday Holiday.

Bethena attended segregated schools in her rural southern town until she was in the ninth grade, riding the bus to school with her cousins and her uncle, the bus driver. She vividly recalls memories of the year she first attended an integrated school. The "parents came and took the White kids out and took them home crying because they didn't want to go to school with us black kids." Bethena remembered details of differences between the Black and White high schools she attended. The White school was a much nicer building and afforded her more opportunities than the all Black high school and attended the integrated high school until she graduated in 1974.

Bethena, was in her fifties during our conversations with three children and one granddaughter. During this time, her son was 16 years old, and her youngest daughter was 19 and had recently graduated from high school. These two children live with Bethena in Detroit but her older daughter with a young girl was reared in her hometown by her mother. This daughter moved in with her grandmother shortly before Bethena's crack addiction "got too bad" and continues to live there with her own daughter. Bethena moved to Detroit in 1975, a year after she graduated from high school, to live with relatives who worked in the automobile industry.

Bethena smoked crack consistently during her second pregnancy with her youngest daughter until she was two years old. Her youngest daughter, who was 19 at the time of our conversations, was born prenatally exposed to crack cocaine and premature at 3 pounds and 2 ounces. Bethena was questioned by the authorities about her crack cocaine addiction but able to bring her daughter home after her aunt agreed to provide support. She reported:

> Well you know, they don't talk to you nicely ... first they come and ask you, Do you use drugs, do you smoke crack? ... What can you say? What I'm supposed to do say no? And knowing when you deliver this baby, it's everywhere. Well, we found crack cocaine all on this baby. This baby was covered in white stuff. Which I knew like I say it wasn't' no prenatal care or none of that, just by the Grace of God honey. She came out with five toes and five hands ... this baby was a crack baby and we can not release this baby to you in your custody without some kind of guardian or somebody that's [going to] help you with ...

Bethena's paternal aunt was notified and agreed to assist with the newborn infant accepting responsibility for ensuring that her infant daughter would be cared for. Interestingly, her daughter was allowed to come home as an underweight drug exposed infant with no early intervention services to monitor her development. Additionally, Bethena was not assigned to a child welfare caseworker to follow-up on her and her newborn infant. When weeks later, she brought her daughter home from the hospital, she does not recall being given any instructions or medicine for her daughter. Three years later, Bethena gave birth to a healthy full-term drug free baby boy.

Once Bethena's addiction took its course, she lost her job at the car manufacturing plant, her house, and several other housing options. However, after kicking her crack cocaine addiction, Bethena managed to purchase the home that she had currently been living in for fifteen years. She was at that moment a manager in the kitchen of her son's local high school and told me "Life is good now. ... Life is good, life is good—I have no complaints."

Ladonna

Ladonna and I spoke at her home located in an area of Atlantic City commonly known as Basin Park (pseudonym). She was 44 years old and lived at home with her husband and youngest daughter (in middle school) during our conversation. Ladonna is very active in her church and Narcotics Anonymous. Ladonna received support from both of her daughters' fathers and her mother when she was pregnant. She lived with her mother and brothers after her first daughter was born but also spent time living with her youngest daughter's father after she was born. Ladonna's mother and/or daughter's father were usually with her daughter once her youngest daughter was in kindergarten. However, at that time, Ladonna was spending less time at home with her family as she begun to engage in more drug use.

Ladonna's family moved to Atlantic City from a southern state when she was in the third grade. Her mother who worked in the medical field believed

Atlantic City would provide her family better opportunities. Ladonna who lived at home with her mother, stepfather, and three brothers believes it was this move that prompted her rebellious behavior as a young child. She had a total of six brothers but two of them and her sister remained in their southern home state. Ladonna and I did not discuss details of her neighborhood or mother's employment. However, she did mention to me she currently lives in the same neighborhood that she did when she was "in da streets" engaged in addiction.

Ladonna's stepfather began molesting her as a young teenager around 12 or 13 years old and when her mother was informed their marriage ended. As a young girl Ladonna believed that her mother resented her because of the molestation. However, she admitted that there was no evidence to justify this and instead now believes her mother was just very strict and expected her to follow rules. Her mother was stern and used corporal punishment when she disobeyed the rules. Ladonna resented her mother for moving their family to Atlantic City and believes this resentment was indirectly related to her path of drug addiction.

Ladonna excelled academically when she first moved to Atlantic City from the south but was constantly bullied at school and had to fight in order to defend herself.

> … And coming from (southern state), … I was a lot different from the kids here … was picked on a lot … I was very smart … an A student. Not a B, but an A student. … one of the kids that was picked on a lot. I guess at some point. I just started to, want to fit in with the other children … I became rebellious at home. You know. Because, I came from a mom. It wasn't alright for me to just do whatever … I had a curfew. It was a certain time that we ate … we did homework after school … I just began to want the other kids to like me. … So I just started doing whatever it was that they were doing … I would be in trouble. … with my mom. … I saw her being mean and strict … I thought she was mean I thought she was strict. Um You know. I fought a lot in school. I had to fight.

Ladonna was constantly bullied until she became the bully and began to get into trouble at school. She "had to fight because … the kids picked on me a lot. You know … I had to fight. You know what I'm saying? I had to fight. Or I would just be one of the kids that was picked on all the time. So I fought back." Ladonna was faced with another significant change that had a major impact on her in the fifth grade. Her family moved to a different neighborhood requiring her to attend a different school that had more children. By this time Ladonna had grown accustomed to fighting and eventually became the bully at her knew school because at first she continued to get beat up a lot. However, through all of the fighting and getting beat up, Ladonna remained an A student because she "was still able to maintain and pay attention and do my work in school."

As a result of Ladonna's rebellious behavior in junior high school, her mother sent her to live with her father in the south. Her father and stepmother lived in a two-family home with her grandmother living downstairs and her father and his wife upstairs. Ladonna and her stepmother did not get along and she eventually moved in with her grandmother downstairs. While in the south, Ladonna was caught shoplifting and her father recommended the police put her in a detention center and she remained there for eight months where she began smoking marijuana.

Once Ladonna moved back to Atlantic City from the south, marijuana smoking was a habit but she maintained her schoolwork and was placed in her correct grade. Unfortunately, she began playing hooky from school and her mother also placed her in a juvenile facility. As early as fifth and sixth grade, Ladonna was interested in older boys. She was mature for her age and by the time she was in junior high school was involved with older boys. Ladonna's mother enrolled her in the federal program Job Corps when she turned sixteen and she was sent to a major Midwestern city. She continued to act out while at Job Corps.

> ... OH. And it was nothing different. It was the same behavior ... I was fighting the other girls, stealing ... Sleeping with this guy, sleeping that guy ... Where I lived. Which was one of the big streets ... the street behind us was the bars and the chicken spot ... You know, the guys knew that this was a Job Corps for nothing but (young) women. So they kind a hung around and stuff.

While enrolled in Job Corps, Ladonna was sexually assaulted after getting into a car with an adult male to go and purchase marijuana. The man sexually assaulted her and left her on a highway far away from the Job Corps campus.

> I was petrified. I was scared ... I was out there in the middle of nowhere ... a guy in um in a tow truck ... he took me to a gas station and he told the guy at the gas station ... I told him where (I came from) and he said oh my God, he said how did you get way over her? Cause (city) is big ... I got back ... I was so hurt ... I just cried ... I never thought about it till later on in life like how I could have died that night ... cause he could have killed me and nobody knew who I was with, nobody ... knew

nothing ... You know and um today, you know I just thank God that he spared my life cause a lot of girls got killed when I was there ...

Ladonna reported how a few girls from Job Corps had been killed while living in the facility, which she described as a refurbished hotel that was converted into a girl's dormitory. She said "during the time that I was there, there was at least 2 that got killed. ... a few of them got beat up real bad. ... From us being out ... Not inside the facility. The facility ... used to be a hotel ... they [redesigned it] into this Job Corps center you know, so many girls on each floor ..." Ladonna never revealed to the Job Corp officials what happened to her but she was ready to come home after her assault and did not speak about it until later when she was in recovery. Job Corps counselors did not allow her to come home until "what made them send me home, cause I told (them) I was gonna burn the place down. ... sent me home and I came back home right back into the lifestyle of the drugs ..."

By the time Ladonna was still only 16, she had already encountered a lifetime of sexual trauma and was well in the midst of her drug addiction. Job Corps, a government program designed to assist "at risk" youth with job training but she did not reap the benefits from the program. Although she made the choice to enter a man's car, it appeared as if there were no safeguards in place to protect girls from adult men in the community. While in the care of Job Corps personnel, not only was she sexually abused and had her life threatened, her addiction to marijuana became habitual without attempts for intervention. It is possible Ladonna would not have been open to rehabilitation. Yet, as a minor there should have at least been attempts to address drug access and addictions when marijuana use was common throughout the live-in female facility.

Ladonna eventually dropped out of high school and never returned after her experience with the Job Corps. Later in 1999, she attended the local community college and obtained her GED also receiving a business administration certificate. At the time of our conversation, Ladonna aspired to continue her education in business education but her current schedule did not allow her the time to commit to school.

Barbara

Barbara and I had engaged in two telephone conversations before we met in person for the first time at a Baptist church function. She greeted me with a hello along with a smile and big hug as if we were already friends. Barbara had several health problems as she was a recent breast cancer survivor, had hepatitis, and diabetes. Yet, what impressed me most was her youthful spirit, bubbly personality and zest for life. In the mornings, Barbara volunteered at a local day care as a foster grandmother and was committed to that job because she loved children. Her active daily schedule and outings with her children and grandchildren often made it difficult to schedule interviews.

Barbara proudly indicated that all of her children were high school graduates and she shares a special relationship with all of her children and grandchildren. Her son has had previous encounters with law enforcement but at the time of our conversation was a supervisor of security and did some carpentry work. One of her daughters has struggled with drug addiction but along with her sister has taken several classes at cosmetology school. Barbara's oldest daughter is a supervisor at the local child welfare agency. She maintains close relationships with all of her children and grandchildren but is very proud of her oldest daughter because "she never smoked, … got high, … never did nothing … always been a lady … Don't care what nobody says, God will give you one if he don't give you no more. That's my one. I drop dead today … tomorrow, that one's gone keep'em going …" Her children continue to call her for emotional support and both her children and grandchildren smother her with love and attention on major holidays. For example, Barbara's oldest daughter and her husband hosted a special Mother's Day celebration at their home in her honor.

> Girl … Them kids … I believe that sun was just rising … phone got to ringing—Happy Mother's Day Mom. Clickup. Another one ring, Happy Mother's Day Mom … all of'em called … every last one of them called. … And (daughter's name) joined the church so it was nice, it was just nice, you know … [son-in-law's name] made lobster, we had filet mignon; he made something with spaghetti with the scallops. What's the lang (linguine) … He made [GIGGLES] little garlic bread … We cut up and danced. I got lil'grandkids too, my grandbabies was there. We laughed and they had their lil'wine.

Barbara was born in a town about fifteen miles southwest of Philadelphia and was the middle child in a family with her mother, father, three brothers, and four sisters. Her father was the children's primary caregiver because her mother was rarely home. Barbara's father worked at Westinghouse and provided a comfortable lifestyle for their family as evidenced by their three-story home in a predominantly White middle class neighborhood during the

1950's. As a young girl, she lived in a neighborhood with only two Black families on the street.

Barbara's childhood was very stressed because her father worked long hours, her mother "... was on the run for the streets ..." and she was responsible for the care of her younger brothers and sisters. She might see her mother on holidays

> Holidays we might see her and she would come in. Like Ooooh, one Easter, I will never forget it. I thought I was the prettiest thing in the world. Me and my sister was dressed a like. She came home and did our hair up. Brought us these pretty dresses.

Barbara's recollection of the Easter dresses, were the only positive memories she shared with me about her mother. In the early 1950's, when Barbara was a young girl, the local child welfare agency attempted to remove the children from their home. After this occurred, Barbara went to live with her father's sister who lived in Atlantic City and her siblings were separated among other relatives. Her father worked long hours and was unable to also care for his children without the support of her mother who was seldom there. He eventually left the small town and also moved to Atlantic City. As a child, Barbara's extended family buffered the stress the children endured in her mother's absence and she understood then her extended family loved them.

Barbara attended school during her early years in her hometown and attended elementary, junior high, and high school in Atlantic City. However, she did not do too well in school once she moved to Atlantic City. Barbara had difficulty adjusting to being separated from her father and siblings. She says: "I was about 8 ... I just grieved myself simple. I just cried all the time. I lost weight and then when they put me in school. I cut up in school. Oh I was terrible." Barbara was implicated in an incident involving a junior high school teacher breaking her arm resulting in suspension and transferred to Trenton State School for Girls. She remained there for about a year and six months. Barbara says the adults in the state school were serious about education. However, she had difficulty following the rules and restrictions and had to fight off bullies.

> ... I was offered like 6 to 8 months. I end up doing a year and six. Cause I got there on them grounds and cut up with them girls. Um telling me what to do. (laughter) taking advantage of me ... In the place. On the grounds. Hell yeah cause I'm little, cause I was little. You know (then) ... they left me alone. I was alright. But I went through

changes in there ... go to school ... I was assigned to laundry ... They was serious there about school there too ... That's where I got my education from.

After Barbara came home from the state school her life drastically changed because her aunt died while she was away. Things for her became more complicated because during this time she became pregnant with her first child and was prevented from attending school due to her pregnancy. In a very sad voice with sad facial expressions she talks here about when she came home from Trenton.

> ... And they sent me away. When I came back, my aunt was dead, my uncle, everything was gone. ... Um Who did I stay with? (15 second pause) my uncle. She (her aunt) had a husband. (But) he didn't last long. Cause he wasn't together after she died ... And then I ended up with this kid's father. (tapping her finger on the table) the oldest kid. And we got married and I went on about my business.

Although traditional school did not meet Barbara's needs, she had an eagerness to learn. She later received her GED and completed computer training to work in the unemployment office.

Desirea

My conversations with Desirea took place in Atlantic City although she was raised in a New York Bourough. I had more conversations with Desirea than the rest of the mothers. We spent most of our time walking the boardwalk, stopping on the north end to finish our conversations. Desirea lived in a one-bedroom apartment on the North side of Atlantic City in an apartment complex located on the same street intersection recognized as a high crime area where drugs are sold. Yet, Desirea walks around her neighborhood day or night freely without fear. Until she moved to Atlantic City in the mid nineties, she lived in the same apartment building in her New York Bourough she grew up in and where her daughter continues to live. Desirea was born in a southern state but her family including her mother, grandmother, sisters and herself migrated to New York for a better life when she was a small girl. She was the oldest of three sisters and described them as "homebodies." Desirea's grandmother worked as a domestic worker for a wealthy White family and as a practical nurse. Her mother worked in department stores and at the Greyhound bus terminal.

Desirea's family celebrated traditional holidays together and had family outings. She does recall though that Christmas was stressful because of finances. She did not always get the presents she requested but received items she needed such as socks or a winter outfit. During summers, her family spent holidays at the beach with cookouts and gatherings at her aunt's house. Her aunt and grandmother coordinated family activities for the summer at Jones Beach and Croton on da Hudson, and Coney Island.

As a child, Desirea lived with both her mother and grandmother and was considered "spoiled" because she spent a lot of time with her grandmother who allowed her to do things her mother would not have without consequences. When living with her mother, Desirea was not allowed to play outside much because she was very strict wanting to protect her daughters from street life and raise respectable girls. Her New York Bourough neighborhood was also more dangerous than her grandmother's home. Desirea emphasized important distinctions between the quality of life when she lived with her grandmother in Manhattan as opposed to with her mother and sisters in their New York Bourough. Things were much nicer for her when she was able to stay with her grandmother. She shared nice memories of spending time in Manhattan as she smiled and enjoyed reliving those moments. Her "fondest memory ... Winter time ... went skating, bike riding, skating, ah sleigh riding ... Ice skating. The A train was 10 cents ... We would have a frankfurter, what's that company? ... Nathans. Ahh yes. We would have a good time." Desirea recalled how famous Black people who were "pretty rich" living in

> brownstones in the neighborhood ... And they would come certain times out the year and ... would take us many places ... did many things with us. ... Baseball games, ah we lived right down from Yankee Stadium. And we would play in the park, softball, with the likes of Willie Mayes and stuff. ... millionaires that lived in the neighborhood. And so we got to meet a lot of the stars across the board. They would come out on Sunday, Carolyn Franklin, Aretha Franklin's sister. ... We had such fun, we just had so much fun.

Although her grandmother was a domestic worker for rich White families in Manhattan, this job allowed Desirea access to an Elite Black community where members supported children who were not as fortunate. Yet when she was with her mother in her New York Bourough, "... My mother never let us go out ... kept us in the house ... a lot of book reading ... my favorite subjects, science, social studies, history stuff like dat. I'm a history buff ... I belong [to] the Audubon Bird Society."

Desirea's narratives about drugs at school and in her neighborhood took place in the late sixties and early seventies, prior to the crack cocaine era but during the height of New York's heroin epidemic. This time frame also coincides with our country's history of the volatile period of desegregation and busing. She describes her school environment as being overcrowded and overwrought with racial tension because Black students had been moved to a school that is "… majority White, Jewish, Irish, … some German … I can remember … like a simmering pot waiting to boil over. OK … you being a teenager, you know, … seeing and hearing about this but … not really knowing this is what you call racial discrimination …" Desirea reported that between the racial tension and the readily availability of drugs, it was challenging for her to maintain her status as a student.

In addition to the racial tension, like Ladonna and Barbara, attending school was such a struggle for Desirea because the adults demonstrated no leadership as she was bullied mercifully. When referring to many of her fellow students, Desirea reported that the teachers were "… scared too … they used to beat them (teachers) up. … You'd come around the school, and you'd think that it's an outside field day or something. Cause you got that many outside that you had in school." Administrators at Desirea's school were unable to keep student dropouts and others from loitering on the outside and inside of her school. "They were the former students that messed up. They had no business in the area but they were. Ok. School had security, but I mean shucks they got beat up too …" On her high school grounds Desirea encountered "… those selling this and those selling that. And those going to this club. … That young lady done been recruited to Go Go dance to make some extra money. …" All of these distractions were in direct competition with Desirea's efforts to obtain a high school education.

Desirea had been the fierce target of bullying ever since she was in elementary school and tells the story of how she grew tired of the assaults and in the 9th grade, eventually joined the bullying crowd. She reported that her "… shoes were taken … was beaten up that was in 9th grade … I sorta got through the 9th grade. I was a little taken back by the way Desirea talked about her bullying history. She spoke in such a matter of fact style as if bullying was a normal and usual occurrence in her school experiences. Desirea says "… In 9th grade after shoes … taken … got my little initiating and stuff … cause from grade school on up … you always had a student or two that would bother you … throw paper at you and hawk at you, and hit you … all of that stuff … behind the teacher back …"

Similar to Ladonna and Barbara, Desirea encountered extreme bullying at school with no safety net and in order to be protected from the bullies, she joined the bullying group. Desirea was "painfully shy" and believes that she was a target for bullying because of her shyness and she was a loner. Desirea's new associates provided opportunities as well as incentives for her to join them to skip classes and use drugs. She was eventually recruited by and joined this group because "… it's high school and you a little scared and stuff. And someone befriend you … and (it's) thank God, I don't have to eat lunch by myself kinda syndrome.

> … you been beat … in the 7th grade, 8th grade and all that. You tired of getting beat up. You getting beat up on your block. … When it comes to the offer about come on and join us. And the benefits … Hey we won't pick on you. You won't get beat up everyday. That sounds good to me. … They would do things like beat up other kids. Girl you wouldn't want to be late. … they would catch you … they would strip you naked. Beat you down … take everything on you. And I never took part in it. But I ran with them … that was a harmful thing. But those were the things that they would do to you.

Through the eyes of a scared teenager bullied throughout her entire school tenure, membership in this new group provided important safety nets offering many social benefits. To the contrary though, involvement with these peers resulted in a downward spiral with long-term negative consequences she would endure throughout much of her adulthood. I find Desirea's perceptions of the concept choice very interesting as she describes her progression of drug use within this peer group. It all began with her effort to fit in with the crowd for protection and she indicates that in the beginning "… all you have to do is very light stuff. Look out. Hold it. And then you graduate. You lost your choice the minute that you decided to get with that." Desirea is referring here to the use of heroin for the first time when she says "get with that" as she shared with me her torment of wanting to stop her heroin use but unable to do so based on her choice and will. She told me it was not until years later when she was in the midst of her heroin addiction she came to understand the power and control of the drug.

Desirea's gender put her at risk for further exploitation at high school because she became pregnant and attended a school for pregnant girls in the eleventh grade. However, when it was time for her to return to her original high school, it was difficult for her to adjust and she simply stopped going. Desirea told me that she became pregnant with her daughter in eleventh grade by the school security guard and by this time was fully engaged in her heroin addiction. However, she did report to me she did not use heroin during her pregnancy. Desirea tells the story of why she eventually left high school.

> ... Security officers, that's watching and fooling (around) with the kids. I was one a those kids that got fooled with. Wow, that's how I got pregnant. And you got that , "better not say nothing syndrome" cause he married and all that stuff. Ahh, alright, OK, took the nocks ... I kept it to myself and God's her father and I raised her the best I can. By this time I am truly up under addiction. Now I done broke totally from the (teenage) crowd. So now I got in with more of an adult crowd then those my age. Cause now they was people up there, let me see. I was like a 17, 18, 19. they was like 29, 30, 40 years.

In spite of her horrific academic experiences as a child, Desirea's had a thirst for knowledge and enjoyed reading books. She completed her GED requirements in the early 1980's before she graduated from American Business Institute (ABI) but realized later that this certificate was useless. Desirea's eagerness to excel academically made her susceptible to financial exploitation from for-profit educational agencies because the certificate she earned did not increase opportunities for employment. She later found out that the school was under investigation for fraud. "... You know it and was a scam, we wasn't going no where. We was just a neighborhood with a hope. And they was just getting money and not really taking us nowhere."

Desirea later attended Touro College for a year and a half but had to stop because of finances and the demands of the methodone treatment centers. She says that "... you get on the program and they wouldn't ... make it easy for you to make your classes or your job. You know, they (job and school) just insignificant to them you know ..." Desirea encountered many obstacles and disappointments when pursuing her educational goals. She wanted to stop using heroin and enrolled in a methadone clinic. However, accommodating the regulations of the methadone clinic often interfered with her attending school or maintaining employment.

The Settings

Bethena, Sharonda, Ladonna, Barbara, and Desirea's stories were collected in Detroit, Michigan and Atlantic City, New Jersey. We have already discussed their home cities with respect to drug businesses and their drug use but this next section provides you with additional background information of Detroit and Atlantic City.

Detroit

Bethena and Sharonda were living in Detroit throughout their addictions to crack crack cocaine during the mid 1980's when Detroit's inner city streets were immersed in the crack business. Detroit, Michigan, a major mid-western city is located in the eastern part of the state just south of Windsor, Ontario. Detroit is known for its once thriving automobile industry and the sound of Motown, the famous rhythm and blues record company. Both of those industries are gone but Detroit now has three casinos. According to the United States Census Bureau's State and County Quick Facts, Detroit has an estimated total population of 680,250 for 2014 and in 2010 82.7% being Black, 11% of their population is White, 6.8% is Hispanic or Latino (of any race), 0.4 is American Indian and Alaska Native, 1.1% is Asian, 3.7% is some other race, and 1.5% is two or more races. The median household income between 2009–2013 was $28,069. In 2000, there were 40, 537 Black families living below the poverty level and 200,324 individual Blacks living below the poverty level.

Detroit houses the largest school district in Michigan. However, during the fall of 2006, Detroit Public School had 116,800 enrolled in its district, which was a loss of 12,350 students from the previous year. The school district expects a declining enrollment to continue and they have planned to close schools. In 2010, Detroit had a total of 220 schools that include 147 elementary, 31 middle, 28 high schools, 10 adult education and 4 vocational education schools. The number of schools have drastically declined as in 2014 they only had 70 elementary, 55 middle (several of which also served as elementary schools, e.g. preK-8th grade), 23 high schools, 2 alternative schools, 2 adult education schools, 6 special education full service schools, and 4 career and technical schools (Detroit Public School Website). Among 50 large school districts in the country, Detroit Public Schools ranked last for students graduating from high school on time (Hing, 2010). Detroit Public Schools has been overseen with a state appointed emergency manager since 2009, gaining national attention for deplorable conditions during the time of writing this manuscript. Educators' protests and strikes due to pay and poor working conditions gained momentum with national news coverage in early 2016.

They must have a lot of hurricanes here

I never really thought much about the physical appearance of cities in Michigan as I left the state immediately after high school. During the 1980's I lived overseas and occasionally visited my hometown, approximately 90 miles north of Detroit. It was during these short visits, I witnessed drastic deterioration of my hometown and observed consequences of increased unemployment. The impact of the sudden influx of crack businesses on neighborhoods and families in my city was jarring as I returned home for visits.

During my first road trip to Detroit to meet with Bethena and Sharonda, it was easy to see the remnants of unemployment, the 1960's Uprising, and the crack business throughout the city. Neighborhood businesses and what were obviously beautiful multilevel brick homes were boarded up and or simply abandoned. After careful observation, it did not take much for me to see that "back in day" these were beautiful thriving Black neighborhoods and communities with Black owned businesses. Driving around Detroit was an interesting contrast to the small Mid Western college town where I was living at the time. The scene of boarded windows and doors was so frequent that as we drove through the city, one day my daughter commented, "they must have a lot of hurricanes around here." She was referring to the alarming number of homes with boarded windows she observed riding around the city linking it to preparation for the onset of a hurricane. The empty buildings and homes would suggest the community was empty, except for the presence of people (almost always Black) walking along the streets. Yet, there was something about the people that I interacted with from Detroit that expressed hope, pride and love for their city.

The spirit of the famed Motown Recording Company was apparent as I drove throughout the city with two huge billboards with a photo of the late great Marvin Gaye's *What's Goin' On* (1971) album cover advertising Hennessy Cognac. The city also proudly houses the famed Hitsville USA, the Motown Historical Museum's whose presence clearly marks their roots in Detroit. Interestingly though, as I drove along streets with abandoned homes and businesses, I also saw life and hope for change. For example, I observed several political campaign signs in residents' yards seeking the support of Martha Reeves from the Vandellas for Detroit City Council. During one visit, the most striking "ghost" of the Motown era was a radio show's discussion of the gentrification of downtown that included The Woodbridge Estates. This new housing division included buildings, streets and parks named after Detroit and Motown artist such as apartments called The Diana, Temptations Street, Aretha Avenue and a Miracles Park for children to play.

Sharonda's childhood Detroit home during the late 1960s and 1970's was located in a predominantly Black neighborhood she described as a nice middle-class neighborhood where most of the houses were "well painted and neatly kept" with manicured lawns. There were two or three brick homes on her block and spoke of her street being a place where special childhood relationships were established. Sharonda's facial expressions illustrated fond memories of "playing four-square and baseball in the middle of the street and children running home once street lights came on." She indicated "right now today, I still hang with some of the people that I grew up with ... we been knowing each other for like thirty-eight years ... were just like family ... a nice neighborhood ... when we moved over there it was really nice and we all just got along ... it was nice, I liked it."

When I first met Sharonda, she lived in a rental home in a residential section on the west side of Detroit. Most of the homes on the block were nice older brick two to three story homes with nice sized front yards. There were a few homes in the neighborhood with similar structures but were boarded up and appeared unkept. The homes on the street were nice but looked worn in need of paint and repairs yet you could tell that at one time these structures were beautiful homes and probably a very nice street to live on a few decades ago.

Atlantic City

Barbara and Ladonna were raised in Atlantic City, a very small town of 11 square miles located on the shores of the Atlantic Ocean 55 miles south of Philadelphia, Pennsylvania. Atlantic City has an estimated 2014 population of 39, 415, with 2010 data indicating the city had 38.3% Black, 26.7% White, 30.4% Hispanic or Latino, and 15.6% Asian alone residents. Between 2009–2013, the median household income was $29, 2000 with 34.3% of their residents living below the poverty level (US Census Bureau). For the 2013–2014 school year, Atlantic City Public School District has a total of 11 schools consisting of 1 preK school, 5 preK- 8th grade, 3 Kindergarten – 8th grade, 1 Kindergarten-5th grade and one high school with a total of 7,311 students (School Directory Information, 2014–2015). However, students from surrounding cities also attend the high school.

Historically, this small seashore town has been a summer tourist attraction with beaches, Boardwalk, and amusement piers. However, since 1978, Atlantic City has been the major hub of beachfront hotel and casinos on the Atlantic shore until recent years when casinos were built in Mississippi, Delaware and Maryland. Now the city is experiencing another economic downfall as several casinos are now closed. Since its inception, Atlantic City has been a haven for tourist seeking refuge at the Jersey Shore. As early as 1854, new railroads allowed travelers from Philadelphia and from afar to come the shore in large numbers (Rubenstein, 1984). Between 1890 and 1920, the city enjoyed success because it was a place where lower class families could travel to and indulge in upper class and elite experiences. The railroads played a major role in allowing out of state travelers to visit Atlantic City (Rubenstein, 1984). On the other hand, entertainment attractions such as mechanical amusements and cheap vaudeville theaters catering to working class drove the upper class away. These cheap thrills led upper class vacationers away from the huge hotels and high-class restaurants. Atlantic City was a resort intended for only upper-class but decades after its inception, was frequented more by working class (Stansfield, 2006). By the 1930's the grand hotels that were built on the land and ocean sides of the Boardwalk had begun to age and deteriorate with no plans to refurbish them.

By the 1970's, the demise of Atlantic City was obvious to anyone strolling along the Boardwalk or the main strip of Atlantic Avenue. Poverty among Atlantic City's residents in 1970 was at 23% and increased to 25% by 1980 (Goertzel & Cosby, 1997). Statistics for that year also indicated 40% of children were being raised in female-headed households increasing to 60% in 1990. During 1970, 55% of the residents were White and 44% were Black and in 1990 increased to 51% Black and 35% White (Goertzel & Cosby, 1997). In 1976 in response to the continuous decline of the, New Jersey residents voted in favor of legalized gambling in Atlantic City and Resorts International Casino opened in 1978. Legalized gambling was intended to provide employment, support for senior citizen residents (Goertzel & Cosby, 1997), and small portions of profits were to be used for reinvestment and development of the city (Rubenstein, 1984).

By 1990, most of Atlantic City residents who were employed in casinos or civilian labor jobs lived in middle-class neighborhoods. Residents in impoverished neighborhoods benefited from enhanced services due to the casino tax base but few were able to move out of poverty (Goertzel & Cosby, 1997). The casinos' role in redevelopment of the city has varied depending on location. In 1984, neglect of parts of the city remain and those areas near the casinos continue to be redeveloped (Rubenstein, 1984). This abandonment occurred and was quite obvious during the height of Atlantic City's crack epidemic.

Redevelopment of the Boardwalk area has historically been the priority as the inner city remained ignored. One effective method of allowing the inner city's decay is the lack of state and local governments' effort to intervene to avoid selective reassessment of personal property and unplanned rezoning.

This unfortunately allowed the rapid change of ownership of prime property and the removal of many of the city's original residents (Rubenstein, 1984). The revival of the city requires a new framework of redevelopment that includes property and areas beyond the Boardwalk. Shifting the perceptions of Atlantic City as being simply the Boardwalk with a "resident service population" (p. 71) is required for real revitalization of the entire community. This was the backdrop of Midget Moley's heroin and crack industries that further dissipated Atlantic City's Black neighborhoods.

Blacks at the South Jersey Shore

Considerable numbers of Blacks in Atlantic City had the privilege of residing in one of the few places in America at or near the shore for 150 years. By 1905, Blacks were 20% of Atlantic City's population and were instrumental in the development of the seashore resort that we previously knew as America's Largest Playground (Goddard, 2001). Historians typically ignore or marginalize the Black presence in Atlantic City's history, yet they helped build the railroads and worked in recreation and tourism though mostly in service occupations. However, though seldom acknowledged, Blacks also maintained a middle-class existence in the city. For example, Blacks were property owners as early as the 1870's, professionals and business owners. In 1898, Black doctors had even established a Black nursing home to accommodate their senior citizens in the community (Goddard, 2001).

Atlantic City also embraces the legacy of important Black historical figures including, artists, business owners, and not to mention entertainers. In 1913, entrepreneur Madam Sara Spencer Washington started a hair dressing business, developed beauty products, and taught students. In response to lack of hair care products for Black women, she later founded Apex News and Hair Company in 1920 that included a lab, school in Atlantic City and an office in New York. Madam Washington expanded her business to beauty colleges in twelve states with 35,000 agents (Goddard, 2001). In response to racial discrimination in Atlantic City, she established her own golf course welcoming those from all racial backgrounds. She even found the nursing home Apex Rest and established the Easter Parade in Atlantic City for Blacks since they were not allowed to enter the annual parade on the Boardwalk (Goddard, 2001).

Early in its history, Atlantic City has been home to Black doctors, teachers, business owners, church leaders, and even summer vacationers. The artist Henry Ossawa Tanner's famous work *Sand Dunes at Sunset, Atlantic City* provides evidence of Black vacationers as early as 1885. This painting, now housed in the Green Room in the White House, was painted when Tanner and family from Philadelphia vacationed at their summer cottage in Atlantic City (Goddard, 2001). Atlantic City is also the birthplace of the Harlem Renaissance artist Jacob Lawrence as well as Black actor James Avery and actress Rosalind Cash.

In spite of their rich Black history, Atlantic City did not escape segregation with the Black community consisting of neighborhoods located on the Westside, Northside and in the Inlet. However, most jobs were only summer jobs, leaving Black residents with access to very little income after Labor Day, thus the saying "three months to hurry and nine months to worry" (Goddard, 2001). Blacks were allowed to work in service professions in hotels and venues on the Boardwalk, however not allowed to frequent the places as customers. From the 1900s to the 1950's, the beaches were even segregated and Black residents were restricted to the beaches located only on streets still affectionately known as *Chicken Bone Beach* (Hooper, n.d.).

The segregated Black community included a wide range of Black owned businesses. Barbara described her neighborhood in the 1950's, along Tennessee Avenue as a booming place. As a young girl, she lived next door to a guesthouse that accommodated famous Black people visiting the city and not allowed to stay in local hotels. She fondly recalls "... I was telling you about Joe Louis ... he was boxing then ... Right next door. He stayed a few days ... We lived right next door. We had the whole apartment downstairs ... the lady that owned it lived over top of us ... kept a beautiful place." Barbara recalled these memories with so much fondness as she shook her head with a smile describing her old neighborhood with pride. She emphasized the fact that these were often famous people and people from out of town who stayed in the guesthouse and also frequented Black owned business in her neighborhood. She said "... they (people from out of town) know where to come ... They come down by the bus loads. Cause you see during them times, the Elks Parade, the Elks, this town was wide open then boy ..."

Barbara had an opportunity to see and meet the boxer Jersey Joe Walcott, Joe Louis and other famous Black people coming in and out of the guesthouse next door to her childhood home. The house is still there and she said "Every time I see that house ... it gives me a good feeling. You know, cause they redoing to whole facing of the house." Barbara spoke about her neighborhood with so much pride as she recalled an area of three blocks within the city where there was "nothing but shops and stores ... All Black ... working

Blacks ... with their own businesses." These businesses included a candy shop, variety store with ice cream counters, army/navy store, restaurants, camera shop, and entertainment establishments. The city's landscape has drastically changed since Barbara's childhood but these same communities set the stage for Desirea, Barbara and Ladonna's narratives in the next chapter. The next chapter illustrates the complexities of Desrea, Bethena, Barbara, Ladonna and Sharonda's lives as mothers with drug addiction.

References

Collins, P. H. (2000). *Black feminist thought: Knowledge, consciousness, and the politics of empowerment* (2nd ed.). New York, NY: Routledge.

Detroit public school website. Retrieved from http://detroitk12.org.

Dunbar, C., Rodriguez, D., & Parker, L. (2002). Race, subjectivity, and the interview process. In J. F. Gubrium & J. A. Holstein (Eds.), *Handbook of interview research: Context and methods* (pp. 279–298). Thousand Oaks, CA: Sage Publications.

Gaye, M. (1971). *What's goin on* [Vinyl Album]. United States: Motown subsidiary label Tamal Records. (Recorded June 1970–May 1971).

Glaser, B. G., & Strauss, A. L. (1967) (as cited in Bogdan & Biklen, 2007). *The discovery of grounded theory: Strategies for qualitative research*. Boston: Pearson A & B.

Goddard, R. F. (2001). *'Three months to hurry and nine months to worry': Resort life for African Americans in Atlantic City, NJ (1850–1940)*. (Unpublished doctoral dissertation). Howard University, Washington, DC.

Goertzel, T. G., & Cosby, J. W. (1997). Gambling on jobs and welfare in Atlantic City. *Society Magazine*, May/June, 62–66.

Hambrick, A. (1997). You haven't seen anything until you make a black woman mad. In K. M. Vaz (Ed.), *Oral narrative research with Black women* (pp. 64–82). Thousand Oaks, CA: Sage Publications.

Hing, J. (2010). 45 Detroit schools to close: Where have all the students gone? *Color Lines*. Retrieved from http://colorlines.com.

Hooper, D. (n.d.). Chicken bone beach historical foundation, Inc. Retrieved from http://www.chickenbonebeach.org.

Johnson-Bailey, J. (1999). The ties that bind and the shackles that separate: Race, gender, class, and color in a research process. *Qualitative Studies in Education, 12*(6), 659–670.

Rubenstein, J. (1984). Casino gambling in Atlantic City: Issues of development and redevelopment, *The Annals of the American Academy of Political and Social Science, 474*(1), 61–71.

School Directory Information (2014–2015). *National Center for Education Statistics*. Retrieved from https://nces.ed.gov.

Seidman, I. E. (2013). *Interviewing as qualitative research: A guide for researchers in education and the social sciences* (4th ed.). New York, NY: Teachers College Press.

Solórzano, D. G., & Yosso, T. J. (2009). Critical race methodology: Counter-storytelling as an analytical framework for education research. In E. Taylor, D. Gillborn, & G. Ladson-Billings (Eds.), *Foundations of critical race theory in education* (pp. 131–147). New York, NY: Routledge.

Stansfield, C. (2006). The rejuvenation of Atlantic City: The resort cycle recycles. In R. W. Butler (Ed.), *The tourism area life cycle: Applications and modifications* (pp. 287–305). Clevedon, UK: Channel View Publications.

United States Census Bureau's State and County Quick Facts (2015). Retrieved from https://www.census.gov/quickfacts.

· 6 ·

"I HAD HELP"

Kinship, Drug Addictions, and Black Family Resilience

Black families in the United States (US) relied on kinship networks for survival. Proof of these networks date back to the presence of enslaved families on plantations in the United States and have African roots (Sudarkasa, 2007) and helped buffer the sting of race, class, and gender oppressions (Anderson, 2003; Collins, 1999; Fordham, 1996; Hill, 2003; Ladner, 1971; McAdoo, 1998; Stack, 1974; Tolliver, 1998). Kinship networks become even more valuable to Black families when navigating crank, powder and crack cocaine and heroin addictions. The mothers' narratives highlight kinship networks as essential child-care, housing, and financial resources. Particular attention is made to guardianship and care of grandchildren, family and Black males kinships, fictive kinships and their costs. Bethena, Barbara, Sharonda, Ladonna and Desirea share stories of legal and informal guardianship of grandchildren and the supportive role of other relatives such as aunts, cousins, and sisters. There is also a focus on the support of Black males in and outside of the family and fictive kin who intervened as important assets for families. Lastly, the cost of kinship networks will also be addressed.

Kinship Networks

The controlled image of the nuclear family structure of a mother, father, and children symbolizes the ideal family in the United States (U.S.). This hegemonic construction of family privileges the ideal family structure as superior (Heilman, 2008) to families with strong kinship networks (Sudarkasa, 1996). The term extended family has been used to refer to family structures based on marriage and include members beyond the nuclear family. This term is frequently used to refer to U.S. Black nonnuclear households and assumes the nuclear family unit is the basic family organization (Sudarkasa, 1996). For purposes of this chapter, the term family kinship is used instead of extended family to refer to supportive relationships with individuals who are related through blood or by marriage. The term fictive kinships will refer to such relationships with individuals who fall outside those categories.

Kinship networks have been the foundation of resilience and survival for families of the descendants of enslaved Africans in the U.S. (Anderson, 2003; Collins, 1999; Fordham, 1996; Hill, 2003; Ladner 1971; McAdoo, 1998; Stack, 1974; Sudarkasa, 1996; Tolliver, 1998). The dominant narrative may suggest kinship networks emerged from the destruction and disorganization of the Black family unit during their capture and enslavement in this country. To the contrary, kinship networks have strong African roots that came along with the Africans as they adjusted to their enslavement in the U.S. (Gutman, 1976; Sudarkasa, 1996). African familial patterns of organization survived slavery and remain present in contemporary Black family life. At the same time, we cannot deny that economic forces and racial ideologies of African based family patterns change across time periods and geographical and political environments (Sudarkasa, 1996). An example of change may be found in many Black neighborhoods' response to the crack cocaine era and so-called war on drugs. Interestingly though, there were periods of history in which Black family structures were actually nuclear in nature during and after slavery as much as and sometimes more than their White counterparts (Gutman, 1976). The key point being, African family values and familial patterns, such as kinship networks were not destroyed by the institution of slavery (Gutman, 1976; Sudarkasa, 1996).

Guardianship and Care of Grandchildren

There was a heavy reliance on family kinships from all mothers in this book during their active addiction. In response to the crack industry's stronghold on impoverished Black communities, Black grandmothers across the US assumed responsibility for parenting their grandchildren (Dunlap, Tourigny, & Johnson, 2000; Haglund, 2000; Zerai, 2000). Grandparents played significant roles in the caring of their grandchildren. Sharonda and Ladonna legally transferred temporary guardianship of their children to their mothers. They describe why they gave their mother guardianship of their children.

> ... I had signed the kids over to my mother. I was like you know what I can't do both, I can't do the kids and smoke too. So mom I'm gonna give you custody of the kids, we go downtown and sign the papers for a two year guardianship ... when I get myself together, I'll get them back and so I had did that.

Sharonda's relationship with her mother was not always pleasant but her mother would always help with her children. Here, Sharonda realized she would be unable to navigate addiction and recovery with custody of her children and her mother was a safer alternative. Her self-imposed time limit of two years to get herself together illustrates her intention to later regain custody of her children.

Ladonna on other had shared a very tight knit relationship with her mother and during her first pregnancy, spent time together every day. Her mother already expressed concerns about Ladonna's living conditions and welfare of her granddaughter before she retained guardianship. Ladonna's mother told her "... if you want to live here ... like this that's fine. But, I am not bringing this baby back." Shortly afterwards, LaDonna moved back home with her mother and eventually became employed demonstrating more personal responsibility. That is, until she developed a relationship with a younger man who was a cocaine dealer and soon lived with him. Ladonna indicated that she had been abstinent from crank for a little less than a year when she developed her addiction to cocaine. She says:

> ... I ended up getting in this relationship with a guy younger than me. ... he sold coke ... was a drug dealer. ... it was always in the house and I said to myself one day ... let me see how it make me feel now. Well I hadn't done the crank in awhile. ... I think I was just smoking marijuana and drinking and stuff. And I tried this coke and I liked it. And from there it was off to the races ...

Ladonna's relationship with her new boyfriend was the catalyst for her new addiction to powder cocaine addiction after she had been clean from crank for a sustained but short period of time. As a young woman just becoming abstinent from crank, her home environment with her drug-dealing boyfriend made her vulnerable to powder cocaine addiction. In her own words, it "was off to the races" after she tried some of her boyfriend's stash in their home. Ladonna describes the scene:

> … Like, I lived right across the street from my mom … people would come to my house and my mom would call … Anyway you know at this time my addiction is progressing more and more. I would stay up all night, I would have company, the house was dark, my electric got cut off. … And um when [my daughter] was 3, I marched across the street to my mother's house one day. And I said to my mom, I said look, I can't take care of this baby, so what you gone do?

Even in the midst of her addiction, she understood her mother was going to pick up the slack and care for her daughter. Regardless of how entrenched Ladonna was in her addiction, her mother had always been there by her side to care for her granddaughter. In retrospect, Ladonna acknowledged the negative impact of her addiction on her daughter as well as the sacrifices her mother made to care for her daughter. She emphasized that throughout her addictions, she remained confident of her mother's love regardless of the circumstances.

Similar to Sharonda, Ladonna also clearly understood the progression and power of her cocaine addiction and its interference with parenting. Ladonna's mother never failed to confront her about her drug problem and responsibilities but was always supportive throughout her addiction. Ladonna shared a story about a confrontation with her mother before she gave custody of her daughter. Her mother gained knowledge about Ladonna's drug use and saw the needle tracks on her arm, "… she tried to take the coat off, she saw. And I let her see it, she could see it. And you know, we cried, and I was gone get myself together you know what I'm saying. But by then I was already in the grips. You know …" In retrospect LaDonna understands the powerful stronghold of her cocaine addiction. Here she talks about being in the "the grips" as she called it and the difficulty with stopping regardless of her desires and intentions to quit using powder cocaine and parent her daughter.

Initiating the legal transfer of custody or guardianship of their children to their mothers were LaDonna and Sharonda's way of cautiously carrying for them during their active addiction. LaDonna's and Sharonda's mothers became primary caregivers of their grandchildren in spite of the horrors that come with having a child involved in the crack and heroin industry. These grandmothers were challenged with stereotypes of their daughters and grandchildren but maintained a sense of obligation and hope for a better life for their grandchildren (Zerai, 2000). Crack and heroin use and sale often diminish resources available from kinship networks with grandmothers (Dunlap et al., 2000). For example, family coping processes become stressed when these drugs are introduced into the household because of the distinct violence accompanying drug and street norms (Dunlap et al., 2000). However, LaDonna and Sharonda's mothers were able to rise above these stressors and obtained legal relationships with their grandchildren remaining as their primary caregivers until the mothers regained custody of their children.

Other Family Kinships

Grandmothers were not the only family members willing to care for children during their mother's active addictions. Desirea not only had the support of her mother, but her sister, aunt and grandmother actively participated in the raising of her daughter throughout her childhood regardless of her drug use. They were key members in her family kinship network that helped care for her daughter during her heroin addiction. Here, she describes how inevitable it was for her female relatives to help raise her daughter.

> ... she interacted a lot with her grandmother and her aunts. A whole lot. Because she was the first grand. It wasn't so much I was active in addiction ... she was the first grandchild and niece. ... I had so much freedom cause I always had either my mother or my sister or my aunts could have had her. ... She could go off to school today decide she wanna go to her aunt's house and call and see could she stay, you know and it's alright. So it wasn't like the system or anything had to move her ...

Relinquishing legal custody of her daughter was never required because Desirea's mother, grandmother, or sister voluntarily shared responsibility in raising and caring for her daughter. Desirea's story also calls attention to the fluidity of roles for women in her family when it came to a relationship with the family's first grandchild. Family kinships emerged smoothly as Desirea presented the first grandchild to the adult women in her family. Her daughter's grandmother, great-grandmother, and aunt were delighted to spend time with Desirea's new daughter ensuring her safety and wellbeing. Unfortunately, this provided ample opportunities for Desirea to resume social activities focused on heroin addiction with no parenting responsibility.

Childcare arrangements for Sharonda included shared responsibilities of babysitting among her friends and her sister during her active addiction. For example, she says:

> ... I ... keep the kids, so you can't get high while the kids there anyway. So basically, I always had somebody's kids or mine would be gone. My sister and my mom kept them a lot ...

Immediate family members were not available to Bethena with her second daughter born prenatally exposed to crack cocaine. However, her two aunts and male cousin were important resources for her. One aunt allowed her to reside in her two family dwelling home rent free. Another aunt was instrumental in her ability to bring her daughter home from the hospital. This aunt intervened so that Bethena's daughter would not be put in foster care.

While at the hospital, Bethena acknowledged her drug addiction and the negative consequences on her new born infant. In spite of potential legal ramifications, she did not deny her addiction. At this point Bethena realized she required assistance because the hospital personnel informed her that "... this baby is a crack baby and we can not release this baby to you in your custody without some kind of guardian or somebody that's gonna help you with this child."

Bethena is really grateful for the support she received for the care of her daughter and would become quite emotional when she would speak about it. Here Bethena tells the story of her aunt's support:

> ... Auntie was the only one, (tears began to fall from her eyes) Auntie was the only one that came and step forward to say well, I don't live there with her. But I'm willin to come on that side a town once a week and check and see how (her name) and that baby ... I don't know what she told them people in that hospital. ... I called her cryin and told her they was gonna take my baby and cause of crack. And Auntie knew we was on crack, but Auntie was the type she never judged any of us. She never judged any of us, even when we told her a lie to get some money ... I guess she just continue praying for us, continue praying, continue praying. And I tell you it worked.

Bethena relied on her family kinship networks and her aunt accepted responsibility for ensuring that Betheana's infant daughter would be cared for. Amazingly, her daughter was released from the hospital as an underweight drug exposed infant with no early intervention services to monitor her development. Bethana was still actively involved in her crack addiction without drug rehabilitation services and was not assigned to a child welfare caseworker to follow-up on her and her newborn infant. When she brought her daughter home from the hospital, she does not recall being given any instructions or medicine for her daughter. Bethena's perception of why this happened is:

> So like I say, they gave me [my] baby at three pounds and two ounces. And I look back and over the years I look back, they wasn't supposed to release that baby at no three pounds and two ounces, knowing you was a crack baby too. ... Oh chile, they was hoping—now that I look back on it, I say they was hoping that the baby probably go out and die so they could charge me with murder. But God look out for babies and fools.

Interestingly, Bethena's ideas resonates with Dorothy Roberts (2003) claim that poverty, racism, and ineffective health care policies set the stage for poor Black mothers addicted to crack to be blamed for infant mortality. States were more apt to prosecute a mother who was addicted to crack during her pregnancy as opposed to offering prenatal health care or drug rehabilitation (Roberts, 2003; Zerai & Banks, 2002). In Bethena's case, no local child welfare or legal institutions became involved in her family, and kinship networks were essential for her daughter's survival and family resilience. Similarly, family and fictive kinships with Black children of alcoholics provided substantial support to their overall well-being. These kinship networks made significant contributions to social and emotional development of Black children when effective parenting was disrupted by parental alcoholism (Hall, 2008).

On the other hand, Marian Harris and Ada Skyles (2008) argue the child welfare system's overreliance of Black children's placements with family kinships undermines goals of foster care. Family reunification of the birth mother and child is the stated goal of foster care. Yet, support for Black mothers suffering with drug abuse or other mental health difficulties is often lacking for birth parents of Black foster children placed with kinship care. Often, once a Black child is placed in kinship care, adequate efforts are not made to provide assistance required for family reunification with their birth mother (Harris & Skyles 2008). Yet, family kinships sustained families in this book throughout the mothers' years of active addictions, serving as important buffers from placement in an already burden system of foster care.

Fictive Kinships

Fictive kinships have also been key to Black family survival and resilience in the U.S. These kinship networks are comprised of individuals who were not blood related but functioned as kin and have African roots (Gutman, 1976; Manns, 2007; Sudarkasa, 2007). Fictive kinships have been important to emotional support and supplementing resources (Manns, 2007; Miller-Cribbs & Farber, 2008; Jarrett, Jefferson, & Kelly, 2010). These networks were also sources of childcare for Sharonda and Bethena throughout their lives of addiction.

Neighborhood kinship networks are not as prevalent today because of the changing institutional fabric of the Black community (Sudarkasa, 2007; Collins 2000). During the 1980's, the influx of crack cocaine forever changed the collective sense of community for many Black neighborhoods in the U.S. (Collins 2000). However, in spite of the harsh realities of crack's neighborhood invasion, Sharonda and Bethena were able to establish strong fictive kinships in Detroit. Sharonda's mother and sister often cared for her children. However, fictive kinship, such as Sharonda's next-door neighbor Lacrecia and her family provided continuous child care support during her addiction. Lacrecia often helped take care of her children as Sharon says when she would "… be wherever … doing what I do …" Sharonda described how much she appreciated Lacrecia:

> … she don't know how much she was … a big support … she'd be like, naw-naw sit down, go ahead. Girl, gone do what you doing, I got this. You know she was a big help to me … Yeah, she was just a blessing, just a blessing. And um, she wasn't judging even when you messed up and you know you messed up … you know she was just a blessing. Well um her mother and her brother lived next door … they just started calling me "oh that's my daughter, oh that's my sister." So they just sort of like adopted me, and so yeah I had help in that aspect.

Bethena established a network of support comprised of her male cousin and others outside her biological family. I was really impressed with Bethena's ability to recall specific details of memory surrounding the events of her daughter's birth as she described support from fictive kin. She was able to recall minute details such as how she was feelings, the time, and dates. Here she speaks about when she was sick and needed to go to the emergency room.

> … I guess … it was nine fifteen, nine twenty. Dey took me to one hospital over on somewhere, (Street A) and (Street B), or (Street A) and 14th, anyway dat was closed … In da next two, three days, I couldn't walk. I don't know what was up I couldn't walk … bein in January, de second and third and fourth, you know January dat's de coldest time of de year. I'm walkin around wit house shoes on … So my cousin (Pseudonym Bobby), he paid dis other lady, dis other crack head, I mean everyday

he would give her ten dollars or five dollars or fifteen to stay there with me for about week and she did, to help me out wit de baby. Cause like I said I had caught cold and when you catch cold, oh God all I could do was crawl. I couldn't even walk …

Bethena's aunt checked on her and the newborn baby weekly as she promised the child welfare personnel at the hospital. However, Bethena also received help with her newborn outside of the family. She came home from the hospital before her newborn was ready to be released. When the hospital called her to come get her baby, she did not have transportation and relied on someone in her circle of friends to take her to the hospital.

> Honey that baby a mines and we all might a been smokin crack and whatever. But I had everybody, men, boys and girls, everybody that smoke crack was helping me with that baby. Everyday they bring some clothes, they would find or milk or this and that. That child be kickin and come the second of January this year she'll be eighteen. I ain't had no problem. Everybody, crack or whatever we helped—everybody help raise that one.

Clearly this was not the optimal or appropriate environment to raise a new baby. Yet, her narrative does illustrate how even in the midst of crack addiction, Bethena was able to create a fictive kinship with her network of friends for support. About a year after Bethena's daughter's birth, she stopped using crack cocaine and later had a son. She continued to be a caring but now a more responsible parent with important goals for her children. Many of these goals involved strict academic expectations and ensuring her children did not become parents until after completing high school. Most importantly, she wanted her children to have better academic experiences than she did and to remain drug free. After high school, Bethena's daughter completed a dental hygiene program at a junior college and worked in a local dentist's office.

Fictive kinships were fundamental to resilience as Bethena and Sharonda navigated their crack cocaine addiction. Sharonda also emphasized that support outside of her family often proved to be an important mental health resource for her throughout her children's lives. She says:

> There was just always somebody that stepped in and just I don't know why the reason somebody would just step in. Even when I didn't need, I mean even if I wasn't doing anything they would be like you need a break, let us take the kids type of thing. It's always been like that for me and I thank God for that, cause that's why none of them, I didn't kill no body (laughter). Cause I got a lot of breaks, yeah.

Black Males: Essential Resources

Black men have historically been significant to kinships and their roles were significant to the resilience of Black families in the U.S. (Gutman, 1976; Staples & Johnson, 1993; Livingston & McAdoo, 2007). Black fathers play active rolls in raising their children enjoying close relationships with their daughters (Staples & Johnson, 1993; Livingston & McAdoo, 2007; Sudarkasa 2007). Barbara's stories illustrate the special relationship shared with her father. She became addicted to heroin as a teen in the 1960's until the late 1990's, when she also picked up a crack addiction. Her father and second husband were primary sources of support and were actively involved in raising her children. Barbara speaks about her father when discussing her first child's father whom she eventually married.

> My father used to say "Puddin" he used to call me "Puddin." You don't have to marry him. Daddy ... and you can take care of that baby. ... He said you ain't got to marry him. They didn't like him. They sensed something about him that they didn't like. And they was right. Cause that fool would get to fighting me.

Barbara's narrative illustrates a quality daughter-father relationship she shared with her father, her main source of support with her children besides her second husband. She spoke fondly of the special bond she shared with him since her early childhood. Even as an adult addicted to heroin, he was always there for Barbara and her children. Barbara did not remain married to her first husband but stayed with her second husband, also a heroin addict, for over thirty years until his death. He was not the biological father of her first two children when they met, however, he loved and cared for them as his own children. For example:

> Christmas girl, my kids had a tree (her face smiling, she looked happy as she recalled) gifts would be from here to da door. And it be different rows. A row for (daughter's name). Each child had a row of presents. So that's how we had to do it. Cause, I only had the two by him, 11 months apart. I told him I was pregnant. He'd just grin. And I cried like a baby. (she laughs) I knew what was coming. (Laughter) He's smilin. I'll never forget that smile on that man's face.

Barbara and her second husband were a very loving couple who cherished their children even in the midst of their years of heroin addiction. As a stepfather, Barbara explained how her husband loved and cared for her children before she became pregnant with his own biological child. She says that he would take the children "… up on the boardwalk. I have pictures with [child's name] up on his shoulders. Yeah he loved the kids. He loved kids. And never had none of his own" until she became pregnant. Barbara explains how excited and proud her husband was about being a biological father.

> … couldn't wait for her to walk. Soon as she walked, he took that baby to New York to see his people. By his self … I said, you gone be able to take care of that baby up in New York. He said look here, I got seven brothers and seven sisters and he said you don't trust me around my baby. I said. I just want you to be careful takin my baby all the way up to New York by yourself. And he took her … for his family to meet her, so you know he was happy.

Barbara's husband was also an important resource for childcare and was confident in his ability to care for his children. They coordinated their work schedules so that at least one of them would always be home, and she was very proud that her children never required a babysitter.

> … Um He got a job at (employment). He was a head bellman at (employment) … He worked in the daytime and I worked at night … This was after my father died. This is how we kept my kids together. So that's why they never knew a babysitter. He worked during the day and I be home. I watch my own kids. And at nighttime, when I'm working at night. He got them. And that's the way we did it … we both had our same two days off. You know. So that's how we did thangs.

For the most part, this childcare system worked well for Barbara and her husband until one of their teenaged daughters would sneak out of house in the middle of the night. Barbara's father was also a childcare resource until his death. He took care of her children prior to meeting her husband, as well as at times when she was at home getting high. She talks about how she did not need a babysitter.

> I told you … had a built in babysitter … they had their father … each other. Now what else did they need? … You know I wasn' out there … like that with my babies. When I had my new babies. … I mean period, when I used it, I was usin it at home. I wasn't no street person, I told you I was a private person … They would be fed, taken care of, you know. And if they needed a bottle my dad would be up here, he'd give it to him. … So my kids wouldn't need … want nothing, you know because we'd all be right there … I put them babies first and they lil'cousins … we'd feed all them babies.

Barbara's home appeared to be the gathering place for her friends, sister and their children during her active addiction. Thus, they created a network of support for their children to be cared for together in the safety of their home. Barbara proudly tells the story of her and her friend's children being cared for at home by her, her family or friends. In spite of the significance of the combination of heroin addiction and parenting, Barbara maintained a strong sense of parental competence about her role as a mother. She prides herself on the idea that her children were cared for just as good as children raised in any other home.

Barbara received support from her father and husband for child-care. The Black men in her family made important contributions to parental decision-making and the socialization and care of all of her children (Staples & Johnson, 1993; Livingston & McAdoo, 2007). Black men outside the family can also serve as significant support for Black mothers impacted by drug addictions. For example, Sharonda found comfort and support from a childhood friend named Lamar who was an essential resource for emotional and financial support.

> Well, there's this guy named (Lamar). I've never kissed him, slept with him or nothing. But he's been, I've been knowing him since I was eight and he was just over to the house yesterday, he sits there. He just comes, he's just my friend. And um, it's basically him, he's the main, main part of my life. And when I'm not with the kids father, he'll come and say oh what they doing, oh what they need, oh well let me go get him some shoes—don't he need some shoes. He's just helpful, he's just a big help to me. … When I was eight, we all grew up together. We'd run up and down the street actin crazy. But we just always kept in touch.

Sharonda's fiancé was also a major source of emotional support for her as illustrated in her comment about him. She says that

> … this man I have is a excellent, excellent, excellent person in my life … And um, and this man I have, he's a big, big, big help. He's a big praying on fire fella. So um if I think something, he'll look at me—you okay? You look like something go on, come on let's pray type of thing … it just helps, a lot of praying

Sharonda talked about how her fiancé as well as her pastor was always there for her whenever she was feeling depressed. The Black church has historically been a place of refuge and support for Black families (Hill, 2003). Sharonda attended a church that welcomed those impacted by crack addiction and provided her meaningful support during her period of recovery. Her pastor also played a major role in her network of fictive kin supporting her during the trails of crack addiction and recovery. She shares that:

> … Cause anytime I even think, well now, I call Bishop too. 'Bishop, I'm feeling a little heavy.' He's like alright woman of God we gon pray right now. Whatever he

doing, he gonna drop it and pray for you and by me believing that this prayer is gonna work it does, you know what I'm saying.

Cost of Kinships Networks

Kinship and fictive networks have historically been vital to Black family resilience as illustrated in the families of Bethena, Barbara, Sharonda, Ladonna, and Desirea. The mothers highlighted how family kinships served as important resources for childcare and housing. However, Sharonda and Deseria found there were huge costs to receiving help from these networks (Stack, 1974; Roosier 2000). In her seminal piece *All Our Kin*, Carol Stack, 1974 illuminates costs associated with the since of obligation or the system of exchanging resources which interferes with the smooth functioning of kinship networks. These costs become evident when reciprocity and respect are absent from the kinship (Dunlap, Tourignt, and Johnson 2000; Stack1974) and not everyone participates in the sharing of resources.

Heroin and crack addictions prevented Sharona and Deseria from contributing to the kinship network with the older women in their families that assumed care for their children. Nonetheless, they both recognized the cost of the support their family provided. Sharonda's mother assisted her quite a bit with caring for her children by gaining legal custody and with providing housing. Their relationship was strained as she reported that her mother mistreated her as a child and demonstrated favoritism toward her sister. Sharonda reminds us of the costs associated with the benefits of kinship networks (Stack, 1974; Roosier 2000). She revealed to me that her mother was overly strict on her and required her to do excessive amount of housework to the point that it interfered with her schoolwork at a very young age. In the interview data, Sharonda discussed how her mother put the total responsibility of keeping the laundry done and the house cleaned and organized on her. This burden was so heavy for Sharonda that her chores compromised her school work and was one of the precursors to her dropping out of high school after the first semester of her senior year. While Sharonda understood the importance of raising your children and teaching them how to clean house, she believed her mother's behavior toward her was extreme. Her mother did not have the same expectations for her sister. She became upset once she began to observe the same parenting practices with her oldest children in her mother's care. This prompted her to begin thinking seriously about recovery. She says:

> ... they was with her for a long time, I was like unh, unh. (no) Cause I went over my mother's house and they had my older kids doin what I used to do and I got so pissed off. ... I said I got to get myself together and get my kids. So I had to get myself together and that's what I did. I had to get myself together and get my kids back.

Sharonda expressed an interest in regaining custody of her children but her mother did not agree that she was ready to have custody of her children and did not support her efforts at doing so.

> But my mother didn't want to give'em back. Because they was givin her like six and seven hundred dollars per child. Why do they do that? ... she got a Lincoln and I was like mom, I'm ready, I'm ready for the kids to come home. She was like oh naw, I don't think you're ready ... she said no, and I had to go to court ... So that got me takin drug tests and all that ... drug tests are nothing, you can beat that ... you can take the drug tests on Tuesdays and Thursday. You get high Monday, Thursday you take your test you're clean. Crack is out your system in three days, so, I did that. I started smokin back a little, but ... My older kids was doin what I was doin. ... I was like what the? You know, so I had to straighten up and get'em back ... So I go to court and then at first I was just tryin to beat the court, but then a after a while I was like, let me get myself together for real and get my kids home ...

In this narrative, Sharonda talks about the drawbacks of accepting support for childcare and housing from her mother. Her major concern of their placement with her mother was that her children were being exploited for not just domestic labor but also financially. She began to "start smoking back a little" and in the beginning, her commitment to staying clean was sabotaged by her crack addiction. However, eventually custody of her children motivated her to stop using crack cocaine. Sharonda's mother was fortunate that their state provided financial support to those with guardianship of their grandchildren. Child welfare laws and policies in Desirea's, Ladonna's, and Barbara's state during the time of their active addictions did not provide financial or medical resources to family members with legal guardianship. Eventually, the child welfare laws did indeed change and their states began to provide financial and medical support to legal guardians.

Desirea also highlights the drawbacks of her daughter being in the informal custody or care of her mother, sister, and grandmother. It was only later in her daughter's childhood that she begin to realize the negative impact of being absent as due to heroin addiction had on her daughter. As result of her absence, her daughter did not really know her as a person or as a mother. She illustrates this realization when she says:

> Didn't know nothing about me. The things she really heard from my mother and sister and others talking bout me too. They do more damage too. You know so, da child looks through what they hear from other people. Especially when "and yo mother ain't no good" [she's imitating the voice of others speaking about her] "yo mother this, and yo father this." You know how they do that thang.

The negative thoughts about Desirea remained deep in the consciousness of her daughter throughout her childhood. Even as an adult, her daughter still questions her based on things her aunt and grandmother said to her when she was younger.

> Sometimes she have questions even right now. She too ... I guess wanna know. Well, I was lookin at it as ... I didn't abandon you cause you was with your family. They would call for you or you'd want to go over there. To me that wasn't abandonment ... she was with them so much she's the only child. OK. They was young and would call and stuff. She wanted ta be with her auntie. She wanted to be with grandma. Well, grandma always wanted her. Grandma acted like it was her daughter. OK. So um weather than do a tug a war over her, it was like. It was alright. I call myself sharing with the family. Come to find out that what I call sharing, they was calling it, sort of like um you was out running ... doing her own thing and stuff like that.

Desirea's thought was that her mother, grandmother, and sister did not provide an accurate or fair assessment of her love and concern for her daughter. Instead, when Desirea was not around, they would tell her daughter "... what she was doing was more important than you, the people she was with was more important than being with you ..." This upset Desirea because she believed that in spite of her heroin addiction, she did assume responsibility for raising her daughter.

> Never mind that I was the one that got her enrolled in early school. I'm the one that got her enrolled in pre-kindergarten. I'm the one that got up and took her to school, I'm the one that helped her with those readings and math and learning how to write. I did it. Um, They might a did a little bit. But they didn't focus on those areas and stuff. ...

Regardless of her heroin addiction, Desirea remained steadfast in ensuring that her daughter achieved academically. She wanted her daughter to have a better life than hers and believed that achieving academically was a key element of meeting that goal. During an interview, Desirea reports:

I'd read to her. And like I told you before I would give her things ... Um. I do it just a little bit, just a little bit above what her grade, what her level suppose to have been. Like with the GED book. She said it was hard. You know. ... I would say answer to the best of your ability, what do you think? And she did very good. Very very good. And. Um again, just because I was into (heroin), well I didn't know it, I didn't know at the time I was an addict. I didn't even know that. That's how naive I was. I didn't know back what I was doing was considered that. It'll be some many a years before I realize the whole total package of what I was doing was actually something I couldn't stop doing when I felt like it. I had to go through the system. ... So I wasn't like a person that had a problem with low IQ or learning disability. So I. So it's natural I would teach my daughter as well as my nieces and nephews. But more so my daughter you know.

Unaware of the full impact of a heroin addiction until it was too late, Desirea still loved learning, maintained a strong academic orientation and tried to pass that on to her daughter.

Family scholars (Jarrett et al., 2010; Stack, 1974) argue that kinships are based on network exchanges that sometimes result in conflictual relationships accompanied with other significant costs for the benefit of support and resources. Sharonda and Desirea's narratives spoke to the cost of support from their family kinships. Their mothers were the primary caregivers of their grandchildren during their daughters' years of active addiction. This was a tremendous sacrifice and gift to their grandchildren as it might have kept them out of foster care. However, Desirea and Sharonda recognized later the vulnerable situation this placed their children in during their times of active addiction. Desirea has tried to move forward to enhance her relationship with her daughter, as she is now very supportive and active in her grandchildren's lives. Her grandmother, mother, sister, and daughter remained close and when able continue to spend family time together. Sharonda eventually retained custody of her children and they too have been able to move beyond the chains of her crack addiction and maintain a close family relationship.

Discussion

Bethena, Barbara, Ladonna, Sharonda, and Desirea were able to cope with the stressors of life as a drug addict and mother with the support of both networks of family kinship and fictive kin. These networks of support provided valuable resources such as care taking of their children, housing as well as emotional and financial support. Unfortunately, as noted above, Desirea and Sharonda incurred significant costs for the benefits rendered from their family kinship networks. However, both family kinships and fictive kin were important to Bethena's journey through crack addiction and recovery. She attributed much of her support outside of the family to being nice to people prior to her crack addiction. She says: "… what kept me going, a lot of people, they knew how generous, how good I was, when I was workin at (automobile company) …" People who knew Bethena prior to her drug addiction assisted her and her daughter in their time of need during her active addiction. They recalled her kind nature and looked out for her when she needed help.

Sharonda also received invaluable support from her neighbor Lacretia and Lacretia's family that helped care for her children and her male friend Eric. While social services in Michigan provided financial and medical resources to Sharonda and Bethena, the other mothers depended totally on the support of their kinship networks. Except for Bethena's experience during her daughter's birth, the mothers initiated the process for removing their children from home. Ladonna and Sharonda initiated contact with the courts to have their children placed in their grandmother's home. This was done as an act of love and concern for their children because they knew that their addictions interfered with the wellbeing of their children. Kinship networks assisted the mothers raising their children throughout their addictions and recovery. In the next chapter you will explore the complexities of Desrea, Bethena, Barbara, Ladonna and Sharonda's lives as mothers with drug addiction and in recovery.

References

Anderson, C. (2003). The diversity, strengths, and challenges of single-parent households. In F. Walsh (Ed.), *Normal family processes: Growing diversity and complexity* (3rd ed.). New York, NY: The Guilford Press.

Collins, P. H. (1999). The meaning of motherhood in Black culture. In R. Staples (Ed.), *The Black family* (pp. 157–178). Albany, NY: Wadsworth Publishing Company.

Dunlap, E., Tourigny, S., & Johnson, B. (2000). Dead tired and bone weary: Grandmothers as caregivers in drug-affected inner-city households. *Race & Society* 3, 143–163.

Fordham, S. (1996). *Blacked out: Dilemmas of race, identity, and success at Capital High*. Chicago: The University of Chicago Press.

Gutman, H. (1976). *The Black family in slavery and freedom, 1750–1925*. New York, NY: Vintage Books.

Haglund, K. (2000). Parenting a second time around: An ethnography of African American grandmothers parenting grandchildren due to parental cocaine abuse. *Journal of Family Nursing, 6*(2), 120–135.

Hall, J. C. (2008). The impact of kin and fictive kin relationships on the mental health of Black adult children of alcoholics. *Health & Social Work, 33*(4), 259–266.

Harris, M., & Skyles, A. (2008). Kinship care for African American children: Disproportionate and disadvantageous. *Journal of Family Issues, 29*(8), 1013–1030.

Heilman, E. (2008). Hegemonies and "transgressions" of family: Tales of pride and prejudice. In T. Turner-Vorbeck & M. M. Marsh (Eds.), *Other kinds of families: Embracing diversity in schools* (pp. 7–27). New York, NY: Teachers College Press.

Hill, R. B. (2003). *The strengths of Black families*. Lanham, MD: University Press of America.

Jarrett, R., Jefferson, S., & Kelly, J. (2010). Finding community in family: Neighborhood effects and African American kin networks. *Journal of Comparative Family Studies, 41*(3), 299–328.

Johnson, C. (2000). Perspectives on American kinship in the late 1990's. *Journal of Marriage and Family, 62*(3), 623–639.

Ladner, J. (1971). *Tomorrow's tomorrow: The Black woman*. Lincoln, NE: University of Nebraska Press.

Livingston, J., & McAdoo, J. (2007). The roles of African American fathers in the socialization of their children. In H. P. McAdoo (Ed.), *Black families* (4th ed., pp. 219–237). Thousand Oaks, CA: Sage Publications.

Manns, W. (2007). The significant other: Type and mode of influence in the lives of Black families. In H. P. McAdoo (Ed.), *Black families* (4th ed., pp. 184–200). Thousand Oaks, CA: Sage Publications.

McAdoo, H. P. (1998). African American families: Strengths and realities. In H. I. McCubbin, E. A. Thompson, A. I. Thompson, & J. A. Futrell (Eds.), *Resiliency in African-American families* (pp. 17–29). Thousand Oaks, CA; Sage Publications.

Meyers, M. (2004). Crack mothers in the news: A narrative of paternalistic racism. *Journal of Communication Inquiry, 28*(3),194–216.

Miller-Cribbs, J., & Farber, N. (2008). Kin networks and poverty among African Americans: Past and present. *Social Work, 53*(1): 43–51.

Roberts, D. (2003). Punishing drug addicts who have babies: Women of color, equality, and the right of privacy. In A. Wing (Ed.), *Critical race feminism: A reader* (2nd ed., pp. 167–175). New York, NY: New York University Press.

Rosier, K. B. (2000). *Mothering inner-city children*. New Brunswick, NJ: Rutgers University Press.

Simpson, G. M., & Lawrence-Webb, C. (2009). Responsibility without community resources: Informal kinship care among low-income, African American grandmother caregivers. *Journal of Black Studies, 39*(6): 825–847.

Stack, C. (1974). *All our kin*. New York, NY: Harper Collins Publishers.

Staples, R., & Johnson, L. B. (1993). *Black families at the crossroads: Challenges and prospects*. San Francisco, CA: Jossey-Bass.

Sudarkasa, N. (1996). *The strength of our mothers: African and African American women & families: Essays and speeches*. Trenton, NJ: Africa World Press.

Sudarkasa, N. (2007). African American female-headed households: Some neglected dimensions. In H. P. McAdoo (Ed.). *Black families* (4th ed., pp. 172–183), Thousand Oaks: Sage Publications, Inc.

Tivis, T. (2013). Self-definitions of daily routines, parent-child interactions & crack cocaine addiction among African American mothers. In E. M. Zamani-Gallaher & V. C. Polite (Eds.), *African American females: Addressing challenges and nurturing the future* (pp. 303–324). East Lansing, MI: Michigan State University Press.

Zerai, A. (2000). Marking a way outta no way. In M. Harrington (Ed.), *Care work: Gender, labor, and the welfare state* (pp. 249–269). New York, NY: Routledge Press.

Zerai, A., & Banks, R. (2002). *Dehumanizng discourse, anti-drug law, and policy in America: A "crack mother's" nightmare*. Burlington, VT: Ashgate Publishing Company.

· 7 ·

"WASN' NO JUNKIE, I WAS A WORKIN' ADDICT ... IT'S A DIFFERENCE"

Self-Definition of Black Mothers' Roles and Responsibilities

> I told you, wasn't no junkie, I was a working addict, you know what I'm saying? It's a difference, it's a difference. ... You know I wasn't out there like that with my babies ... Ain't no getting high and falling all on top of my babies wit no hot water and food and stuff. You know. They be eating. We feed them all.
>
> —Barbara

Ideas of motherhood in the literature is often based on the controlled image of a mythical ideal family with white middle-class norms and values. This hegemonic construction of motherhood privileges the parenting standards, values and practices of white mothers as superior to non-white mothers. Biased understandings of motherhood becomes even more exacerbated for Black mothers addicted to illegal drug addictions. Existing paradigms of Black mothers parenting their children with drug addictions limit our understanding of families navigating the stressors of crank, powder and crack cocaine and heroin addictions. This in part is due to the fact many academic theories across disciplines that frame Black motherhood remain silent on race, class, and gender oppressions. Knowledge claims are typically based on quantitative research methods that ignore family resilience and parental strategies used to circumvent negative neighborhood effects (Jarrett 1997; Jarrett, Jefferson, & Kelly, 2010).

Our basic understanding of Black motherhood becomes inadequate when these knowledge claims and negative controlled images of Black mothers direct our thinking. As previously mentioned in Chapter 3, our understanding of Black motherhood overwhelmed by powder and crack cocaine, crank, and heroin addictions has been high jacked by the crack ho.' This powerful stereotype contributes to the notion Black motherhood and addiction is simply an oversexed mother fiending for her next high (Meyers, 2004). More than twenty years have passed since the crack ho' and her baby came on the scene but their images remain steadfast. Yet, Sharonda, Bethena, Barbara, Desirea, and Ladonna provide counternarratives of parenting between the 1970's and the 2000's that disrupts the controlled image of them ignoring their children's need during active addiction.

Deconstructing theories based on norms of universal parenting expectations for "good" mothering and consequences for Black motherhood is essential to understanding prenatal and postnatal drug addiction (Collins, 1994; Glenn, 1994). Mothering is a social construction described as a historically and culturally variable relationship where one party nurtures and provides for the needs of another (Glenn, 1994). However, Black women experience mothering/motherhood as a subjective experience directly connected to their racial ethnic community. Survival, power, and identity formation are key themes in mothering experiences with women of color shifting in meaning when different voices become central to theorizing about motherhood (Collins, 1994). The mothers in this book uniquely define their individual mothering roles as they weather the storm of crack, powder cocaine, crank, and heroin addictions.

Barbara, Desirea, Bethena, Ladonna and Sharonda provide stories of survival, power, and identity formation as they navigate the dreadful terrain of powder and crack cocaine, crank and heroin addictions. Their counternarratives provide a broader picture of family values and beliefs at the core of their mothering. This chapter provides insights on family resilience as the mothers provide self-definitions of parenting, parent-child interactions, and discipline. Their stories highlight maternal roles as active and recovered drug addicts across their children's life span.

Motherhood for Black women has traditionally been co-opted by institutional powers since our arrival on these shores as enslaved Africans on southern plantations. Historically, Black mothers often succumbed to the requirement to serve as breeders of children for plantation owners and nurturing and caring for White children at the expense of their own children's well-being. At the same time, Black mothers have been blamed for the demise of their families and communities due to inadequate parenting. This is the historical context as discussed in Chapter 3 in which Black mothers addicted to crack, powder cocaine, crank and heroin are often judged and deemed unworthy of motherhood.

Together with Black maternal roles and responsibilities, their children's social and economic spaces provide important context for understanding their lives impacted by illegal drug addiction. Maternal and environmental factors such as geographic locations and socioeconomic levels are important to the analysis of interactions between Black mothers and children impacted by drug addiction (Griffith, Azuma, & Chasnoff, 1994). This book allowed for the mothers' neighborhood, school, and family backgrounds to enter their story as they provide self-definitions of parenting children within the context of drug addiction.

Protection from Streets

Many Black mothers are challenged with the task of buffering the dangers of drugs and violence in their neighborhoods (Collins, 1994; Shaw, 1994; Cook & Fine, 1995; Roberts, 1997; Jarrett, 1997; Jarrett & Jeffereson 2004; Jarrett, et al., 2010). Barbara, Desirea, Bethena, Sharonda, and Ladonna were not only tasked with providing typical day-to-day mothering but with the dual responsibility of preparing their children for survival in an oppressive society that does not value them (Collins, 1994; Shaw, 1994; Cook & Fine, 1995). Embracing an idea of family difference (Rosier, 2000) and attempting to keep their children away from neighborhood dangers (Jarrett, 1997) are specific strategies used by mothers to accomplish these dual responsibilities. Black mothers who are low income are able to shield their children and themselves from neighborhood dangers using strategies that were nonconfrontational and family focused (Jarrett, 1997; Jarrett & Jefferson, 2004). Barbara and Bethena made concerted efforts to keep their children safe from the violence in their neighborhoods.

Barbara stood her ground as a mother when it came to safeguarding her children from the dangers of their housing complex. Barbara and her husband illustrate below the extent to which the implemented family protection and child monitoring strategies (Jarrett, 1997; Jarrett & Jefferson, 2004) . Their housing complex was considered a very dangerous housing area and here Barbara talks about why she did not allow her children to play outside of her home.

> Got'em up out of Shore Homes to get them a boyfriend. They didn't have to play around them kids and stuff ... in Shore Homes (pseudonym). Baby, ... Shore Homes was a piece of work. They be fighting, slicing, and killing, drugs flying everything else. Naw, they didn't have to stay in there, naw I mean when they got dressed to go out, I mean they went down my steps and out the Shore Homes. You don't look out your window and your door and see my kids playing in the Shore Homes cause I didn't allow it. ... I did not like the people in the Shore Homes. I did not like the people that I ... raised my kids around. I didn't like them.

Bethena also kept a tight rein on her children's activities and social life in the neighborhood where they have lived for fourteen years. Her daughter had been friends with some neighbors since elementary school. She says:

> ... they might move away and then move back in and maybe move and move back. Some of them are drinking, smoking weed, having sex, have babies. Then they want [daughter's name] to come over to their house spend the night ... ain gonna have it. No, uh uh, I don't let them do that. No, I never, unless they really close relatives, to let my kids go to anybody house and spend the night, I don't do that. And ain't too many come to mines (to) spend the night. You keep that mess over there where you live. I keep mines here, you know. I guess I don't try to expose them to all this stuff ... Good as gold, I love them, but uh uh (head gesturing meaning no) We got other plans, we ain't got time for them.

Barbara also spoke about what might have happened had she not enforced strict rules for her children. She believes her children would have never left Atlantic City and function as independent adults had she allowed them to play in Shore Homes. She says "I might a had them dead or whatever, the way them fools was cutting up over in there." Interestingly, in spite of their very own street drug addictions, all of the mothers believed that a significant part of their role as a parent was to protect their children from the dangers and influences of street life.

Healing Relationships

Mother-daughter relationships among adult children and their recovering parent are complex. Once Ladonna became abstinent from drug, her daughters twelve years apart returned home to live with them. Desirea's daughter lived off and on with her but as an older child had an opinion about her mother's addiction. They both spoke about their mother-daughter relationships once they stopped using drugs and believed it was important to heal relationships with their children who were young during their active addictions.

They worked hard to manage their guilt as they moved forward in healing their relationships.

In this next narrative, Ladonna speaks about her struggle with her oldest child once she stopped using drugs. Ladonna's daughter was 15 years old when Ladonna became drug free and attempted to resume her role as a mother. Prior, Ladonna's mother had custody of her daughter, functioning not only as a grandmother, but also primary care giver playing a mother's role. This resulted in Ladonna's feelings being hurt when her daughter challenged and even questioned her authority as a parent. At the same time, through Ladonna's healing, she was able to understand her daughter's feelings and anger.

> You know I had a struggle in the beginning with my oldest daughter cause when I got clean, she was 15 ... I wanted to be this, you know, I'm mom. ... And my daughter said to me one day. She said well where was you in 15 years? And I was like woaa ... that hurt ... But what I had to tell my daughter, I understand how you feel. ... And at that time, I said to her, I understand, but I really didn't. I do now. But I really didn't. But what I told her was that I am your mother, and you will respect me. And it took a while of us building a relationship. See, let me tell you something about children, that I find that being in recovery with my own children. I don't care how rotten a parent you have been. Kids want their mother.

Ladonna's mother was the primary care giver for her oldest daughter and says "she'll still tell me now, that's her baby. That's her daughter you know ..." However, in spite of Ladonna's drug addiction and absence, once she became drug free and back home, her daughter still wanted to be close to her. She says:

> But when I got clean, my daughter clung to me even through our fighting and stuff. Wherever, I lived she came. ... Um they just want they parents ... it was a struggle with her. Cause she was angry ... full of resentment. You know just like I had grown up (anger), you know what I'm saying and I'm real mindful of that. ... I tell my daughter, all the time ... I can't help you. Like I go somewhere, where I have a 12-step program. Where I get my help. ... I can nurture you. ... I could love you, I can be the example for you.

Through her own healing process and recovery, Ladonna has accepted responsibility for years of addiction and the negative consequences for her daughter. At the same time she maintains a strong sense of her identity as a mother. Ladonna believes her role as a mother is to nurture and demonstrate love as her daughter learns how to become responsible for her own healing.

Desirea and her daughter now share a special relationship but she is sometimes reminded of her years of indiscretions as a drug addict. She acknowledges the negative consequences of her addiction on her daughter. Yet, she draws on her faith and explains she is confident God has forgiven her for being a drug addict and mother. Desirea proclaims this belief keeps her from long-term self-loathing as she reminisces about her past as a heroin addict and mother.

> ... I still understand why you do what you do (referring to daughter). It's not about a guilt trip. I ain't guilty but ah you know, cause the Lord say you know I'm forgiven. When you are ignorant and as a child, living as a child that didn't know better but you was an adult. You (God) forgive me for that. I've wept, I've changed, I've transformed. But still be able to love.

Here Desirea illustrates how she relies on her faith to remind her that she has been forgiven during times in which her daughter brings up the past. She also describes how God's forgiveness has even allowed her to love again. This passage illustrates the continued need for mother and daughter opportunities to reconcile the past days of heroin addiction.

In spite of Sharonda's addiction, she has relationships with her adult children who were at the time of our conversations now 18, 22, 24, and 25 years old but were young when she was on crack. She talks about their reflections of her life as a mother and addict. Sharonda reports they share no resentment against her and comments about what her 25-year old daughter says about her.

> ... we was sitting down talking one day and they was like one thang we can say, this was my oldest daughter. She was like one thang we can say, ma and I bet you (other daughter) and (son) could say it too, I don't care what you was doing, if you ever told us you promised, we knew we had it. But if you said we'll see, we wasn't getting nothing. [LAUGHTER] She was like I don't care if you was drunk, high or what if you said I promise I'm a do that for you. She was like yeah, my momma gon do this, you can bank on that. But if you said we'll see, we was like naw she ain't getting us them shoes this time. So yeah they know the difference, and um I was glad of that. At least I was good for a promise. So that really meant a lot to me.

Here, in spite of the seriousness of Sharonda's crack addiction, her children still recalled fond memories of her functioning as a mother during her active addiction. She also spoke about her daughter who at the time was in middle school demonstrating challenging behavior at school and home. Sharonda really became frustrated and did not know how to handle her behavior. However, she put forth an effort to change her interaction style with her daughter by reminding her that she loves her but does not like her behavior. Sharonda noticed a difference in her daughter's facial expressions and positive responses to her constructive comments as opposed to when she used to scream.

Sharonda also believes that her relationships with her children are improving because she is growing spiritually. She says:

> I think spiritually I'm getting better ... by prayin to God and asking him to give me what I need to give them what they need. So I think He's helping me and it's helping me help them. So I think we're just all getting better.

Ladonna and Desirea have come to terms with the consequences of their addictions on their daughters and their relationship. Their religious beliefs and faith informed them of their forgiveness from God as he continues to heal their families. All mothers expressed sentiments similar to what Sharonda says as they seek God's help with raising their children.

Daily Routines

Kinship networks were vital to the care of the mothers' children throughout their childhoods. However, there were times when the mothers also cared for their children independently during their days of addiction. Sharonda talks about daily routines with her children when she was pregnant with her fifth child. During this time of her active addiction, all of her children were in elementary school. Part of Sharonda's morning routine included getting her children ready for school and making sure they were fed.

> Get them up for school ... while they was gone that was my party. If they came home, cut the party. ... Because you know the kids came home now, so the party had moved. ... They come home you'd fix them something to eat ... I'm the type where I don't like anything to bother me ... especially when I'm getting high. I don't want to have to think about, oh you have to cook. So before I get high, I'm gon have to cook, cause I'm not finna think about that later. So I would um, ... cooked an every thing before, like right before they got home ... we basically calmed it down before they got home ...

With laughter, Sharonda jokingly emphasized the fact that she prepared meals for her children. She says "if we didn't do nothing—through all my addictions. If I ain't do nothing else, they ate ... Cause you just know, a hungry kid is gon get on yo nerves till he's filled, so they'll shut up."

Desirea also cared for her daughter when she was not with her mother, grandmother or aunt. She provides an account of a typical day for her and her daughter.

> ... If it was a school day, we would rise early, get her prepared for school. I would prepare breakfast as she would wash and dress her-self. Which she been doing that since she was about 3 years-old ... Then um. School would start for her around 8:30 but we'd be out there round 8 o'clock. She was in kindergarten. She started pre-kin and um. I'd do her hair and she'd be dressed all pretty. And we'd take a moment to sit down ... we'd usually be getting dressed with ... all those educational, um programs they had on the public television station. And her favorite was um Seasame Street ... watched Seasame Street while eating breakfast and I'd be getting dressed and get her out by 8:00. ...

I would like to point out Desirea's reference to her daughter's independent dressing skills at three years old. Typically developmental delays are attributed to Black children living in poverty and female-headed households. Yet, Desirea highlights her daughters' mastery of self-help skills usually seen in older children.

Desirea continues to describe her daily routine with her daughter on school days once she gets home from school.

> ... So, she was there until 2:30 and um. ... And um after school, she again would have her little broadcasts lined up that she liked. And um. I had a big pool table. ... An um we would have dinner, watch TV and play with her things together. I like to paint ... antique and she would help me on stuff like that. I'd read to her or let her read to me.

Desirea admitted to me these routines were quite a bit to juggle while she was using heroin. Yet, she states without question when her daughter was with her, they read together daily. She also pointed out that during that time she did not realize the full impact of heroin addiction but maintained a strong faith in God. However, the tone of her voice changes as she discusses this and begins to speak slower as her mood became more somber.

> I might didn't have that kind of energy ... even then. I had a strong sense of faith and connection with God, Tierrra. And um anything that I mighta been feeling it had to be put on hold if she was with me at that time I had to do the parental duties as far as the addiction. I mean you put the addiction first. Not in the early years, um but maybe on down in her junior high school and early high, maybe then. Because like I said I had so much freedom cause I always had either my mother or my sister or my aunts could have had her.

It appeared as if Desirea was able to care for her daughter on the days she stayed home with her and tried her best to make her parental duties a priority when she was in pre-K and kindergarten. She used her faith in God to negotiate her addiction and parenting duties when her daughter was young. However, she admits that during her daughter's middle school years, her daughter often stayed with her mother, grandmother, and aunts. Throughout her daughter's life, they were important resources when it came to caring for her daughter's daily needs.

Similar to Sharonda, Barbara proudly pronounces that she took her duties as a mother seriously by establishing a routine that consisted of cooking for her children before she got high.

> I told you, wasn't no junkie, I was a workin addict, you know what I'm sayin? It's a difference, it's a difference. ... You know I wasn' out there, out there like that wit my babies. ... Oh yeah. Ain't no getting high and falling all on top of my babies wit no hot water and food and stuff. You know. They be eating. We feed them al. ... Like I take it and I'd had to time it knowing I'm gone have the kids out the way ... I'm telling you, you feed one kid, you feed them all ... Right now today. They walk in that door today, they could tell you what I'm telling you. Right now. If that phone rings and it's one of my kids. You can talk to them. They'll tell you. Yeah they'll tell you. Sho would.

Barbara candidly spoke about her routine of getting high but taking care of her children first with motherly pride. She spoke with laughter as she explained how she "had to take it and ... time it ..." describing how particular attention had to be made to the scheduling of her drug use. Barbara had to ensure her children were taken care of within a certain time frame so that she would not risk getting "sick." Barbara explained to me that getting sick meant to "jones" for the drug causing her to become dangerously sick if she was without her next hit.

Barbara talks about how she cared for her children's needs before getting high and also shared stories of her husband (also addicted to heroin) playing with the children and helping them ride their bicycles. Barbara fondly recalled special girl talks she had with her daughters and nieces as well as talks with her sons. These were precious times for Barbara as demonstrated by her facial expressions of enthusiasm and smiles telling the following story with so much passion.

> ... Yeah, they go out. They'd be hurryin up, they'd clean up and do what they had to do—cause they had to be in at a certain time ... Um, the girls would get up in the bed with me ... I'd talk about life with them. Whatever questions that they wanted answered, I'd answer for them. I had two little nieces that would come over just for that. I tell you, my little nieces and nephews they took my house for theirs. You know what I'm saying, yeah, naw, I ain't never had no problem. And they ain't never had no problems, cause they know Aunt (her nam'll) take care of them.

Barbara was especially proud of the fact that she taught her nieces familiar lessons "… Tellin'em … they can do bad by they self, they don't need nobody that's gonna pull them down …" She emphasized that it was important to also have special moments with her sons and nephews. Barbara says "… you boys … need to learn … same things … so he ain't got to go through no changes with … [women] … we would teach them how to iron, cook, clean, you know. "Barbara told this story with expressions of such joy while smiling and enthusiastically recalling each minute detail of the event she was describing with the children. She had a strong sense of parental competence and her nonverbal communicative expressions clearly illustrated she loved her children and nieces. More importantly, she knew she contributed to the development and maturity of her children, nieces, and nephews and that she mattered to them as well.

Desirea and Barbara were the two oldest mothers in the study and used heroin who self-defined themselves as working addicts distinguishing themselves from street addicts. This is illustrated when Desirea also referred to herself as a working addict as she described how: "… Sometimes I work 2 jobs, along with that (meaning doing heroin), I was also still active. I was one of those working addicts. I wasn't no street addict. I always kept something going …" Desirea and Barbara inferred that heroin did not totally disrupt daily routines for their children or their role as working parents.

All mothers provided examples of adhering to daily routines with their children when they were sober and some during active addictions. Daily routines are often the context for measuring expressions of warmth, responsiveness, and love during parent-child interactions. Therefore, it is important Black mothers have an opportunity to self-define social interactions with their children especially within the context of street drug addictions.

Expressions of Warmth, Responsiveness, and Love

Parent-child interaction quality with young children is often measured by educational researchers based on standardized notions of warmth and responsiveness. Historically positive infants' mental health and developmental outcomes are suggested to occur when parents are responsive and sensitive to prompts and communications from their infants (Landry, Smith & Swank, 2006; Taylor, Anthony, Aghara, Smith, & Landry, 2008). These knowledge claims continue to inform early childhood practice. Good mental health and overall development are considered key readiness skills required for children to do well once they enter school.

Most early childhood practitioners would agree positive parent-child interactions result in positive developmental and academic outcomes. However, this common knowledge within the field becomes problematic when ideals of parenting and child development ignore family diversity. Black mothers' responsibilities for preparing their children's survival in a hostile society require unique parenting sometimes inconsistent with universal standards for "good" mothering. In this section, the mothers self-define their ways of demonstrating concepts of warmth, responsiveness and love to their children.

The quality of warmth and responsiveness of parent-child interactions are measured, usually with a standardized instrument in families with young children considered to be at risk (Carta et al., 1997; Krauss et al., 2000) and in need of intervention. These tools are normed and based on communication and interaction styles with young children from the dominant culture. My intentions were for the mothers to focus on their children's early childhood. However, that was not always the case and instead, I followed their lead as they provided rich self-definitions of the concepts. Nonetheless, they still provided important perspectives of parent-child interactions.

Desirea is now a major source of support for her only daughter and five grandchildren. She believes she demonstrates warmth to her daughter illustrated by providing emotional and financial support. Desirea self-defines warmth as

> I guess, I have to say through material things, it was hugs and kisses and I love you ... a lot of positive things to make them feel special ... daily base. But um ah my mother didn't ... If a parent did this and it was a negative you didn't do that. You did this. So I showed and told (her) daily ... (But) you'd never hear it outta my grandmother either ... I didn't, um she didn't say words of encouragement, and build self-esteem ...

Desirea was determined to stop the generational practice of ignoring children's emotional needs as she realized her mother and grandmother were unable to support her as a child or an adult. Desirea puts forth an intentional effort to encourage and build her daughter's self-esteem and says:

> I would let her know she was a spiritual star of God ... that's how she's gonna have ... a dream within her, that one day if she focus and you know keep herself ... walking with the Lord ... But I always let her know to always walk with the Lord cause that's where her strength would be at.

Desirea's daughter was teased in school as you will read about in the next chapter much like her mother. She used those opportunities to teach her daughter to lean on her religious faith to self comfort herself. For example:

I would share ... if she had a particular rough day with a child that has said something outta the way to her to make her feel bad. I would have to build her up to make her feel special. That she was not an ugly child. She's a beautiful spirit. Things like that. Yeah. I still do that today. I have to try to build her up ... That He didn't make anything that wasn't beautiful. I let her know ... her strength was in the love of God.

Desirea had her own ideas about what the concept of warmth meant in relation to her interactions with her daughter. Providing emotional support and making her daughter feel special with positive words of love and encouragement were Desirea's methods of showing warmth. She also indicated to me that you are unable to demonstrate expressions of love to your children unless you love yourself first.

> You have to first love yourself ... you have seen, have been in my presence you see that I smile a lot ... I smile from my heart ... Love flows because no matter what you do, the Lord is within you ... Listen, I don't know too many mothers that go through the extent of giving the ATM card to make it easy on that side (in New York) and call and saying is you alright? How's your little pampers? You got enough food? You know. Where you at? Well here an extra 20 in there for you. Well OK I'll put this bill on hold and let you, cause I know ...

Desirea would put the majority of her paycheck on an ATM card for her daughter who still lived in New York with her five children. She believed it was important to be supportive of her daughter financially, emotionally and spiritually because she had experienced the fallout of her mother's negative interaction style. Desirea made a concerted effort to interact differently with her daughter and challenged stereotypes of low-income Black female-headed households innately producing family dysfunction across generations. Instead, she put forth effort to change the family legacy so parent-child interactions among her, her daughter, and grandchildren are more positive.

Sharonda demonstrates warmth and love to her children by giving them hugs, kisses, and compliments. She also believes it is important to build her children's self-confidence and show them she loves them. Sharonda gives:

> ... all of my kids are kissies and huggies. Even the big twenty-two-year-old I love you momma. I don't care who around, I love you ma. ... No, I don't do any special things with the kids—never have ... we just all get together talk, crack jokes, and just have a good time ... we did that a lot at my daughter's house because most of us was there a lot ... that's all we do just sit down and have fun, talking and laughing and, oh, like I remember when you used to drink ma ... you know reminiscing. But they'd be like thank God you ain't drinking no more, cause it was a hard time for them and I realize that. But um, they all good now. They all good, ain't no really no special

occasions. We just do it all the time, we just always somewhere sitting up talking and my sons think their comedians so, they always have us laughing. So, we don't do much together. Cause I never have, my kids probably just could count the times they was in the grocery store with me, cause I don't do kids like that.

Like Desirea, Sharonda puts forth an effort to be more loving and emotionally supportive to her children than what she experienced as a child. I find it interesting here, that Sharonda illustrated very special times with her children. Yet at the end, she indicated "we don't do much together" and appeared to link demonstrating love by taking her children places and being in the grocery store with her children. Sharonda also relied on her relationship with God for guidance on how to demonstrate expressions of love and warmth.

A mother's expression of love toward her children can be manifested differently depending on family make-up and the mother's personal interaction style. Bethena is not the type of mother that demonstrates typical signs of love and warmth in an outwardly fashion. Yet, it is obvious that she loves her children. The following narrative is an example of this contradiction.

> What do I do to show my kids that I love them? Oh, oh, I don't know, I don't do nothing special. Always doing something. I might tell them, ok ... let's do this or let's do that, I'm paying for it. You know I don't know, I'm always showing them any little little pieces how I want to love them, so. I don't just necessarily always come out and express it to them. ... Cause I show no warmth, I show no love. They say, all I do is fuss, I'm mean. [Laughter] So, I don't know, I don't know. I'm not one of them type of mothers that come in and always hugging them and telling them I love them and all that. I'm not one of them type of mothers. So I don't I don't. ... I just don't show it. I just don't show it. They know I love them. ... How ... would they know? Well, could be a Monday Tuesday Wednesday any day of the week and I say you all come on I got some money, let's go to Red Lobster [to] eat and I pay for everybody or come on you all let's go ... I'm in a good mood come on I'm going out to the store and buy all us a outfit, pay for it. There's stuff that I do, you know, just little stuff I do. We come in they get in my bed and we have a little family talk, discussion, we talk end up playing and whatever, so you know. That's kinda the way I show.

Yet, according to Bethena, she does not believe she is responsive to her children's needs.

> Oh. I told you I'm mean. So I don't care nothing about their needs or this and that, they cook their own food, done leave me alone. Between 12 and 2:00 and we at home, I'm looking at my stories so uh. Responsive to their needs? ... I guess it (the question) make sense, but I'm not responsive. They say I'm a cold hearted person, kids say, you know.

Bethena described her understanding of warmth and responsiveness during interactions with her children now that they are older. She was unable to relate the concept of responsiveness to interactions with her children but it was clear that she valued the gift of quality time with them. However, Bethena was able to clearly explain how she demonstrated love to her children when they were young.

> ... get them in the car, that time my eyes weren't too bad ... would get my kids in the car, just me and them and plan I might say this week uh me and the kids going to Cedar Point ... to Six Flags or whatever, it was just me and my two kids. I didn't take the man, nobody have my car, I planned it for me and two kids. Got the little road map thing from AAA they had, in the hotel and me and my two kids get in the car, we do the drive. So that's bonding getting there ...we stay at Six Flags for two, three days just me and the kids ... they were like seven, eight, nine, ten, eleven, twelve. I fill my car up, my 2 get in the car, we done hit 75. We'll go there, find out where we're at, find us a hotel check us in and go to the amusement park, so and that you know I did all that kinda stuff. So that ain't showing you love either I don't what showing it is ... I done took em to Florida. I went down to Florida stayed 5 days ... we went on a bus trip that time.

Here, Bethena is able to link her actions with her children as a demonstration of love but was unable to provide examples of the concepts of warmth and responsiveness. Bethena did not believe she demonstrated warmth and responsiveness to her children. Yet, she shared stories of providing gifts, dinner at restaurants, and creating opportunities for quality time with her children. Bethena also believed going on family vacations is one way she demonstrated her love to her children.

Barbara believed that spending time together as a family was important and family gatherings occurred often. She points out that even as adults, her children continue to celebrate each others' birthdays and get together as a family for traditional holidays. These birthday celebrations are big events in Barbara's family. She believes it is important to acknowledge her children's birthdays.

> Birthday parties, I'm just giving you a piece of the cake now. We keep things rolling as best we can for each other. One don't forget the other's birthday, now I got another's birthday coming up the twenty-first of next month. You know (daughter's name) was the twenty-first of this month for the other one and (another daughter's name) was June the tenth. So I had all mine right there together, yep. [GIGGLE} And they jealous, trust me they jealous. ... Yeah, you can't get one and don't get the other one now. I mean you give that one a birthday party, the other one's [gonna] look

for it so you might as well get ready, you know I mean that's the way we had to do things ... if you [gonna] give me, why don't you give her. If she [gonna] ask, why can't she get it. You know and they [gonna] tell you about it later if you don't, ... you know what I mean, yeah. And I ain't believed in that kind of stuff. ... What I did for one, I did for the other one. Or I tell one, you won't go because that one didn't go. So don't ask me. Mom ain't go let you go, cause Mom ain't let me go. I mean that's the way ...

In order to be perceived as being fair to her children, Barbara established specific criteria to use when deciding on hosting birthday parties and providing privileges. However, family celebrations were important and she has passed on this legacy of getting together as a family on holidays and birthdays to her daughters.

Family outings were important to Barbara and her husband when her children were small. Barbara worked the night shift and she would often be sleepy during the day. When she or her husband were unavailable, the older siblings would be responsible for taking the younger children on outings. Whenever Barbara spoke about her children, she would be so passionate and excited about sharing another story about them, the following story was no exception.

> We went to picnics, um during that time it was Great Adventures. We'd go to Great Adventures; we'd go to picnic areas. Yeah, we'd take um the Boardwalk in the Wildwood. Yeah we would hang out with them. ... I'd be cookin, I'd cook for like two days almost. You know gettin the food and stuff ready, yeah the kids be helpin me ... Yeah because I know, I knew that a couple of my nieces and nephews once they heard they Aunt (Barbara) was goin, they was [gonna]e want to go too. Had to make extras cause that's the way my kids was. They were with their aunt like that, they was close with my nieces and my nephews. I'd take them and I'd take them all. ... Yeah, some of'em spend the night girl. So we don't get away before we leave'em. ... Girl I tell you how things, stuff like that I be cooking. Cookin, my table be full of food and cakes and stuff and they friends be like, eh, eh, eh. [LAUGHTER] ... we walked the boardwalk, get on the rides, you know.

Barbara believes in spite of her drug addiction, she was able to not just meet their needs but also cater to their desires.

> Ah man, whatever your kid had my kids had too. You know what I'm saying, they didn't have to beat your kids up to take what they got, cause they want what yours got—mine had it. Other people might want to beat mine up for what they got. They had everything else everybody else had ... I ain't never had that problem. ... I wish [daughter's name] ... I knew what she was doing now so she could tell you what they Christmases and holidays was like. But she, she'd tell you. I mean ... had everything,

I mean and something that they would want or didn't get, that I didn't give'em and if I didn't have it, I would a got it. I betcha I get it. You know what I'm saying, it might not be then, but I'd get it, you know. That's how responsive I was. I felt as though, they needed it and I see they really wanted it, girl, yo bett'a get out my way and let me go get it, yeah.

Here, Barbara describes "how responsive (she) was" to her children's needs. At the beginning of this chapter, Barbara makes important distinctions between being an addict and a junkie. She explained to me that she was "no junkie" and let me know that as a working addict, she was capable of being a good mother and caring for her children. As Barbara talks about expressing love to her children, she is confident that she has been a good mother to her children.

If I tell you I love you, I love you. If I don't, I don't. If you want something and I got it, you got it. All kids is not alike. Some want attention and some of [them] don't. Some of [them] want you to hug and kiss them and others one don't ... each individual, each one of my five kids is different. You know, I got one, like I was telling you about that would crawl up in the bed with me, aww, that girl. I love my child though, when she had her two cousins and they be asking all kinds a questions, I be wrestling and tussling with [them]. They was a piece of work. But they never forgot what I [told them]. Even now, you know, even now, Aunt [her name] didn't you tell us we could do bad by, her hands on her hips too [LAUGHTER], we could do bad by ourselves. I said that's right, what did Aunt [Barbara] tell you? Now you know it's the truth, yeah you can do bad by yoself. Aunt [Barbara] been by herself for years now ain't she. [LAUGHTER] Ain't nobody helping me.

In the last part of this narrative, Barbara must have been referring to a time after her second husband's death because she was married to him until he died. As a mother though, Barbara knew her children well enough to discern their diverse needs depending on the child and circumstances. Thus, she carefully considered who and when she decided to show expressions of love and support.

It's different times and different occasions that calls for hugging or kissing, you know ..., come on and give me a hug. You know your mom love you. You know ... somebody hurt their feelings or if something happens, or I got a break [them] up from fighting outside, or something you know ... You just can't stay out there and just gonna fight cause you want to fight. I say come on and give your mom a hug now and get yourself undressed and go get in the bed. Now you can't be out there fighting like that, alright. I mean they growing, you know sometimes you got to give it to [them] when you think they should have it to help [them] along to get what you want. You know, I wanted him off that street, off that porch, you know fussing or whatever it is they getting ready to do. You know come on in the house, go lay down, you know get [them] in the house. ... Oh you got to, you got to know what you doin' and ... do it, you better. Cause they get to cussing and fussing and all up in your face, I ain't never. Oh God, thank you Jesus [LAUGHTER] I ain't never had to go through that baby.

Barbara's survival texts reveal a tremendous amount of motherwit with an awareness of her children's individual unique needs. Her story below explains how her keen observations of her son's motor development prompted her to seek help.

> ... my son (son's name), um I didn't like the way he walked. Took him a long time and I didn't like it. I took him to uh Grossley Shoe Store, they had a ... doctor in there to check him out. And his ankles was weak and we had to strap him on boot shoes [with] a piece a metal. And he wasn't allowed to run, every time I turn that boy was gettin up off the ground [LAUGHTER] cause he'd be runnin and that metal would be too much of a weight for him, they be tellin me he could not run in them shoes. And I had to keep [them] on him in order to keep his lil'legs, lil'ankles together, you know ... About four, three to four (his age), something like that ... for a coupe of years, but I kept him in them, cause I wanted to make sure that he would be ahight. But he's (OK). I didn't have no problems [with] my kids.

Barbara said that except for her son's problem with his ankles, none of her children had any health problems and with laughter, she says to me "Girl, I tell you God been blessin' me ... He knew I was a fool and I needed his help." Here, Barbara describes an act of mothering that required close attention and critical observation of her son's motor development. Not only did she have the parental competence to become aware of the problem, she responded appropriately by taking him to a specialist. Again it is amazing that Barbara was active in her heroin addiction throughout all of her adult children's lives. This parental behavior is clearly inconsistent with the behavior of a stereotyped Black mother on heroin only focused on her next fix. This narrative also illustrates how Barbara again acknowledges God's presence in her life. She jokingly refers to God blessing her for with healthy children.

Warmth and responsiveness are constructs typically used to measure the quality of parent-child interactions with young children prenatally exposed to cocaine (Bolzani Dinehart, Dice, Dobbins, Claussen, & Bono, 2006; Carta et al., 1997; Krauss et al., 2000). Sharonda, Desirea, Bethena, and Barbara presented stories of loving their children and articulated their own understanding of how they demonstrated warmth, responsiveness, and love to their children.

Although not identified specifically during their early childhood years, these expressions of love, responsiveness, and warmth would not have been noticed using standardized measurement tools. Here the mothers' narratives were not compared to predetermined definitions of warmth, responsiveness, and love. Instead, they self-defined these concepts on their own terms, in unique ways that challenge predetermined definitions of warmth, responsiveness within the context of crack cocaine addiction. The mothers' stories inform us of how the meaning of the concepts of responsiveness, warmth and expressions of love vary when Black mothers are allowed to self-define their experiences with their own ideas, from their perspective and in their voice.

Discipline

Black mothers have typically relied on discipline strategies unique to their family, social and historical contexts. Discipline practices with their children are sometimes considered to be harsh but should be examined within a cultural context (Dodge, McLoyd, & Lansford, 2005). After all, Black mothers are burdened with added responsibility of teaching their children survival in a racist society that does not appreciate their well-being (Collins, 1994; Shaw, 1994; Cook & Fine, 1995). Historically, respect for authority and strong orientation toward obedience and conformity have been the foundation of Black mothers childrearing practices (Staples & Johnson, 1993). Barbara, Sharonda, Desirea, Bethena and Ladonna's narratives illustrate they share the same philosophy when it comes to parenting their children.

Desirea provides an historical perspective of discipline strategies implemented from the women in her family and spoke about how the traditions were not so pleasant. While speaking of harsh discipline she experienced as a child, she was very quick to offer a rationale for the adults' practices. She says:

> ... But I had to realize that came from an element, when you coming from the tale end of slavery, my grandmother did. She was born in 1918, and um my mother seen a many a hangings down there cause we come from the south. (state's name). So you come out a time their grand, her grandmother, kept their kids hidden. Kept them quiet you know what I'm saying. It was a child should be seen and not heard.

Barbara, Sharonda, Desirea, Bethena and Ladonna implemented a variety of discipline strategies they felt were effective with their children sometimes including corporal punishment. Bethena and Sharonda share how they feel about using punishment as a way of discipline.

> I wish I could ... put a little more punishment and all that. I never had time for all that, I forget all about that. You know, so instead when you go and you do something, find me a stick or switch or something, right now, let me come and you get your butt whooped and it's all over with. Over with, ain't no punishment no none of that and whatever. I always forgive and I say OK I'm taking the TV away for a week, 2 hour, 3 hours. I'm back in my room doing something they getting on my nerves. You all leave me alone, go on [and] listen to the TV they get their TV back (Bethena)

> I will beat'em down! [LAUGHTER]. ... Sometimes, most of the time it's punishments. But if you go overboard, I will whip you. I will get a belt and I will whip you. ... But I basically put them on punishments and that's another reason why my house stay real clean, cause somebody's always on punishment. (Sharonda)

In the past, Sharonda has gone to her daughter's school and spanked her in front of the class when she was misbehaving at school. While Sharonda believes and sometimes uses corporal punishment, she admits:

> But my bark is bigger than my bite. ... I yell at them, I do. I yell and scream, I'm a, if you don't sit down—I don't curse and so that's a good thing. But I used to curse'em out, but now I don't curse. I'm [gonna] knock you out—but they know I won't do nothin. Even my little baby, I was like [youngest son's name], if you don't sit down I'm gon knock you down. He said [SNICKERS LIKE A CHILD]. I was like see they know I ain't finna do nothing, cause he laughing ... The older ones ... their punishments were a little more severe. Those younger ones, I'm tired. They was like look at ma, you let him get away with everything. I'm tired, I been doin this for twenty-four years. [LAUGHTER] I'm tired. So no, he don't, they don't the boys you know they get a tap or I'll tap'em up a little bit. But they don't get no whippings and they don't clean up.

Sharonda's older children complain that she allows her younger children to get away with things that they did not get away with. This may be common for many families with a large number of siblings. Sharonda admits that her four- and seven-year-old children do not get spanked or have to clean up like her other children did at their age. As mentioned earlier in the chapter, Sharonda relied on God for assistance with discipline and began using more positive strategies to modify her children's behavior.

In spite of their drug addictions, the mothers were able to sustain a sense of responsibility and authority over their children. They maintained their stances as mothers with expectations for their children's behavior. Even though Barbara and her husband were drug addicts they still demanded respect from their children and expected them to follow their rules. When talking about showing respect and enforcing rules, Barbara says:

> I made it and I demanded that. And if somethin happened to the other one and the other one didn't tell me, then I was, I'd be on all of [them] see. You know ... one of [them] got pregnant and they was scared to death then cause they knew I had to find out. ... kept respect from my kids, because I demand respect from them, you see. What they know was their business, what I did was mine.

Barbara tells about an encounter with her older daughter who was disrespectful.

> Once that oldest one, she was about eighteen ... it was time for her to leave ... she shoved me, my back hit the corner of the refrigerator and dislocated some pieces back here in my back. And um, by time [her husband] got down to the bottom of the steps, we had her up and outside, so she never came back in my house since, not to want to live, she just kept on goin' ... she was eighteen ... it was bout time, you know cause you ain't gon be standin up in my face telling me what you [gonna] do and what you ain't gon do, you know. Not in my house, go get your own, and that's what she did.

Ladonna was sensitive to her daughter's needs and understands why she might be angry but stood her ground and did not allow her to be disrespectful.

> I told my daughter that if she ever tried to fight, I would probably kill her. ... God is so good. And at the time that it happened, I'm talking 'bout, He had me in a place right where I understood. I understood that my daughter wasn't fightin' me cause she don't like me, or just to be disrespectful, she was angry enough at me to try to fight me. You know what I'm saying even in all of that though, I still had to take a stand. And I put her out and like cause when she was livin' with me, she wasn't paying no bills, I was paying her car note, I was ruining her. ... This was only maybe, [daughter's name]'s 24 ... This happened maybe 4 years ago. Yeah ... You know, I took a stand and you know, I'm watching my daughter become productive and responsible. You know ... I still um, you know talk with her. You know what I'm saying and tell her. And I tell her like you can talk to me but you not [gonna] give me everything because all of your issues are with me. You only [gonna] give me some. But you need to get it all out.

Professionals from the dominant culture may mistakenly take Ladonna's comments literally as an actually threat to kill her daughter if she ever tried to fight her. However, "I'm a kill you" is often a figure of speech used to express extreme displeasure in someone's actions. Like with Sharonda's "bark (that) was bigger than her bite," Ladonna came to understand the basis of her daughter's anger and behavior was linked directly to her drug addiction. Nonetheless, Ladonna maintained expectations for her daughter living in her house and believed her daughter would not become independent as long as she had no financial responsibility.

Barbara did not have discipline problems with her children when they were young. She explains why:

> Cause I never pulled no punches with [them]. I was straight up... Just keep that relationship you got, keep'em on a nice level ... Stay like that, that keeps that respect. ... I would want them to listen. ... Tell them how I felt. Tell [them] what to do and what not to do and I meant it. And they knew I meant it, there's a difference. They got to know. Honey these kids out here, don't know nothin' but DYFS [Division of Youth & Family Services], mine workin' for DYFS now, yeah. But I tell [them] when I get through whippin yo behind, you gon need DYFS [LAUGHTER]. Yeah I used to tell'em that, I wasn't no joke. They ain't play [with] me. (Barbara)

Ladonna and Barbara understood the consequences of their children becoming undisciplined. They were familiar with the dangers of the streets and implemented protective strategies as a means of preparing their children for adulthood.

Crack and heroin addiction presents a different circumstance for understanding parent-child interactions among Black mothers. It is important to distinguish here between these interactions when they were active drug users or when they were sober. Parent-child interactions are culturally based occurrences that vary across race, class, and gender. There is a gap in the educational literature about parent-child interactions among Black parents and their children in general. The number of either research or content articles becomes even scarcer for work that explores crack and heroin addiction and parent-child interaction in Black families. Typically, educational researchers (Carta et al., 1997; Kraus et al., 2000, Bolzani Dinehart et al., 2006) rely on the mothers or adult-child performance on standardized assessment to understand parent-child interactions and drug addiction and from an outsider's perspective. However, these mothers articulated perceptions of social interactions with their children as they mothered and presented the complexities of their lives as drug addicts. My intentions here are for their self-definitions to help to expose the 'crack ho' and Black mother who is "just a junkie" for who the really are, racist myths.

Clearly effective parenting can be compromised in homes stressed by crack, heroin, and crank addictions. I argue though, that parenting in those homes is no more challenged than in those burdened with chronic maternal mental or physical health problems. Desirea, Barbara, Ladonna, Bethena and Sharonda realized this and accepted responsibility for the negative consequences their years of active addiction had on their children. Yet, they were firm believers they were not bad parents and did what they needed to do to care for their children (Baker & Carson, 1999). The mothers self-defined their abilities to establish and maintain routines, express love to their children, and engage in positive parent-child interactions regardless of the difficulties of their lives. The mothers resisted stereotypes of them as bad mothers due to their addictions, who did not love or care about their children. They were confident in their capacity to mother and at least fulfill their children's most practical needs (Baker & Carson, 1999). In the next chapter, you see the mothers' counternarratives not only challenged the controlled image of the "crack ho" but also her crack baby as they discuss their children's educational experiences. The mothers' stories of parenting provide important context for the next chapter about their involvement in their children's school. However, first I discuss the construction of the crack baby myth and its educational implications.

References

Baker, P., & Carson, A. (1999). I take care of my kids: Mothering practices of substance-abusing women. *Gender and Society, 13*(3), 347–363.

Bolzani Dinehart, L. H., Dice, J. L., Dobbins, D. R., Claussen, A. H., & Bono, K. E. (2006). Proximal variables in families of children prenatally exposed to cocaine and enrolled in a center- or home-based intervention. *Journal of Early Intervention, 29*, 32–47.

Carta, J. J., McConnell, S. R., McEvoy, M. A., Greenwood, C. R., Atwater, J. B., Baggett, K., & Williams, R. (1997). Developmental outcomes associated with in utero exposure to and other drugs. In M. R. Haack (Ed.), *Drug-dependent mothers and their children: Issues in public policy and public health* (pp. 64–90). New York, NY: Springer Publishing.

Collins, P. H. (1994). Shifting the center: Race, class, and feminist theorizing about motherhood. In E. N. Glenn, G. Chang, & L. R. Forcey (Eds.) *Mothering: Ideology, experience, and agency* (pp. 45–65). New York, NY: Routledge.

Cook, D. A., & Fine, M. (1995). "Motherwit": Childrearing lessons from African American mothers of low income. In B. B. Swadener & S. Lubeck (Eds.), *Children and families "at promise": Deconstructing the discourse of risk* (pp. 118–142). Albany, NY: State University of New York Press.

Dodge, K. A., McLoyd, V. C., & Lansford, J. E. (2005). The cultural context of physically disciplining children. In V. C. McLoyd, N. E. Hill, & K. A. Dodge (Eds.), *African American family life* (pp. 245–263). New York, NY: Guildford Press.

Glenn, E. N. (1994). Social constructions of mothering: A thematic overview. In E. N. Glenn, G. Chang, & L. R. Forcey (Eds.) *Mothering: Ideoology, experience, and agency* (pp. 1–29). New York, NY: Routledge.

Griffith, D. R., Azuma, S. D., & Chasnoff, I. J. (1994). Three-year outcome of children exposed prenatally to drugs. *Journal of American Academy of Child Adolescent Psychiatry, 33*(1), 20–27.

Jarrett, R. (1997). Bringing families back in: Neighborhood effects on child development. In J. Brooks-Gunn, G. J. Duncan, & J. L. Aber (Eds.), *Neighborhood poverty Volume II: Policy implications in studying neighborhoods* (pp. 48–64). New York, NY: Russell Sage Foundation.

Jarrett, R. L., & Jeffereson, S. M. (2004), Women's danger management strategies in an inner city housing project. *Family Relations, 53*(2), 138–147.

Jarrett, R. L., Jefferson, S. R., & Kelly, J. N. (2010). Finding community in family: neighborhood effects and African American kin networks. *Journal of Comparative Family Studies, 41*(3), 299–328.

Krauss, R. B., Thurman, K. S., Brodsky, N., Betancourt, L., Giannetta, J., & Hurt, H. (2000). Caregiver interaction behavior with prenatally cocaine-exposed and nonexposed preschoolers. *Journal of Early Intervention, 23*(1), 62–73.

Landry, S. H., Smith, K. E., & Swank, P. R. (2006). Responsive parenting: Establishing early foundations for social, communication, and independent problem-solving skills. *Developmental Psychology, 42*(4), 627–642.

Meyers, M. (2004). Crack mothers in the news: A narrative of paternalistic racism. *Journal of Communication Inquiry, 28,* 194–216.

Roberts, D. E. (1997). *Killing the Black body: Race, reproduction, and the meaning of liberty*. New York, NY: Pantheon Books, a Division of Random House.

Roberts, D. E. (2002). *Shattered bonds: The color of child welfare*. New York, NY: Basic Civitas Books.

Rosier, K. B. (2000). *Mothering inner-city children*. New Brunswick, NJ: Rutgers University Press.

Shaw, S. J. (1994). Mothering under slavery in the antebellum south. In E. N. Glenn, G. Chang, & L. R. Forcey (Eds.) *Mothering: Ideoology, experience, and agency, 1–2,* (pp. 237–258). New York, NY: Routledge.

Staples, R., & Johnson, L. B. (1993). *Black families at the crossroads: Challenges and prospects*. San Francisco, CA: Jossey-Bass.

Taylor, H. B., Anthony, J. L., Aghara, R., Smith, K. E. & Landry, S. H. (2008). The interaction of early maternal responsiveness and children's cognitive abilities on later decoding and reading comprehension skills. *Early Education and Development, 19*(1), 188–207.

Tivis, T. (2016). *I had help: Kinship Networks, Crack/Powder Cocaine and heroin addictions and Black family resilience*. Manuscript in preparation.

· 8 ·

CRACK BABY AFTERMATH AND NAVIGATING EDUCATIONAL INSTITUTIONS

Construction of a Crack Baby

In the second section of this chapter, the mothers provide counter narratives that continue to deconstruct the crack ho' and her baby. The mothers' perceptions and academic orientation as well as educational implications are presented in that section. First, this chapter highlights the social and medical construction and myth of the crack baby in response to the epidemic of crack cocaine. More specifically, children of the mothers in this book born prenatally exposed to crack cocaine demonstrated no long term permanent developmental delays as promised would occur in the 1980's news reports. A select few of medical scholars and sociologist agree the social construction of the "crack baby" has been a powerful tool across disciplines in advancing ineffective laws, policies, and practices based on negative stereotypes. These scholars have challenged the legitimacy of the crack baby's existence, as there is no persuasive evidence prenatal exposure to crack alone results in permanent adverse child developmental outcomes (Frank, Augustyn, Knight, Pell, Zuckerman, 2001; Hurt et al., 1995).

Unfortunately, pregnant mothers using crack often refrain from seeking drug treatment for fear of incarceration because they are not granted the same options as Jessica and Casey mentioned in Chapter 1. They also experience violence and seldom have access to prenatal care and good nutrition resulting in premature births. It is recommended that the "care of families affected by substance abuse should be comprehensive and not irrationally shaped by social prejudices that demonize some drugs and drug users and not others" (Frank et al., 2001, p. 1621). The medically constructed at risk label based on myths and assumptions of prenatal drug exposed infants like their mothers gained popularity during the crack era. Resulting from a highly publicized crisis and media images of the "crack baby," the at risk prenatally crack exposed infant and their mother has been assigned a Black face (Swadener, 1995). These print and television media reports assaulted their viewers with consistent images of Black pregnant women using crack cocaine, describing their children as born with permanent disabilities requiring expensive, lifelong government assistance. The brown crack baby's mothers were not granted the same compassion and respect from media or society as Jessica and Casey mentioned earlier in the book.

More recent news reports (McDonough, 2013; Winerip, 2013) have acknowledged the misrepresentations of the infamous 1980's crack baby. In his New York Times (May 20, 2013) online article *Revisiting the 'Crack Babies' Epidemic That Was Not*, Winerip presents a video clip with excerpts of the 1985 reporting on crack. This included a *48 Hours* episode focused on crack, with mugshots or court appearances of mostly Black prenatal crack cocaine users and Black babies. Images of Black infants as crack babies in Neonatal Intensive Care Units (NICU) cribs immediately after birth while going through drug withdrawal were featured. This show even included an image of then President H. W. Bush holding one of these poor Black crack babies.

This video clip illustrates the media frenzy reporting on crack cocaine and the Black bodies associated with the drug. It was feared and reported crack babies would cost the government millions of dollars for their care. This cost was impart due to the belief they would be "mentally retarded" with permanent birth defects their entire lives. Winerip (2013) highlights how these reports were widely dispersed without solid medical research backing claims made about prenatal crack cocaine exposure. Instead these were images of the sick babies in the NICU with illnesses/symptoms resulting from premature births (Winerip, 2013) and not crack. Premature births occur across racial lines and various medical conditions. Yet, Black mothers and their babies negotiated the crack ho and baby images while healing from drug addiction and putting their families back together.

Crack Baby Backlash: Labels and Stereotypes

> Sometimes I go back to my old neighborhood and see some of the kids from that class where I got labeled a crack baby … I still feel really angry … Those two words almost cost me an education. It's crazy how powerful two words can be. I won by not letting them hold me back.
>
> —Garcia (2004)

Black children in general are more likely to be identified as at risk but those prenatally exposed to drugs are much more easily classified than their White counterparts (Roberts, 2002; Zerai & Banks, 2002). Negative implications of the prenatal drug exposure label like crack baby on Black children have long-lasting effects more detrimental to their well-being than helpful (Frank, 2003; Roberts, 2002; Swadener & Lubeck, 1995). No medical evidence indicates children prenatally exposed to crack cocaine and heroin demonstrate developmental outcomes much different than those who are not prenatally exposed to drugs (Chasnoff, 1992; Frank, 2003; Frank & Zuckerman, 1993; Frank et al., 1988; Frank et al., 2001; Griffith, Azuma, & Chasnoff, 1994). In a *The New York Times* (2003 November 28) editorial letter also signed by 27 American and Canadian researchers, medical doctor and Professor of Pediatrics at Boston University School of Medicine Deborah Frank says:

> During years of studying addictions and prenatal exposure to psychoactive substances, none of us have ever identified a recognizable condition, syndrome or disorder that could be termed "crack baby." Some of our published research finds subtle effects of prenatal cocaine exposure in selected developmental domains, while other of our research publications do not. "Crack baby" is not a medical diagnosis but a media stereotype. Such pejorative stigmatization of children is not only scientifically inaccurate but also dangerous.

Program quality should be emphasized as opposed to a focus on linking programs to children's labels. Improving quality and level of services for all children instead of confining services to only "crack kids," will better meet all families' needs in communities who have the same needs but are not effected by drug addiction (Frank & Zuckerman, 1993). During and after the crack scare, educational professionals were confronted with the dilemma of whether to label young children prenatally exposed to crack cocaine or not. With limited funding and resources, even well-intended educators have capitalized off of public hype regarding crack babies (Frank & Zuckerman, 1993).

Educational programs should be planned based on family's strengths and needs as well as children's developmental and academic needs, not a label. This is particularly true for poor Black children attending schools in neighborhoods haunted by illegal drug industries. There is no educational or medical basis for specialized instructional programming for children born prenatally exposed to crack or other street drugs. Nor is there reason to blame a child's behavior on prenatal crack exposure. This would necessitate a labeling process, potentially rendering some additional funding but with a huge human cost.

Casey, Jessica's drug exposed infant mentioned at the beginning of the book, had medical problems at birth due to this exposure but both were presented through media as a family in need of a safe clean place for both to heal. Jessica makes no mention of her fear of incarceration or Casey being placed in foster care. Unlike images of Casey, an infant addicted to "heroin in a pill," images of Black children born addicted to crack represented lifelong dependency on American government for survival. Thus, draining our country's financial resources to provide specialized educational and other required supports to sustain their lives (Roberts, 2002; Zerai & Banks, 2002). Numerous Black children born prenatally exposed to drugs were routinely placed in foster care (Roberts, 2002). Several adult children trapped in the foster care system because of their mothers' crack addiction endured heartbreaking life experiences. However, it was the shame of being a crack baby most agonizing for many of them. Although these children are now productive and talented adults, some continue to believe that crack had left them "retarded," "slow," or "damaged" (Blake, 2004). Many adult children born prenatally exposed to crack have internalized society's stereotypes about themselves in spite of their fruitful lives.

The controlled image of the crack baby has had lasting effects on adults like Antwaun Garcia (2004), who was a college student pursuing an Associate's Degree at the time he wrote this article. In his online article, *They called me a crack baby. So why am I in college?* he says:

> As I struggled trying to read, the other kids began to giggle. Then this one kid, who lived near me and know about my living conditions said, "He can't read because he is a crack baby." Everyone turned to stare at me. I had never heard the expression "crack baby," so I sat there looking plumb dumb, trying to figure it out. I thought, "What, babies who sniff crack?" I knew I didn't do things like that ... The next day no one wanted to sit next to me during lunch ... I was embarrassed and ashamed of myself and where I lived ... I started to believe those things about myself ... I felt stupid and worthless. So I stopped going to class ... I started staying out in the street ...

Antwuan was eventually placed in foster care at 10 years old, moved to a different city and began a new life. When Antwuan wrote this article he was finishing his Associates Degree with the intentions of continuing his education. The title of his article, speaks volume as he forcibly challenges the crack baby myth.

As was illustrated by Antwuan's story, children labeled as crack babies at school endure devastating effects of being ostracized by peers. These experiences result in social emotional problems sometimes leading to behaviors (e.g. skipping school, drinking and using drugs) not directly resulting from prenatal drug exposure. These children also encounter negative teacher attitudes and lowered teacher expectations during their K-12 school experiences (Lardner, 1997). Keep in mind this occurs regardless of the lack of evidence supporting prenatal crack exposure alone is related to developmental or learning difficulties (Chasnoff, 1992; Frank & Zuckerman, 1993; Griffith et al., 1994).

The negative impact of labeling is evidenced even with children in the toddler age range enrolled in early intervention programs. When 179 early intervention personnel (EIP) were shown 3 different video scenes of two 24-month old boys playing, they were told both children were cocaine-exposed or only one child was cocaine-exposed. No child was actually prenatally exposed to cocaine. Yet, EIPs rated children more favorably when told children were not cocaine-exposed and less favorably when told they were cocaine exposed (Thurman, Bribeil, DuCette, & Hurt, 1994). Here, the EIP's perceptions of crack-exposed toddlers illustrate the power of the crack baby image and important implications for developmental programming for young children and their families.

Unfortunately, labeling young children prenatally exposed to crack also has implications for the overrepresentation of Black children identified as in need of special education. This labeling practice only exacerbates an already big problem of overrepresentation of Black children in classrooms for learning disabilities and emotional disturbance. As an educator and a teacher educator, these research findings are not surprising. I recall a professional experience as a special education multidisciplinary evaluation team member in a predominantly Black low-income inner city school district. Part of my evaluation included classroom observation and teacher interview. As I asked the teacher standard questions about students on my caseload, the teacher informs me he is not learning and will not behave in her class because "his mother was on that stuff," referring to crack. This information was irrelevant and did not inform my evaluation plan or interpretation of assessment results.

Yet, based on my classroom observation, there was a lack of classroom structure, organization and management. There were specific but basic strategies I offered related to classroom management I was sure would help facilitate learning with the student she referred for special education. Many professionals today working with young children continue to believe prenatal exposure to crack cocaine alone results in negative developmental and behavioral outcomes. However, as you will see in the next section, Bethena's daughter born prenatally exposed to crack cocaine had no long-term developmental delays. Also, in spite of their drug addictions, all of the mothers valued their children's education.

Black Mothers' Perceptions and Academic Orientation

> I wasn't good in math, even till this day I'm not good ... that's why I teach my kids ... if you fail a subject ... if you not good in a certain subject, that's fine, go back till you get it and get it right ... I can't do long division, multiplication—I can't do that ... some kind of way I got through the cracks, I got through the cracks, ... through life, nobody never showing me how. I don't want my kids to do that, I want them to learn everything you know, not just get by.

Historically, Black families value educational achievement as illustrated by enslaved Africans willing to risk harsh punishments and sometimes death for secretly learning how to count, read, and write. High valuation of education is considered an important characteristic of strong Black families (Hill, 2003). In this chapter Bethena, Barbara, Sharonda, Ladonna, and Desirea's narratives dispel the dominant culture's myth that Black families do not value education (Sudarkasa, 1996). The mothers in this book challenge the idea Black families do not engage in efforts to establish and maintain academic achievement for their children. This section of the chapter illustrates the mothers' intentional efforts to change their children's academic trajectory due to strong desire for them to be effective and successful students. I present stories about encouraging and supporting academic achievement, perceptions of their children as students, and problems encountered at school. I also give attention to the mothers' values regarding education and home/school partnerships. It is important to note that unless otherwise noted, much of the mothers' attempts to support their children's academic achievement took place when mothers were not active in addictions. The most noted exception is Desirea who proclaimed she did a "remarkable job" contributing to her daughter's academic achievement.

The mothers' generational cultural knowledge informed their values and beliefs about educational attainment being a requirement for upward economic and social mobility. Sharonda and Bethena grew up in homes where their educational achievement was not valued or supported and experienced negatives consequences on their professional options as adults. Thus, they were driven to do things differently by encouraging their children to succeed academically and present high valuation of education. These two mothers wanted more for their children academically than they achieved as children.

The mothers in this study were involved in their children's educational experiences at varying levels. Bethena was the only mother in the study that received a traditional high school diploma. Desirea, Barbara, and Ladonna received their GED and other certificates for additional educational programs during their adulthood. Sharonda is the only mother who has not received her high school diploma or GED.

Intentions, academic difference and hope

The mothers' negative personal experiences with academic support helped shape attitudes about supporting their children's achievement. Sharonda did not quit high school completely until twelfth grade and was not encouraged by her mother to stay in school, but instead to babysit for her younger sister. Her younger sister was born when she was 16 years old, and she "… just stopped going to school cause she had this baby. And I used to stay home and take care of the baby, and she'd be gone …" She reports her mother "didn't tell me girl, get up and go to school—you in the tenth grade, go on to school, girl … when you get out you can do this. She was just glad I was at home and she wasn't …" College was a foreign idea to Sharonda because she was an "excellent student" but "… never knew about the college thing." She poignantly spoke about not being encouraged to excel academically by her mother but passionately voiced her desires for her children when she said

> I'm pushin'em for they schooling … telling them how important it is as nobody told me … I want them to go to school and know the value of going to school … I push my kids like [daughter's name], she went to college … And then the second girl, I got with her so bad till she went out to NIT (National Institutes of Technology). She just graduated that and um I trying to instill in them now, it's not too late either.

Sharonda also tries to balance support of her children's musical talents while emphasizing her value of academic achievement.

> She has a excellent voice … she can sing … has recorded … and she has all Fs on her report card … But with her, I'll encourage the singing, but still, you can't be a dumb singer either. You got to know how to count, know how to speak properly so you still have to go to school. Cause she was like, I don't really need to go to college cause I'm gonna sing. Yeah, you going to college, you gonna sing in college.

Bethena is the only mother that completed traditional high school but did not attend college and wants her children to excel academically as she provided them guidance. Bethena references the bible "… Well they say without the vision the people shall perish" as a way of supporting her focus on her children's educational future. She was very passionately because as a student, she was never encouraged to think about her academic future beyond high school. She says "… when I was coming along I left (state), I didn't have no dream. My momma had no dream for me … She didn't tell us, oh you finish school. … go to college … None of that. …" Bethena shared her comments about school with a sad expression when she said "… So she didn't tell us none of that kind of stuff. … Supposed to go to school. … get a husband … you know settle down. … We had no dreams … none of us."

Bethena believed she missed out and did not consider college because she was never encouraged to think much about school. As a result, she has thought quite a bit about her children's academic future and put a plan in place. During our conversations, Bethena's son was entering high school and her daughter was a high school senior when she said:

> I got it planned out … They want to take me off of my plan. But I ain't, I ain't moving. No, I got a plan all figured out. … Ok, she'll be 18, Monday, January the 2nd. So she took 2 years of vo-tech as a dental assistant. So we been looking for a job really in a dentist's office … in January and I'm gonna sit down with the Navy people. She wants to go into the Navy and become a dentist. So I said okay, go ahead and let them pay for it … they can send you to school. … So ah hopefully everything work out with her being a dentist and (her son) want him to be an engineer but at church … at church my pastor got him running the TV. … But he said … he likes the computer, he can find anything on that computer. So, the camera thing he know, how to do that and the computers.

Bethena focused so much on her children's academic future she even considered options for their future careers. She considered their work experiences and interests as she encouraged them to focus on school and consider her dream for their future careers. After high school, Bethena's daughter, her child born prenatally exposed to crack cocaine completed the community college dental hygienist program and did indeed worked in a dentist office. While she did not join the Navy and pursue dental school she does have a career after high school. This was in part due to access to career training in high school and Bethena's determination she would have a different academic trajectory than her. While Bethena's job provided her a middle-class life style, she did not consider that a career and spoke with so much pride about her daughter's experience in the dental hygienist program at her school.

Sharonda and Bethena both believed that they were slighted for not being encouraged to advance academically beyond high school. Thus, they purposefully encouraged academic success and attempted to create a home environment with a strong academic orientation. These narratives illustrate Bethena and Sharonda's effort to change their family legacy by intentionally doing things differently than their own mothers and encouraging academic achievement. Their involvement in their children's academic achievement is similar to Head Start mothers in Jarrett and Coba-Rodriguez (2015) who came from families with little or no parental engagement. Like Sharonda and Bethena, mothers in this qualitative study were active in their children's school regardless of their own history of parental engagement.

Desirea, Sharonda, and Bethena described their children as students capable of learning. Desirea believes her daughter was a very good student but her academic potential was not recognized in her neighborhood New York public school.

> I believe she was at least an A sometimes B student. OK I won't say ... she didn't get a couple a C's but she definitely was up on A, B still is up on A B status when she takes the tests. She had her hopes and dreams and she just got caught up in the peer pressure. And I hadn't been there too, no one, not even her aunts had ever discussed the peer pressure or we did in a rushed manner.

Desirea believes her daughter was a bright girl but did not succeed academically because of negative peer influence and dangerous school environment. She never provided specific information but always pointed out peer pressure interfered with her daughter's academic success. Desirea also accepts responsibility with regret for being unavailable to support her daughter while negotiating peer pressure at school.

Bethena's high school son and Sharonda's middle school daughter were often in trouble at their Detroit Public Schools. In spite of the children's problems at school, they maintained unwavering hope and belief in their potential to be good students. Sharonda described one of her daughters who displayed behavior problems as "… smart as a whip, she was just bad … B in your grade three in citizenship … gets B3s … A3s come on … she's a lot better … nothing was wrong with her. … cause she's making As and Bs and Cs …" Bethena's son was often in trouble at school because of poor attendance and bad grades. Yet, in spite of these problems, she still sees possibilities for him to change. She says "… My son, he a leader all the way. He ain't following you no damn where, he wants to learn, wants to do, but you know …"

Problems at school

All of the mothers had trouble with their children in school ranging from disruptive behavior, skipping school, poor attendance and grades to bullying. One of Sharonda's daughters really struggled with acting out causing her much frustration with numerous suspensions. These suspensions took place in December and January with only two weeks of class due to holidays but was suspended six times. Sharonda did not believe her daughter needed special education but did threaten learning disabilities class placement attempting to change her daughter's behavior. She was eventually placed in a different school and her behavior greatly improved.

Bethena's son was also getting into trouble at school. He was skipping school, making poor grades but she described his poor choices as "temptations" that were normal for 15-year-olds. Bethena often worked in the same schools her children attended and describes how boldly her son defied her expectations for school attendance.

> Well my son is at the age right now, he 15, that being a boy at 15 you know is so much temptations … they wants to get into. … And he is the type of child … I work in the lunchroom so we go in the back way. So he go in with me in the back way, and chile he go out, keeps straight on, keeps straight on down the hall, out the door. Out the door … security says … I seen your son, I had to bring your son back in. Oh (Bethena) the police had your son, they had to bring your son back in. Teachers, oh I seen your son ran by the gym, I mean ran by the swimming pool and … they going out the back door … we done got two report cards, he haven't got not one report card … he haven't got a progress report … cause he don't go to class enough for them to know who he is.

Bethena's son began smoking marijuana and continued to fail school yet she still describes him as a "Good kid, he don't get in no trouble or anything, but he just at the age where he just gonna get through life, like you know he started smoking weed. ..." Even though her son began smoking marijuana, she continued to believe in his potential to be a good student. She says

> ... started smoking weed so he wants to do nothing. Nothing you know, he doesn't want to go ... to class, doesn't want to do homework. I done bought him three book bags already this year and (son's name) lost them. So that's my baby. The rest of them graduate, you must do something, I can't let you get through the system like this here. So this is why I'm putting him in another school as of Tuesday.

Bethena's son continued to get in trouble but from her perspective he is still a "good kid" and she believes that all he needs is a different school environment. She did not waste any time and quickly enrolled him in another school that was similar to a "boot camp" for students with difficulty succeeding in traditional high schools.

Following the logic of the master narrative of pathology transmitted across generations in Black families, the assumption would be Bethena was to blame for her son's academic problems. She would be the reason her son did not do well in school, began to smoke marijuana and both of her children would be doomed to drug addiction. To the contrary, Bethena used everything in her power to keep her son from street life and addiction to more powerful drugs. On more than one occasion, Bethena told me her major parental goals were to prevent her children from becoming parents or drug addicts at least before completing high school.

Desirea's problems at her daughter's school were quite different than what Sharonda and Bethena experienced with in Detroit Public Schools. Desirea's daughter attended the same schools she attended in her New York Bourough and did not believe her daughter was challenged academically. She believed teachers allowed her daughter to "pass on" with inflated grades when she was given an A or B yet the assignments were worth a C or D. As she said in other words "... it didn't make no difference if you got the A, B, C, everybody was being passed on ..." Desirea established high standards of academic excellence for her daughter and did not want her to receive grades that were not rigorously earned.

Desirea's daughter's academic orientation unfortunately kept her in trouble with her peers. Like Desirea, her daughter endured bullying from grade school until high school. Similarly, intense bullying in high school forever changed her school years, forcing her to leave traditional high school. Desirea even reports that her granddaughter who also attends the same neighborhood school is experiencing bullying that begins on the playground during recess.

> ... The same thing my granddaughter going through now, same thing I went through. ... recess time and that problem. Then ... junior high school was a whole new experience ... had it rough (with) the bullies ... from 7th and 8th by the time 9th grade came ... Woaaa ... adds to the trouble cause she's starting to fight back. OK and um so she would go through a period up there in high school that ... you get those threats and you cut classes and um. (her voice softens and becomes sad) ... That says you gone get your butt kicked if they see you in school. Or if they get you again. And stuff like that.

Her daughter began to cut class and lost interest in going to school and Desirea sadly comments "... I know that's where it come in at. I know cause that's what happened to me."

Desirea spoke with such emotion and passion as she sadly described bullying experiences in her neighborhood school across generations in her family. She told the stories of her daughter and granddaughter getting bullied with such pain and sadness on her face and in her voice. Desirea recalls a story of when her own class was interrupted by a telephone call about a final incident causing her daughter to leave high school. Here she shares her daughter/s life threatening experiences as a high schooler.

> I'm in Torroh now ... was called one day. Up at the transit at the token booth, that elevator change man I was talking about. He called my mother and say that the kids had chased her and ... she ran up there for protection ... this is up in (Bourough) ... they had chased her. She ran up to the token booth and asked them for help. So they told her to stand here and told them they better not bother her and ... they called the transit police.

Desirea met her mother at the train station to get her daughter and brought her back to the school with her. Her eyes were so desolate when she reflected on what her daughter must have felt and experienced. Desirea said "She musta been really scared. Lord Have Mercy (with sad voice) brakes my heart ... have my daughter out there running round in fear like that. But we ... spent a mother and daughter day together."

This bullying episode was sparked by Desirea's daughter correctly answering a question during class and the teacher "made a big thing over it" but another classmate had a "jealous streak." This bully and her friends put the word out that they were going to "get" Desirea's daughter and her friends. Desirea painfully notes

> They was gone whop [her daughter's name] behind. What she said was because she thought she was cute. She thinks she so damn smart. My daughter is running for trying to have an education y'all say us Black people need to have. But y'all ain't in control of the other ones that ain't trying to get it ...

As stated in previous chapters, Desirea had similiar experiences with bullying at the same exact school by students who were not interested in learning and disrupted other student's efforts to learn. This would consistently happened with no school officials to intervene keeping students enrolled at school learning or safe. The threats toward Desirea's daughter never stopped and she eventually had to leave high school "… Cause it just got worse in each grade until (she) just started cutting and playing hookie." Her daughter was in a precarious situation as she consistently received threats from the bullies but adults were insisting that she attend school but she "know somebody's out there waiting to beat (her) up. And you know. … ain't nobody going through all that to survive. … And um along with the threats …" Desirea indicated alternative high school was a better match for her where she eventually earned her General Equivalency Diploma (GED).

> … she'd rather find an alternative school she could go to. Which she did. She fared better when in the class … you have young people and adults maybe a GED or continuing education class, it's so much easier. Cause now (she) finally can concentrate and you will see that we're all education material. It's just that all we had to go through …

Desirea's story provides a counternarrative of reasons some Black students might drop out of school that have nothing to do with academic abilities. Across generations, both mother and daughter, attending the same school encounter the same bullying problems resulting in life changing events and dropping out of high school. During my conversations with Desirea, she emphasized that irrespective of ongoing bullying, her daughter was also never challenged academically. I found Desirea's commentary about Black children being "education material" intriguing once her daughter experienced a more academic enriched classroom setting. This is significant because some may argue that obtaining a GED is less preferable than completing a traditional high school diploma. Yet, it was this educational program that was more conducive to academic achievement allowing both Desirea and her daughter to thrive becoming a successful student.

Mothers' home school involvement

As mothers, Sharonda, Bethena, and Desirea were aware of and able to articulate their children's academic problems. Bethena and Sharonda requested support from their children's school to assist with their children's problems. They advocated for better school placements for their children and received support from Detroit Public Schools. Once Bethena became abstinent from crack cocaine, she was often employed at her children's' school allowing her to remain aware of her children's experiences during the school day. Sharonda spent so much time at one of her daughter's school addressing behavior problems that they offered her a job as a classroom and cafeteria aide. The school psychologist and administrator at this school provided Sharonda with caring and nonjudgmental assistance for her daughter. In collaboration, school personnel and Sharonda found an educational program that better matched her daughter's needs. Her daughter was eventually transferred to this school where she performed much better socially and academically.

Bethena recognized that her son needed a different academic setting and initiated a transfer for her son to an alternative high school that is considered a "boot camp" high school. She believed this school would be better for her son by positively influencing his choices enhancing opportunities for high school graduation. During this process, Bethena was supported by school administrators and other key personnel and kept her aware of her son's behavior at school. Before the school ended for winter vacation, Bethena worked zealously to identify a school setting that would support her son's school success. Her persistence and hard work paid off because she was able to enroll him in an alternative school beginning immediately after winter break.

> But I have something for him. As of Tuesday when we go back, ... I'm gonna drop him from that school, cause we got 2,100 kids ... Compared to last year we had 1,500. So I'm gonna drop him from that school and put him in (school name). It's a smaller school 500–600 kids, and they kept the kids, it's a boot camp type school where they got to wear uniforms, you go in, you gotta do what you're supposed to do, and once you get in they lock the doors, you can't get out. He need that kind of thing. ... it's a academy, a little private school but it's still Detroit Public School. ...

Bethena recognized that the sudden increase of 600 students compromised her son's schooling and realized he would benefit from smaller class sizes with a focus on discipline. She also uses her social capital within the school district to learn about and take advantage of other educational options for her son.

> So (school principal), we got a couple of principals at (high school name) that I like ... like me ... they told me the same thing, (Bethena), get him outta here. If I was you I would get him outta here, get him outta here ... [cousin's name] she always help me with the kids ... she say ... when I go and talk to Ms.(Name), Tuesday ... tell her that's my nephew he coming over there. So I got a couple people that know her at the school I'm going to. So it should be no problem getting him in. And then besides, ... I come right by that school every single day, ... he wants to go.

She established supportive relationship with staff in Detroit's school that was invaluable to her. When asked if she received support from Detroit Public Schools, she says:

> Oh God, it did. Oh it did, it did, it did, it did … work in there and they know who he was … 9th grade wasn't too bad, he went to class but he didn't do anything, still got Ds and Fs. Then we go to summer school, … you gotta pay for summer school, $100 a class. So [the principal], he my little buddy at the school [the principal] … he waived that for me, he paid that for me, $200 for him to go to summer school. And he went and still failed that. Still failed summer school. So he got all the 9th grade classes to redo, we in the 2nd quarter of the 10th grade …

Bethena never gave up on her son and his ability to complete high school in spite of continuous academic failure. She spoke passionately about her son's academic experiences and refused to acquiesce, as she remained focus on her future goals for her son. Bethena hoped that his placement in the new school would allow him to develop the discipline that he needed to be a productive adult. She wanted her son to go to "… vo-tech, get him a little kind of trade for one year, get a little job, a couple hours of schooling you know, in a trade …" At that time, even though Bethena's son was not college bound based on his current academic performance, it was still important that he consider future goals. She believed it was her responsibility to actively pursue alternative avenues for her son to complete high school and encourage him to establish goals for his future.

Bethena was able to establish and maintain effective home/school partnerships with professionals at various levels with her children's school district, which helped her monitor her son's academic problems. Her narrative illustrates in spite of her efforts and support from caring school personnel, her son continued to struggle academically. Further inquiry about the context of his schooling experiences from his perspective would greatly enhance our understanding of his failure to conform to the structure at school. One thing for sure, her son's poor academic performance is truly not the fault of a stereotyped single ex-crack addicted Black mother. Instead, Bethena's ideals and concerns about her son's academic progress is no different than any other mother trying her best to fulfill her dreams for her children. Her son eventually obtained his General Equivalency Diploma (GED) and at the time of writing this manuscript is taking college classes.

Unfortunately, Desirea did not receive the same kind of support from her daughter or granddaughter's school for bullying. During our conversations, her granddaughter was experiencing bullying at the same school that her and her daughter attended. Desirea was very emotional and passionate when she pointed out the school system's failure to keep students safe across three generations in her family.

> That's what happened to you and that's what happened to me and we know better now. I seen them, same school, might be different teacher, same school ... she's nerdy. The nerdy kids always got picked on. So what they call nerdy, is ones that the teacher calls on all the time. And that labeled her as nerdy. ... And um. Outside, (you have) class bullies. And the jumping down and the fear of guns ... It really got hard ... I notice my granddaughter do the same. Because they try and draw attention to it (but they) don't seem to believe. ... She told you, She done told her mother ... the teacher ... told the counselor ... principal. Y'all all seem to believe I done made this up. There's no kinda way can you see them mocking her, this laughter that's goin on and this pickin and this pullin and taking her stuff and beatin up on her? ... So by the time she get to a certain grade ahh you don't care anymore.

Considering her and her daughter's treacherous bullying experiences, Desirea had great concerns for her granddaughter's safety and believed it might be better for her to move to Atlantic City. Desirea believed that it would be easier for her to intervene because Atlantic City was a smaller school district than her New York Borough and she would be closer. However, Atlantic City had the same problems as big urban cities, just more concentrated because the city is so small. Unfortunately her granddaughter also experienced bullying at the elementary school in Atlantic City. This was actually the same elementary school Barbara and Ladonna spoke about when they discussed their experiences with bullying thirty years ago. Her granddaughter did not stay long and after a short period of time, returned to New York.

While her granddaughter attended Stateside Elementary School (pseudonym), she was bullied her first day at her new school. At seven or eight years old, her granddaughter would not fight back but would speak out about what was happening to her but believed adults in charge would not listen to her.

> Why you keep telling her she have to have proof and they can't do nothing until she have proof? ... Transferred her down here in January and enrolled her in Stateside School (pseudonym). Day 1. Boy choked the hell outta her. She came home. All this, round here, fingerprints where he had choked her and all. [she pointed to her neck area] What did they do? They didn't even call. ... Ain't nobody call and say that nobody choked the chile. So when I called ..., they say well it coulda been something she said. ... Everyday she done been there. (School personnel) said: Listen, we don't know about it so we don't know who was at fault and what she might a said or done. ... Well then ... she try and defend herself ... And she's the one steady getting written up. ...

Desirea and I had several conversations about her encounters at this school and her interactions with school personnel. She also believed they were prejudice against her granddaughter and stereotyped her because she was from New York, suggesting she was more streetwise and rough. Desirea was upset because they immediately concluded her granddaughter was the problem, ignored bullying and would not communicate with her. Instead of meeting to discuss the problem, they dismissed the bullying claims and blamed her granddaughter for the problem. When her daughter fought back, they wanted to refer her to special education. Her granddaughter eventually moved back to New York and attended the same school she left because of bullying.

Contributions to academic achievement

Throughout their addictions, Sharonda and Desirea attempted to support their children's development or academic progress. On days when their children were with them, they followed routines that supported academic achievement. Sharonda was able to make sure her children ate when they were with her while she was still getting high. However, when asked about helping with homework, she admits "I'm not gon lie and say all the time. Not all the time, sometimes. I was either too tired, didn't feel like it or didn't even thank about it." Sharonda interacted with her daughter's school to address her behavior problems previously discussed in this chapter. However, prior to that, she rarely interacted with schools.

> I really didn't even when I'm sober, I really didn't interact with the school. The only reason I um got (to) associate with the school was … cause the girl was just so bad. … So um, every time I had to put her back that's how I come across with them. But I really didn't ever do too much with the schools. Usually I was always pregnant and couldn't hardly, and I didn't have a car so I was walking. So no, I didn't interact with the school very much.

Sharonda, the mother of ten children illustrates here how transportation is sometimes a barrier for mothers attempting to establish partnerships with their children's school. This is even more pronounced if a mother has several children under eighteen and lives in a state with brutally cold winter seasons. Thus, as she reports, the likely hood of Sharonda visiting her child's school was slim even if she was not active in her addiction.

Although Desirea was using drugs when her daughter was school aged, she supported her daughter's academic achievement by establishing daily routines related to school. On the days Desirea's daughter stayed with her as a preschooler, they would read to each other daily. Observing her daughter's classroom, attending Parent Teacher Association (PTA) meetings, and buying educational materials were things she believed supported her daughter's academic achievement. Desirea brought her daughter a GED book to help her with her 4th grade silent reading and had a system at home for facilitating her daughter's academic skills.

> Like I'm doing with my grandchildren. Umm. They got a globe, telescope, things that when they do these in class, they can do them at home. I took her to arts and cultural things. Ahh um. ... Fourth grade when she started the silent reading ... always remember this cause I got her [her daughter] the GED book. ... She had chalkboards and she had all the um workbooks and stuff to try to further what it was she learned. I tell you, the GED book ... was in 4th grade. When she took her 4th grade testing. (Her daughter's name) was found to be on the 6th grade level. By the time she got to 6th grade, she was already between 8th and 9th grade level. And when she did get to high school, she was already in en route to half of the college level. OK. That's how much the GED and other materials and things I was doing. She was ahead of herself.

Desirea believes although difficult, she was capable of juggling her heroin addiction and parental responsibilities. She says with confidence she did a "remarkable job" supporting her daughter's academic achievement.

> Yes I was on drugs during all this, this whole time period. I was in and outta millions of rehab and just kept getting caught up and stuff. But I would keep up with her schooling. I would go. She was always dressed nice. Her hair was nice. You couldn't tell. ... I would go to the PTA meetings ... I had permission to come in and sit in the back of the class ... I did a remarkable job as far as trying to guide her. It's just that the things. You know it's one thing to tell a person how to go and it's another when they see you doing another thing. So it was kind of hard for (her) to believe. But I didn't know that.

Desirea admits here it might have been difficult for her daughter to understand the contradictions of her mothering. She was teaching her daughter the value of education but at the same time engaged in her heroin addiction. However, Desirea accepts responsibility for her inconsistent presence in her daughter's life because of heroin. She says she "... wasn't involved with just me ... she was left to fend a lot within the family and outside for herself and um she um holds that against me." Desirea's daughter's recollection of her absence during her childhood caused strain on their relationship. Although she believes that her daughter is "coming around ... and is proud of (Desirea's) accomplishments," she acknowledges

> Still it did damage to her as far as all she had to go through. With all she had be teased about, all she had to fight about ... I was part of the teasing ... your mother's ... a whore, she's a this, she's a that. You know what I'm sayin. She didn't understand that I could a been a saint. They was gone say something about me anyway. ...

Although crack was not around, she describes how a crack ho' image was the blunt of her daughter's bullying and feels badly about the hardship it caused. Desirea realizes regardless of her contributions toward supporting her daughter's academic achievement, they will always be viewed under the cloud of her years of heroin addiction.

Bethena's contributions toward her children's academic achievement is based on the assumption her children's future is directly related to their academic experiences. She was not so involved in her children's academic achievement when she was using drugs but since Bethena has been clean, she has put forth much effort in supporting their schooling. In order to facilitate academic achievement in her home, Bethena's established a daily routine consisting of getting homework done when they were young. Her job as a noon hour aide at their elementary school kept her to informed of their educational activities at school. Bethena speaks about the schedule she had for her children when they were young.

> ... bring them home, help them with the homework. After do our homework then we put our clothes on, they usually (watch) TV or go outside and play and whatever, then come back in about 9, 9:30, wash up, change clothes, get ready for bed. Next day we start it all over again. ... I like to do the homework soon as you come in the house ... from school let's do that right now and get that outta the way see ... when you let them go and play first then come back and do homework, can't get them to settle down ... So we did that first. While school is still fresh. ... Well it worked through elementary. It started fading in middle. You could hang it up in high school. ... I don't know how we got off track. I don't know how we got off track. Honey, I couldn't tell you. I couldn't tell you, but (my daughter) she still come home sometime do hers.

When her children were young, Bethena was diligent in trying to instill academic values in them, by prioritizing school with scheduled homework time. Her family maintained a homework routine throughout elementary school and sometimes during middle school. This routine seemed to vanish in high school, however, her daughter still has a rigid schedule. She talks about her daughter who at the time was a high school senior's that was closely monitored ensuring she stays out of trouble.

> ... So when she come home now most evening, Monday, Wednesdays, Thursday and Friday and Saturday, she work at Taco Bell, from 4 to 9. So it just Tuesdays and

Sundays she off. And ... when she come home from Taco Bell she go straight into, 9 we get back home, time I go pick her up 9 get in the house 10, she go and do her homework. Then she got to try on her clothes for school tomorrow. I guess time she settle down to get into bed it's about 12, 1:00.

Black families across class lines value their children's educational achievement and believe home-school involvement is key to acquiring the best educational opportunities for their children (Rosier, 2000; Rowley, Helaire, Banerjee, 2010; Toliver, 1998). Bethena, Sharonda and Desirea's perspectives of their contributions to academic achievement defies negatively controlled image of the crack ho,' or in Desirea's case, junkie whore who could care less of their young children's education. The mothers shared stories about encouraging academic achievement, perceptions of their children as students, addressing problems encountered at school, and their means of supporting educational experiences.

Regardless of Desirea and Sharonda's own failed attempts at completing traditional school, all of the mothers desired their children excelled academically making efforts to support their achievement. Bethena and Sharonda felt obligated to stimulate an interest in and encourage academic achievement. They had firsthand experience with what it was like not to be "pushed," encouraged or supported to excel academically or plan for your future. The mothers' own negative school experiences did not taint their optimism for considering goals and expectations for their children. Instead, their stories suggest in spite of their educational experiences, they still valued educational attainment and made a conscious effort to support their children's school success. They recognized when their children were not thriving and sought assistance often to advocate or support their children's academic success. Sharonda, Bethena, and Desirea were able to clearly articulate their children's school problems and school related concerns. These mothers also knew what changes were required so their children would do better in school and made intentional responsible efforts to act accordingly.

The mothers' stories provided important counternarratives of Black mothers, drug addiction and parent involvement in schools. Many factors interfering with children's academic success were totally unrelated to the mothers' drug addictions or efforts to support their achievement. For example, Desirea's neighborhood school historically failed to keep children safe while learning and in spite of her efforts, she unfortunately watched females in her family bullied across three generations. The bullying was serious, often life threatening and directly related to dropping out of high school. The inner city public school environment contributed more to Desirea's daughter's academic failure than her heroin addiction. Her daughter did not have access to a safe effective neighborhood school or financial resources for private school where she might have obtained a quality education.

What Does All of This Have to do With Education Now?

I charge educational professionals and policy makers to think critically about "evidenced-based practices" used for designing and implementing policy and practice related to Black families living in poverty. Currently not much education research informs us of maternal crack, powder cocaine, crank, and heroin addictions or family resilience from the Black mothers' perspective. However, drug use in impoverished Black communities continue. When educational research and policy ignores race, class and gender oppressions, stereotyped images like the welfare queen, junkie, crack ho' and crack baby prevail and our knowledge of Black motherhood remains limited. It is my hope that Bethena, Sharonda, Ladonna, Desirea, and Barbara's self-definitions and experiential knowledge of maternal drug addiction and parenting are validated and respected as legitimate sources of information (Collins, 2000; González, 2005; Solórzano & Yosso, 2009) as we learn more about the topic. When their voices are ignored, stereotypes are advanced and their child's developmental or educational problems are blamed solely on them and family resilience is overlooked. Thus, there is no need to examine the social structures (e.g. schools, legal systems, dangerous neighborhoods) impeding Black children's developmental and educational growth who are impacted by the illegal drug industry.

The crack ho' and her crack baby stereotypes continue to shape the minds of many professionals across disciplines in medicine, education, and the social services. As an early childhood teacher educator, I typically encounter at least one graduate student who describes her job as working with "drug exposed children." Many of them also share their students live in poverty as if those children required lower expectations because they are poor or born drug-exposed, which are often code words for black children. Throughout the semester I attempt to relay the message the label of being poor or drug exposed has very little to do with children's innate abilities to learn basic early childhood concepts. Instead, I suggest they focus on getting to know families and become culturally responsive. I remind them they are to meet student's developmental needs in a respectful manner beyond the welfare queen and crack ho and baby stereotypes. Recently, I have had conversations with school administrators who continue to believe that crack cocaine is currently responsible for children's behavior problems in schools.

My intent here is not to paint a rose-colored picture of the home environment for children impacted by crack, powder cocaine, crank, and heroin addictions. However, knowledge claims about prenatal drug exposure from the perspective of the mothers in this book deepens our understanding of family resilience. Educational scholars and scholars of color have a responsibility to challenge epistemological racism and frameworks privileging one perspective over others. New theories will then be created and provide space for those that have been historically excluded (López & Parker, 2003). It is my hope, Bethena, Barbara, Desirea, Ladonna, and Sharonda's narratives expose structural and systemic forces providing alternate understandings of why Black children stressed by parental addiction do not always excel academically. They share experiences and perspectives about their children's education providing new insights about their children's potential. Thus, professionals may approach their work with mothers typically considered (whether intentional or not) a welfare queen or crack ho' and baby with more compassion and care. Hopefully resulting in professional practices that eliminate residuals of negative controlled images and embraces families as they would impacted by any illness.

Home environments burdened with drug addiction are obviously not optimal settings for healthy development and parent-child interactions, which are considered to be precursors for academic achievement. However, neither is being bounced around in foster care systems or living in homes impacted by alcoholism or prescription drugs. Stressful home environments do not always result in children doomed to lifelong problems and singling out Black children impacted by addictions only impairs opportunities for family healing. This can be offset with a focus on resilience and hope supporting all children and families' victory over hard times. Black families impacted by drug addiction should be understood and supported without risks of parental rights being automatically terminated only after one year of trying. Except for Sharonda, the mothers had children born before the Adoption and Safe Family Act of 1997 was enacted that only allows mothers one year to get off of drugs. Otherwise, if their child/ren are in foster care for more than a year, their rights are automatically permanently terminated. Yet, as you will see in the following chapter drug recovery is often complex often requiring more than one year.

My work has important implications for expanding educational policies and practices targeted at schools serving Black students in neighborhoods with a high prevalence of crack and heroin abuse. When considering these policies, it is important we do not plummet into the pitfalls of labeling children. As we saw with Antwaun Garcia (2004), children suffer when they are identified and labeled prenatally exposed to crack-a crack baby. The stigma and stereotypes of such labels are more detrimental to the children than the intended support (Lardner, 1997). Labeling and relying on standardized test scores to make educational decisions for these children has proven to be ineffective. Instead, policies should be in place that facilitate learning climates with high expectations for academic achievement for all students. School climates should be a place where families are respected and able to learn regardless of their structure, problems or neighborhood. Students have a right to attend school in loving environments operating from a belief that high academic achievement is obtainable for all children and are not blamed for poor academic performance (Scheurich, 1998). The stigma of Black mothers recovering from drugs has to be disrupted so mothers like Bethena, Sharonda, and Desirea, are validated and supported as they realize their children's academic goals.

As young girls, educational practice did not acknowledge and reinforce their academic achievement or potential. Assuring Desirea and Ladonna's safety while attending school would have supported their academic endeavors. As early as elementary school, effective policies should be developed and implemented in order to protect children from bullying, sexual assault, and exposure to illegal drugs both in and around school. Although signs are now posted, that does not always prevent them from entering school. With the exception of doubling the penalties for possessing drugs near schools, these topics are seldom addressed in the so-called war on drugs or the drug problem in poor Black neighborhoods. Bullying and sexual assault were clearly a precursor for Desirea and Ladonna's introduction to drug abuse as teenage girls.

All of the mothers valued academic achievement and believed they were involved in their children's schooling. Desirea's stories highlight how even in throes of heroin addiction, she maintained a sense of responsibility for supporting her daughter academically. Regardless of addiction, Desirea consciously made efforts to support her daughter's academic progress and believes her daughter's GED reading workbook was key to her high performance on reading tests. Once they weaned themselves off of crack, with no help from agencies, Bethena and Sharonda were so involved in their children's education that they both became employed at their children's schools. Thus, suspicion of substance abuse when working with families should be addressed in collaboration across disciplines without fear of incarceration or loss of custody.

Bethena and Sharonda had nothing but positive things to say about educational personnel in Detroit Public Schools reporting a high level of support. Recent changes in this school district present a different system than when Bethena and Sharonda's children attended and now receives a lot of negative media attention. However, recent news stories chronicle their teacher's care and concern for their students. Enhancing home/school partnerships with families impacted by illegal drug business can only materialize when they are redefined and inclusive of diverse families. Expanding the meaning of involvement with parents typically marginalized is useful when understanding their perceptions of involvement at school especially when they are labeled uninvolved by school (López, 2001). The home school involvement of parents outside of the dominant culture is minimized when schools only acknowledge traditional parent-involvement activities. This is especially true for families with maternal drug abuse. For example, when discussing findings of her longitudinal qualitative research, Barone (1995/1996) points out: "... stories of Jennifer, Jamal ... Danny demonstrate ... these children are like all others ... respond to supportive school and home environments ... do best when both the home and school environment support them as worthy individuals who are trying to learn." (p. 288) Only then will efforts of mothers like Desirea to support her child's education become validated and supported.

Bethena, Ladonna, Barbara, and Desirea had been drug free for more than five years and offer school administrators opportunities to utilize their experiential knowledge of drug addiction and recovery. Mothers with this length of sobriety are important school resources for educating students about dangers of drug addictions. The mothers also provide important facts on the exploitation of young people manipulated into becoming addicted. Thus, the mothers are viewed positively contradicting negative images of welfare queens and crack ho's.

Bethena, Ladonna, Sharonda, Desirea and Barbara's stories provide opportunities for pre-service, teacher educators, researchers, and teachers working with children in illegal drug industries new insights about Black families. Education personnel can be challenged to become reflective about their own perceptions and biases that might interfere with partnerships with families impacted by drug abuse. Teachers can strive to become more familiar with their students' funds of knowledge, family values and experiences at home. Only then will they be able to provide a culturally relevant education to all students, building upon their strengths (González, 2005; Ladson-Billings, 1994; Moll & González, 2004;).

The mothers' strong spirituality also helped them resist the crack ho' and junkie image as they relied on God to help them through their addictions while caring for their children. Their spirituality and religious practices were instrumental in sustaining their abstinence from drugs as discussed in the following chapter.

References

Adoption and safe families act of 1997. Retrieved from http://www.acf.hhs.gov.

Barone, D. (1995/1996). Children prenatally exposed to crack or cocaine: Looking behind the label. *The Reading Teacher*, 49(4), 278–289.

Blake, M. (2004, September 9). Crack babies talk back. Columbia Journalism Review. Retrieved from http://www.alternet.org.

Chasnoff, I. J. (1992, August). Cocaine, pregnancy, and the growing child. *Current Problems in Pediatrics*, 302–321.

Collins, P. H. (2000). *Black feminist thought: Knowledge, consciousness, and the politics of empowerment* (2nd ed.). New York, NY: Routledge.

Frank, D. A. (2003, November 28). Crack baby syndrome? [Letter to Editor]. Retrieved from http://www.nytimes.com.

Frank, D. A., & Zuckerman, B. S. (1993). Children exposed to cocaine prenatally: Pieces of the puzzle. *Neurotoxicology and Teratology*, 15, 298–300.

Frank, D. et al. (1988, December). Cocaine use during pregnancy: Prevalence and correlates. Pediatrics, 82(6), 888–895.

Frank, D. A., Augustyn, M., Knight, W. G., Pell, T., & Zuckerman, B. (2001). Growth, development, and behavior in early childhood following prenatal cocaine exposure. A systematic review. *American Medical Association*, 285(12), 1613–1626.

Garcia, A. (2004). They called me a crack baby. *Represent: The voice of youth in care*. Retrieved from http://www.representmag.org.

González, N. (2005). Beyond culture: The hybridity of funds of knowledge. In N. González, L. C. Moll, & C. Amanti (Eds.), *Funds of knowledge: Theorizing practices in households, communities, and classrooms* (pp. 29–46). New York, NY: Routledge.

Griffith, D. R., Azuma, S. D., & Chasnoff, I. J. (1994). Three-year outcome of children exposed prenatally to drugs. *Journal of American Academy of Child and Adolescent Psychiatry*, 33(1), 20–27.

Hill, R. B. (2003). *The strengths of Black families*. Lanham, MD: University Press of America.

Hurt, H., Brodsky, N. L., Betancourt, L., Braitman, L. E., Malmud, E., & Giannetta, J. (1995). Cocaine-exposed children: Follow-up through 30 months. *Developmental and Behavioral Pediatrics*, 16, 29–35.

Jarrett, R. & Coba-Rodriguez, S. (2015). "My mother didn't play about education:" Low-income, African American mothers' school experiences and their impact on school involvement for preschoolers transitioning kindergarten. *Journal of Negro Education*, 84(3), 457–472.

Ladson-Billings, G. (1994). *The dreamkeepers: Successful teachers of African American children*. San Francisco, CA: Jossey-Bass.

Lardner, T. (1997). Training teachers to educate drug-affected children. In M. R. Haack (Ed.), *Drug-dependent mothers and their children* (pp. 236–245). New York: Springer Publishing.

López, G. R. (2001). The value of hard work: Lessons on parent involvement from an (im)migrant household. *Harvard Educational Review, 71*, 416–437.

López G. R., & Parker, L. (Eds.) (2003). Conclusion. *Interrogating racism in qualitative research methodology* (pp. 203–212). New York, NY: Peter Lang Publishing.

McDonough, K. (2013, July 23). Long-term study debunks myth of the "crack baby." *Salon*. Retrieved from http://www.salon.com.

Moll, L. C., & González, N. (2004). A funds-of-knowledge approach to multicultural education. In J. A. Banks & C. A. Banks (Eds.), *Handbook of research on multicultural education* (2nd ed., pp. 699–715). San Francisco, CA: Jossey-Bass.

Roberts, D. E. (2002). *Shattered bonds: The color of child welfare*. New York, NY: Basic Civitas Books.

Rowley, S. J., Helaire, L. J., Banerjee, M. (2010). Reflecting on racism: School involvement and perceived teacher discrimination in African American mothers. Journal of Applied Developmental Psychology,*31*(1), 83–92.

Scheurich, J. J. (1998). Highly successful and loving, public elementary schools populated mainly by low-ses children of color. *Urban Education, 33*(4), 451–491.

Solórzano, D., & Yosso, T. (2009). Critical race methodology: Counter-storytelling as an analytical framework for education research. In E. Taylor, D. Gillborn, & G. Ladson-Billings (Eds.), *Foundations of critical race theory in education* (pp. 131–147) ,. New York, NY: Routledge.

Sudarkasa, N. 1996. *The strength of our mothers: African and African American women & families: Essays and speeches*. Trenton, NJ: Africa World Press.

Swadener, B. B. (1995). Children and families "at promise:" Deconstructing the discourse of risk. In B. B. Swadener & S. Lubeck (Eds.), *Children and families "at promise": Deconstructing the discourse of risk* (pp. 17–49). Albany, NY: State University of New York Press.

Swadener, B. B., & Lubeck, S. (1995). The social construction of children and families "at risk": An introduction. In B. B. Swadener & S. Lubeck (Eds.), *Children and families "at promise": Deconstructing the discourse of risk* (pp. 1–16). Albany, NY: State University of New York Press.

Thurman, S. K., Brobeil, R. A., DuCette, J. P., & Hurt, H. (1994). Prenatally exposed to cocaine: Does the label matter? *Journal of Early Intervention, 18*(2), 119–130.

Toliver, S. D. (1998). *Black families in corporate America*. Thousand Oaks, CA: Sage Publications.

Winerip, M. (2013, May 20). Revisting the 'crack babies' epidemic that was not. *The New York Times*. Retrieved from http://www.nytimes.com/2013/05/20/booming/revisiting-the-crack-babies-epidemic-that-was-not.html.

Zerai, A., & Banks, R. (2002). *Dehumanizing discourse, anti-drug law, and policy in America: A "crack mother's" nightmare*. Burlington, VT: Ashgate Publishing.

· 9 ·

"I WAS JUST CRYIN' OUT TO GOD"

Recovery and the Spirituality of Struggle

So I'm crying, you know hyperventilating type of crying [LAUGHTER]. I was just crying out to God and um I think when I woke up in the morning he just gave me, I had this peace all over me. And He was like I heard your cry and I will answer. And it was fine ... He just, He speaks. And He'll tell you, I heard you.

—Sharonda

Resiliency is often achieved in Black families through strong religious beliefs (Hill, 2003) and the Black church has always been "a refuge in a hostile White world" (Lincoln, 1964; p. 50) for decedents of enslaved Africans (Staples & Johnson, 1993; Robinson, 2006). Christian religious values and beliefs are the foundation of Barbara, Bethena, Sharonda, Desirea, and Ladonna's lives and they attend church regularly. They credit what they consider God's love and power for their recovery and overall safety. This chapter presents Desirea and Barbara's perceptions on recovery and critiques of methadone clinics. The mothers' share narratives about God's overall protection, intervention during life-threatening moments, and how He spoke to them during their active drug addiction.

All mothers spoke about their reliance on God for personal safety and daily living. I became emotionally affected the most when they shared these stories about their experiences. Occasionally, during our conversations, I worked hard to hold back tears as they spoke so nonchalantly about horrific circumstances but there were also occasions when we cried together. Sometimes after interviews, my psychological response was so intense I would experience sadness into the next day. However, nothing prepared me for the unexpected feelings of overwhelming fear as they shared stories of danger. It was similar to fear a young child might have from watching a scary movie and I thought to myself, what have I gotten myself into? I just wanted to learn more about drug addiction, parenting, and children's academic achievement. Yet, here I am listening to stories from the mothers that mirrored movie plots and scenes right out of movies like *New Jack City* (1991). I did not anticipate hearing gut wrenching stories about the dangers of illegal drug addiction and the industry. I guess this also speaks to my suspect space as an insider and naïveté of the realities of heroin and crack businesses. My relationships with the mothers helped dispel this fear as they acted as loving teachers and we very proud and happy to share their stories with me. I was not a neutral researcher or unattached, but another Black mother experiencing emotions during our conversations. After I went through the full range of sadness and fear, I then became in awe of the mothers' resilience and strength. Their faith and relationships with God were moving and inspirational. On a few occasions, I attended the same church services with Desirea and Barbara. I found my spiritual life changed by my relationship with the mothers, as I believed that my interactions with them and their testimonies increased my own spiritual faith. I also attended church more while visiting my research sites than I typically did prior. One cannot help but be inspired and moved spiritually by the mothers' testimonies of faith, resilience and hope.

Desirea and Barbara's Take on Methadone

Lessons learned from the mothers about rehabilitation centers completely shifted my thinking about drug treatment and rehabilitation for poor Black mothers. Prior to working with the mothers, I thought that access to rehabilitation was the only barrier to recovery. Desirea's recovery from several years of heroin addiction was complex and involved several attempts of federally funded methadone treatment centers. We often spoke about her addiction and recovery outside of the audiotaped interviews. Here, she references the struggle with her heroin addiction

Like I was telling you the first time we met. ... You go ... try to make a real effort at stopping ... putting your life back in order ... you find you weren't in control of your life. And it's not as easy ...

Desirea presents a valuable critique of procedures and policies used in methadone treatment centers to encourage clients to remain enrolled in the program. Instead of supporting her abstinence from drugs, she believed the methadone program "... was the system's way of combating heroin. So now, it's just ... for them to generate another dollar. They call themselves controlling the guy that's on (heroin) ..." Desirea suggested that methadone clinics were designed to manage street level drug addiction and simply a way for individuals to "get high legally cause they'll provide it, but they want us outta sight ..." She argues though "their" attempts to keep drug users off "... the street ..." was not effective for all street drugs. Desirea says

> ... But it didn't happened that way cause you had another group, that got coke, crack, ... and the old groups that's always gon have the heroin. So what happen was, you start getting it legal from the government and you still buying it illegal.

Desirea and I had several conversations about her distrust of most government agencies charged to support those on the margins of society, including the methadone clinic. She knew changes in methadone dosages administered to clients required careful monitoring. However, with facial expressions of disgust and lowered voice tone she reported personnel simply kept the methadone dosage at the maximum level. She described it "... In other words they're locking in a person for a lifetime. Do you know that they have had seniors on the program? I mean people that was grandparents on high dosages of methadone ..."

Desirea explained with so much passion why she does not believe the methadone program was designed to help people recover from heroin or drug addiction. Being a heroin addict since she was a teenager and throughout her adulthood, she understood the time frame for being weaned off the drug but observed patients' methadone doses not being reduced appropriately. Even worse, indicated the dosage would be increased as would the patient's reliance on the methadone program. Desirea's comparison of the methadone program with alternative schools is very insightful. She says:

> ... It's pretty much like if you get a grant to keep an alternative school running ... you need that kid in there. OK, and you know without them kids, you don't have no school right? Alright then. So you going to have counselors, and nurses, and doctors,

all these people came from out of the medical community ... But it was all designed to keep you right in that circle. So the biggest question, how you get out of there?"

In order for Desirea to become totally heroin and methadone free, she devised a plan to strategically manipulate the system in place at the methadone clinic. For example, she would accumulate absences beyond the limit allowed in an effort to be removed from the program. Desirea would receive her "weekend take home" methadone and put it in the offering plate and just pray on Sunday morning during a Catholic church service. She also just walked in this same church that was opened during the day and just pray, believing this was the beginning of her healing from heroin. Although, it would be a few years later before she would be completely heroin free, these church experiences were the catalyst for her recovery. Desirea relied on her faith and relationship with God for spiritual guidance as she attempted to get off of methadone and refers to this experience as a "real spiritual war."

Prolonged absences were frequent but Desirea was still not disqualified from the methadone program so she allowed her Medicaid card to expire.

> ... I refused to get ... Medicaid. You have to have medical insurance ... if you lose it, they carry you over for what they call a grace period. Cause you suppose to get your paper work and run here and run there. Please, I refused to. Sick n tired, of being sick n tired ... I know I didn't sign the papers for another 3 months or 90 days so that happened about 3 times.

She refused to renew her Medicaid hoping her lapse in medical coverage would make her ineligible. Unfortunately, that did not stop the staff from pressuring her to stay in the program.

> But I remember the director told me. 'We don't know why you don't won't to go and get your paper work like you're suppose to. You know, now she's Black, you people can't take no pain. ... You know, you (says with emphasis) people. That's coming from a Black director ... You people using drugs can't take pain ... why y'all do what y'all do because you can't stand pain. Now why would you wanna leave and have to start all over. I said, I'm not starting all over. God has something for me. Now release me like you suppose to. I stood and said a prayer. Oh she was furious (said with emphasis) I wouldn't go get that paperwork. Well they threw me into St. Barnabas, it's a detox. Now, do that make sense?

Desirea, a Black mother poor addicted to heroin was very much dependent on the system for resources, including her opportunity to get drug free. She did not believe the methadone clinic was committed to helping her become drug free. Desirea reasoned "the system" was only interested in keeping her under their control by maintaining her prolonged and unnecessary enrollment in government funded methadone program. As a heroin addict with no financial resources or access to private health insurance, she was prone to what she perceived as exploitation from structural systems charged with eradicating heroin addiction from the community. Even more troubling, her human rights were violated by placing her in St. Barnabas for detox against her will. This system of detox completely disregarded her reduction of heroin use through her religious practices, spirituality and her relationship with God as she understood Him to be. Desirea had made up her mind that she wanted to be free from heroin but this required help and the only help was from programs who did not value her personhood.

During our many conversations, Desirea mentioned negative experiences with major institutions set out to help poor Black people resulting in her lack of trust and laden suspicion. This was particularly true for systems and agencies tasked with addressing illegal drug industries in Black communities. Drug recovery requires not only resources across disciplines, but a societal commitment to prevent drugs from entering our communities. Below, Desirea provides another critique of drug recovery opportunities and limitations of participation in these programs.

> Now let me run it down to you, Tierra. You out there on the street drugs. You go into a program. A methadone program in order to get off of that. And now they gone put you into a government run hospital. Now you come outta there. The people that they done busted and let out along with your (bad) police. You got them people standing around the hospital. So before you can ever get 2 or 3 blocks from the hospital, you done started the cycle all over again ... you have what they call dealers ... coming out after you as soon as you leave the hospital.

Desirea's story of her attempts to kick her heroin addiction challenges existing stereotypes and the dominant story of heroin addiction leading you to believe that mothers like Desirea are not interested in recovery and is then blamed for her inability to stop drug use and revolving stays in rehabilitation. However, Desirea was simply trying to become totally drug-free and did not believe that would happen if she stayed in the methadone program. She was committed to recovery and had access to what appeared to be drug rehabilitation for her heroin addiction. The irony here is that she had to become noncompliant with the methadone program in order to become free of heroin and methadone addiction. Her indictments and criticisms of these treatment centers in our country speak to the hypocrisy of the government's claims at attempting to eliminate drug addiction. Also, the requirements of the methadone clinic often competed with her goals for employment and educational advancement. Her attendance to mandatory meetings for the methadone clinic would often conflict with her work or class schedule resulting in her each time eventually stopping school and being fired from her job.

After being caught shoplifting, Barbara was mandated by a judge to seek drug treatment and enrolled in an inpatient facility in Atlantic City. By this time, she was also addicted to crack. She understood her heroin addiction required medical supervision and explained to me it was the fear of "getting sick" that kept her using heroin. This was a new concept to me, while I understood (at least I thought I did) the idea of craving the drug or needing a fix, it never occurred to me that a person could really die from trying to kick a heroin addiction cold turkey.

> I was out there long enough. 30 years is a long time. To get out there and scared to come back. Scared to come back cause of what it was gone do. I was scared to get sick. So rather than (she taps on the table) to get sick. I kept going. ... Yeah cause that can kill you. ... Kill you dead. Don't have no back up, will kill you dead. Ohh Lord. You got to have some serious help for that.

Barbara was aware methadone was a required drug for her heroin recovery but also understood the dangers of transferring addictions from heroin to methadone. Upon entering the methadone clinic, she made a point not to switch her chemical dependency on heroin to methadone. Like Desirea, she desired to be drug free and was determined to be free from heroin and methadone addiction. Below Barbara critiques the methadone clinic in Atlantic City and equates the tobacco industry with the methadone clinic. She believed that her experience as a long-term heroin addict awarded her the knowledge of understanding how to wean herself off of the methadone.

> You'd be on methadone for the rest of your life if you want to just continue on, in and out of doing the drugs. ... It didn't help coke. It helped me when I was on the dope and I used. But I had sense enough to stop because I was scared of getting (she kept hitting the table as she tried to recall) heroin, I mean a um whatcha call em, jones. ... Methdone jones and that's worse then the heroin. ... Yeah. Ooohh Wee. Yes. ... I've experienced everything and know ... how, when ... You know how long it should be done. When to come off of it. ...

"God Looks Out for Babies and Fools"

Barbara, Desirea, Ladonna, Sharonda, and Bethena all believed very much that God's presence, love and protection has been a constant in their lives throughout their years of active addiction. Their religious beliefs and spirituality gained from their Christian upbringing were heavily relied upon as important coping mechanisms (Gregg, 2011) during their addictions. Below, Bethena, Barbara, and Sharonda share their thoughts of God's continuous presence in their lives across their life spans, even outside of their addiction.

Bethena:	Okay once I come here, like I say I was eighteen. Eighteen when I come here in June, but my birthday was in July so I was turning nineteen. I come here and like I say, God has always had His hand over me since I been in Detroit.
Barbara:	My birthday was November. And the kids wanted to know what I wanted. I didn't know what I wanted. I don't need. I have everything. If I ain't got it, I done had it. God been good to me like that.
Sharonda:	… That's God, it is, cause I should have lost my mind a long time ago and um, I thank God I didn't.

Here, Bethena, Barbara, and Sharonda talked about God's goodness so nonchalantly as if their world-view of God was common knowledge. They credit God for everything including protection as an adult, material things, and mental health. The mothers speak retrospectively of how their faith and connection to God kept them resilient and courageous during some of the most difficult times.

The mothers also refer to God as a powerful source of safety (Kupor, Laurin, & Levav, 2015) for them while in dangerous environments during their active addictions. Sharonda is real clear God protects her daily and depends on this safety when she is alone at night because "… in our neighborhood you hear gunfire all the time … there was a lot of shooting over there …" She explained to me the house she was renting did not have back windows and a man had been murdered that day in a house on her block and someone else had gotten shot closer to her house. Sharonda emphasized to me that this living environment did not frighten her though and said that "… it was just like, just danger all around. But always, God always let me know I was well protected and my family was protected. It's just, I don't know, you know it's just a lot of gunfire …" Sharonda explained she experienced this type of protection from street violence long before her crack addiction. Here, she describes an incident in her early twenties when she was "just smoking weed," that helped shape assurance that God would always keep her safe. It is interesting here, Sharonda minimizes her using marijuana as "just smoking weed" and less serious than her smoking crack.

> ... walking home high one day and I just I prayed because. ... I was raised in the church. So I prayed Lord, protect me as I go. I know I ain't got no business out here by myself, but protect me. And um this still voice just came to me and said you are well protected in Jesus name ... and um, say like I wanted a beer and it's late night and I'm like oh Lord, I'm out here by myself. And that still, that same voice still come to me and say you're well protected in Jesus name. It's been saying it for years and nothing ever happened. And I know that was God ... just anytime. I mean just folks shooting and you'll hear that voice, you're well protected in Jesus name. I was like, ahh, well you really here and you really looking out for a sister cause for years. ... Well you now bullets ain't got no name, but after I heard that voice, I knew I was okay. And I am, I am and I love Him.

While one might question Sharonda's feelings of safety under these circumstances as simply "weed logic" justifying irresponsible behavior while high on marijuana, her faith is impressive. At the same time regardless of what she was doing wrong, she always believed she had God's favor.

Barbara and Bethena also provide testimony to what they interpret as God's protection being divine intervention during life threatening circumstances. Heroin and crack cocaine addictions sometimes placed the mothers in dangerous life threatening situations. Each time, they gave God credit for saving her lives. For example, while out by herself on the street during a dangerous encounter, Barbara proclaims that "... God, given me grace, God is so good to me girl. Um Guns have been put to my head, pulling the trigger." Barbara was in a life-threatening situation as the man with her intended to kill her but once she realized that the gun did not fire, her instincts caused her to hit him back. Barbara said

> I was scared, girl. I knew I was dead. He meant to kill me ... Knocked the happy hell out of him. Yes I did. ... Girl, he hauled off and knocked me back. I hit the ground so hard I bounced back up and these 2 guys that was walking pass ... it was my nephew. ... [Nephew's name] fired on the boy ... I tell you God been watching over me [she starts laughing and says] when I didn't even know it.

Heroin was Barbara's main drug of choice for most of her years of addiction, that is, until crack cocaine came on the scene. She says "... crack ... I'm so sorry I got hooked up on crack, I don't know what to do. Heroin and coke I'd been all right with that. That crack is something else ..." On numerous occasions Barbara spoke about how crack cocaine was vastly different than any other street drugs she had ever used before. She once told me "crack was ... a caller and for young folks" and that is "what brought me down." Her addiction to crack spiraled out of control very quickly and was more intense than with her heroin and pill addictions. Barbara was using both crack and heroin at the same time when she believed she experienced God's protection during a trip to New York to purchase drugs. She shared several stories of how God's protection saved her life when there was no other explanation for her survival from such dangerous circumstances.

The next narrative involves the self-imposed danger she encountered when she traveled alone from Atlantic City to New York to purchase some heroin. To illustrate her unquestionable belief God saved her life, she would begin her story with comments like "... OK. This is where I should have been dead. God's just been God to me. He was guarding me and I didn't even know ..." Barbara then proceeded to describe the details of this trip to purchase heroin and powdered and crack cocaine. However, once she arrived to New York, the people that usually made the purchase for her were no longer available and she unwittingly decided to go by herself. She said "... I didn't have time to stop and think about what I was doing ... You know. I take a whole lot for granted don't I? That's cause you don't be thinking. You don't be thinking ..." As Barbara told the story, she admitted her actions were not well thought out and would not be something that a "thinking" person would decide to do.

In order for Barbara to make her purchases, she had to go alone to "... The big house, is the dope house ... where they manufacture ... girls be walking around with no clothes ... They mask themselves up ... then on (the) other side they had the bosses ... would be bagging and packing getting things together for the pickups ..." As she described her experiences, they sounded like a familiar scene from the motion picture *New Jack City*. I mentioned my observation to her and she agreed that was exactly how it looked once you got inside the building. Barbara had accompanied her friends in the past when they purchased drugs for her and "... (She) took the chance on going up there. Cause I seen him do it. I say oh if they can do it, I can do it ..." The problem was that there was a secret code for entering the building involving a trap door embedded on the doorsteps and if you did not know which step to avoid, you were in trouble. Once again, Barbara credits God for saving her

> ... and I jumped over the right step. God was with me ... Yeah, going into the building ... it was a big boobie trap ... But if you didn't know what you was doing. You go

down and that was it. That would be the end of you. They be waiting for you down at the other end ... I jumped over that step ...

As if Barbara's story of entering the "Big House" was not adventurous enough, the story becomes even more terrifying once she gets inside beyond three armed guys and step boobie trap. Barbara reports

> ... And they had 3 guys in the front. Out in front of the door once you got inside ... 3 of them be right in the front with the guns ... The guy opened the door and I just went on in and I told him what I wanted. But don't you know they was being held up when I got in there. That's why the ones outside was waiting for the people to come up inside and take all their money too.

Barbara's instinct and careful observation or as she puts it, God gave her a "feeling" that something was wrong

> ... Girl, when I seen what I seen, it was nothing but God's gift that God gives me that feeling. You know. I seen the way they had all these people bond up, and taped up to the couch (she laughs and says girl with emphasis) and girl I looked, when I turned around and looked again, I turned around and shot (claps her hands together) back down the steps. And instead of shooting (her dope), I split, I just kept right on walking and went right on down them steps and I got up running ... (Missed that secret step?) ... Yep. Yep. I tell you God's good (she hits the table with her hand) I don't know, girl. ...

I find it interesting here that regardless of her heroin addiction and desire to use heroin that evening, it did not trump her observations of danger and intuitive will to live. This is contrary to the dope addict image who is only concerned with their next high. However, Barbara credits all of that to God's divine protection while she was in a place that she "had no business being."

Bethena also shared stories of life and death situations where she believes God who spared her life each time. One story in particular sticks out to me as she described in detail how she "should have died that night" shortly after her youngest daughter was born one cold Detroit January winter. She starts the story off with "... They always say God looks out for babies and fools ..." Bethena went with a drug user she had just met to purchase crack in an unfamiliar location. She never purchased drugs from this house but they had been known to have larger crack. Bethena says "... should not have went in there from the beginning because I really didn't know these people. But they had the bigger crack at that time, you know every so often you find a new dope house that had big rock ..."

When Bethena paid for the crack, she was given an extra rock by mistake but the dope dealer accused her of stealing the extra and made her go inside a room in the house. The man that took her inside the room beat her with a two by four board "... saying that I stole the crack. You gave it to me, I wasn't going to stand up arguing with these people cause I didn't know them, so I just took whatever you know they gave me ..." My heart dropped when Bethena told me that she accepted what they did to her as her story here describes the inhumane treatment often associated with crack addiction. The beating with the board was not enough punishment for the so-called theft of extra crack rock, the drug dealer tortured her more.

> While we sitting there ... made me put my hands out like this here (held both hands out in a flat position) hit my hands with the stick and ... then they turn around and did Russian Roulette with the gun ... kept putting it to my head and ... the gun kept jamming on them. Then they had a Rottweiler Dog sitting over in the corner ... tried to make the dog bite me ... The dog—I know there is a God!, I know He is good!—cause the dog wouldn't have no parts in this. Like I said I know I didn't do anything wrong, I just got caught up at that time cause he gave me too many and like I say new people ... dog wouldn't do anything. Every time they get the dog out to sick 'em on me, the dog wobble and go on back in the corner like he was high or something. [LAUGHTER]

Bethena believes without a doubt it was no coincidence the gun would not work properly when the drug dealer put it to her head during Russian Roulette. The fact that the dog would "have no parts in this" was a clear sign to her that God was unmistakably there protecting her.

Bethena also knew one of the drug dealers in observance of her torture because his father was the minister of a big local church. Once the other men left the room for a moment she said to him "... now you know this is wrong, you know me and you know I wouldn't steal ..." Bethena attempted to appeal to the man's good conscious but to no avail. However, she began to plead for her life once the other drug dealers reentered the room. She begged them "... I said, y'all, kept pleading—I just had a baby, I just had a baby, she at home crying. Y'all please don't kill me, please don't kill me—just let me go home and see bout my baby ..." Bethena told me the drug dealer continued to beat her but this time he hit her on the face with the butt of the gun. "... I got this scar right here, right here and they took the butt of the gun and hit me in my face right there—that's what they did hit me right here and got the scar."

The drug dealer told the man Bethena knew from church to go to her house to determine if she really had a baby. He reported back that she in deed did have a baby at home but they continued to "… torture me for another half an hour or whatever, and then they say put your coat on—I had my coat and they say well you can go. After that they let me go …" It appeared as if the horror of this story would never end even as she left the dope house

> … while I'm running up the streets and we out in the streets they behind me, a couple of streets behind me, they were going to shoot at me, the bullet went (she motions on the side of her face) I don't know. Like I say I guess God is good. The bullet went zoom right past me. I'm here and the bullet went you know, [motions on the side of her face] could a shot me, went right in my back or anything … I went on home to my baby ohhh. … When I got in the house, oh I picked her up, held her in my arms and cried. Thank God didn't nothing happen to her, thank God for me too, you know.

What begun as a trip to the dope house to purchase $100 worth of crack, resulted in a hostage situation where Bethena narrowly escaped with her life. As I reflect on this story, I wonder about the lasting psychology affect of experiencing that level of trauma. She told me she knew for sure there was a God, God was real and had been with her throughout her crack addiction and other instances of trauma.

Barbara and Bethena share graphic details of dangers they encountered while addicted to crack cocaine and heroin. Their stories illustrate the power struggle between satisfying their addictions and being a responsible mother placing themselves in life threatening situations. Bethena often shared with me her guilt, how much she loved her daughter, and how she wanted so bad to change but the crack addiction had such a strong hold on her. As the mothers reflected on their lives, Bethena and Barbara believed that even when they were engaged in darkest days of their addictions, God's veil of protection saved them from death.

Hearing and Listening to God's Voice

Desirea, Barbara, and Bethena also proclaimed God spoke to them directly or indirectly about their drug addiction and heard his plea for them to stop using drugs. Desirea shares her first encounter with God actually speaking to her about the recovery process while she was visiting Atlantic City before she moved there. In 1996, she spent 90 days in Atlantic City and believed those three months put her on the road to recovery. She said "… In other words, I say it was a spiritual and divine intervention that worked. And then He said that if I went back, seriously and He spoke to me again, and said if I go back to it, I will die. So I didn't go back to that …" This is why Desirea was so adamant about leaving the heroin treatment center mentioned earlier when she realized that they were not trying to wean her off of methadone.

Earlier during her years of active addiction, Barbara heard the voice of God warn her "… to get my life together. Get it together. And I put it in one ear and took it out the other ear. And then he gave me all of this [pointing to her breast area]. And that's what happen …" Barbara was referring to breast cancer when she pointed toward her breast because she was a new breast cancer survivor and recently had a mastectomy. Barbara was diagnosed with breast cancer after she had completed drug rehabilitation for her heroin addiction and believes this was in some ways a consequence of not listening to God's earlier warnings.

Desirea, Barbara, and Ladonna presented other stories illustrating God speaking to them either through someone else or to them directly about their drug addictions. The mothers believed these experiences were the precursor to their recovery. Desirea tells of another experience when visiting Atlantic City from New York on a casino trip. Visiting Atlantic City was significant to her recovery from heroin addiction because the change of scenery took her mine off of the heroin because "… to break that habit, outta sight, outta mind. Come down here, and it was this new thing. … I didn't do anything … God was preparing my feet for a change …" During this conversation, Desirea and I were walking along the boardwalk and as she opened her arms out toward the ocean, she said "… We came down and enjoyed the air. I call it open rehab … I got all this fresh air, you got the boats and all kind a things going on … the casino was helping also …" After returning to her New York Bourough from this trip, she encountered God's voice

> I can't forget it, it was 1996 cause I said in January 1996. … He literally called my name. I was home by myself and I heard this, [her name] [She calls her name imitating a voice with authority]. And I looked around the house, I knew I was home by myself … The second day it was a little louder [her name] [she calls it in a loud commanding voice]. And it was so loud. … The 3rd day when I heard it, and remembrance came and you hear someone call you and there's no one there, you drop to your knees and bow yourself in humbleness cause you in the presence of God and that's just what it was. And from that point on it would become the struggle of knowing God has something for me to do. He has something for me to do. I was on the (methadone) program at the time.

Desirea's encounter with God speaking to her enhanced her faith and clarified her vision for a life free of heroin and methadone. This is the same faith and vision fueling her strength and resilience to challenge the methadone center and detox hospital's efforts to keep her on methadone.

It is interesting to note here, that while Atlantic City was were Ladonna and Barbara's drug addiction began during their adolescent years, it was the birth of Desirea's recovery. Desirea was enrolled in her methadone program but was able to leave New York on weekend trips to Atlantic City. Then the weekends resulted in longer stays with friends and relatives. She indicated to me being around the beauty of the ocean, boardwalk, boats, and breathing the ocean air helped her realize there was so much more to live than heroin addiction.

Barbara and Ladonna also shared stories about God planting the seed for their recovery through His presence when they were getting high or buying drugs. Barbara believed God spoke to her about her addiction in a dope house when she went to purchase drugs from a drug dealer that was the caretaker of a man she knew sick with AIDS. Her sick friend had a nurse caring for him during the day and was there each time Barbara would come to his room to say hello. One day the nurse approached Barbara and asked if she could pray for her. Barbara questioned why she needed to pray for her and the nurse replied, "The Lord wanted me to ask you if it was alright that I hold you and you allow me to pray for you …" Barbara replied to the nurse with "the Lord said that to you Miss?, she said yes. I said alright, pray …" While in her sick friend's bedroom, the nurse held Barbara in the same position as if she was to administer a Heimlich Maneuver and began fervent prayer. When Barbara came to the dope house, there were about nine people in the living room that left during the nurse's prayer and afterwards "… wasn't no body in the bedroom but he was in the bed, his nurse … myself. Everybody was gone … And I believe that boy would have got up and walked if he could walk … He was scared to death …" Barbara recalled during this prayer she screamed, hollered and jumped up and down and believed that is why the nurse held her in Heimlich position. Barbara also reports as the nurse spoke in unknown tongue, she heard

> a voice, continue on to me in my head in my ears. [She's touching her ears]. … And it was God talking to me. And … I was telling Him what they were doing to me, cause I was going through changes and He was going to take care of all that for me. And He told me in the mean time He wanted me to straighten up and get my life together. He said, I'm taking you, taking me where? You got nine years. I said nine years by myself and alone? I was to be, by myself and alone. Nine years to get myself in order for Him … The Lord was ready to do something for me, He's about ready to do something with me.

This prayer occurred during the time when Barbara's husband was still alive but was very ill. She told her husband about the prayer in the dope house and how the Lord spoke to her but he laughed at her. Barbara's husband's response saddened her but believed "… it's the devil, devil didn't want him to believe me, cause he didn't want him to stop bringing them drugs and stuff through that house …" She shared with me that "… The Lord gave us a little time, it wasn't much after that, it was only a matter of months after that, the Lord took him away from me …" It was during this time that she got off of heroin and remained drug free. Barbara truly believed God's presence was in the room with her as the nurse prayed for her and that "… He came in that dope house …" and spoke to her. The angelic presence of the nurse facilitated a divine intervention for Barbara as this began her road to recovery from heroin addiction spanning over four decades.

Ladonna had a similar experience while she was getting high at friend's house in the bathroom. She believes the following conversation with her friend was no accident and God spoke to her through her friend. Ladonna considers this encounter with her friend as a true blessing from God as it planted the seed of recovery in her mind.

> So the night … I made a decision … I had a girlfriend and like we were arguing one day … I was just sitting on the toilet … We were all in the bathroom. You know, I got the needle in one arm and the tear coming out this eye and um my daughter's father we had had a fight. He hit me like on my toe with a gulf club so my feet is this big. You know, I'm talking bout, just a mess. And my friend was telling me, she said you need to get yourself together … you know if you go to them meetings. And I was cursing her out. I said I don't need no meetings. I don't need nothing, if I want to stop getting high, I can stop getting high. That was not the truth you know … and she passed on last February … But I'll never forget her cause what she did was planted the seed … she gave me some information, somewhere even in the mist of my hooping and hollering and arguing with her, somewhere I heard something she said.

Shortly after this incident Ladonna enrolled in a rehabilitation center and still faithfully attends 12 step meetings remaining drug free. After doing cocaine continuously and crank intermittently from 16 until she was 35 years old, Ladonna was ready to stop. She believes God spoke to her through her friend about recovery prompting her decision to go to drug treatment. After Ladonna finished treatment, she began attending church and credits her drug abstinence to her relationship with God. She attended church as a child but only because she had to now she says "I have a personal relationship with God … over these last 9 years my life has been enhanced so much. You know, I um, I'm in recovery, I make meetings."

Conversations with Bethena during our time together were also dominated by the idea of God saving her life and being directly responsible for her current lifestyle. She too heard God speak to her in a manner that scared her straight and initiated her recovery process. When in the deepest trenches of Bethena's crack addiction, she received a word from God reminding her of a better life and that she "... couldn't continue to do this. I knew this wasn't right ... Knew it was gonna have a bad ending ... God talked to me, He told me ..."

> ... used to sit there in the place, me and [daughter's name] in a 2–5 flat, and God said ok, I'm gonna clean you up, I could hear Him just clear as day, ok I'm gonna clean you up but ... when I clean you up if you go back again and a starting smoking the stuff, it's gonna bust your heart, ... I be scared as hell, cause He talked to me that night. ... Oh yes He did!

Bethena reported it did not happen instantly and the next day she was clean but it took six months to a year. Without professional help, she "... kept going back ... getting high, kept going back ... oh Lord I'm so sorry, I'm so sorry, ... Lord please help me get clean, just help me again ... I might wait another 2–3 months. For me that was good considering I was doing it every day ..." What really struck me about these conversations with Bethena, as with all of the mothers was her passion and eagerness to let me know that "He talked to me that night ... Oh yes He did!"

"Church and Cryin' Out to God"

Bethena's narrative not only illustrates God's role in her recovery but also it required several attempts for her to stop using crack cocaine. Unlike heroin, traditional inpatient rehabilitation was not required for detoxification. Both Bethena and Sharonda refrained from smoking crack without formal intervention and instead, God sustains their recovery. Sharonda did speak about the importance of avoiding triggers as if it was a simple process as long as she carefully considered and self-monitored her social settings.

> ... Cause, I mean even when I was smoking, if I didn't go around the people that did smoke, I wasn't smokin ... you know there's these things they call triggers. Beer is a trigger and (friend's name) was trigger. So those are the two things if you didn't want to get high, you just didn't go around them.

Sharonda had a clear understanding of the power and functions of those things and people that would quickly trigger her use of crack cocaine. She knew that

"... it was the people I hung around and I knew when I'm around [person's name] what I was going to do when I got around them ..." It appeared to be so simple for Sharonda

> ... somebody'll call or just sometimes you just want to get out I then been here for four days straight. Let me call (friend's name), what you doin? I'm comin over there. And it would start, and then when you should stop, you just don't, you know what I'm sayin ... you know it's just the people you hang around with. If you know that certain people, person get high, I mean what is you doing, what you over there for if you don't want to get high. So you just don't go.

My conversations with Sharonda were interesting in that her disposition was so calm and collected, yet passionate and confident of the God's role and her relationship with him. She spoke about her efforts at becoming crack free as if it was something simple as just "getting tired" of being tired and wanting to stop.

> It really wasn't just a process, it was just I'm tired and I quit (she snaps her fingers). It didn't, it wasn't like, oh I'm tired and I'm gonna quit next week. I just said I was tired and I just quit. I don't want no more dope, I don't want no more to drink. Just take it and I quit. And I did quit and I just quit. ... Well it actually the high wasn't getting me high no more. It just wasn't for me anymore; I wasn't even getting high no more. I was like oh no I'm wasting money now, ... I don't think my mentality was there anymore. You know I had a focus somewhere else and this getting high wasn't fulfilling it.

Unlike Bethena, Sharonda says she stopped because she wanted to stop. She describes how she eventually just stopped smoking crack because she was tired of using and the type of lifestyle required from crack addiction. She came to this realization without a formal rehabilitation program, therapy or support groups and relied strictly on support of her faith, pastor and church for staying clean. The church that Sharonda was attending during the time of our conversation was run by a pastor she knew before he was her pastor and was key to recovery. She described the pastor as a man who did not judge and accepted her as she was even though she was still drinking and using crack.

Sharonda says she was able to stop using crack with the support of her church and pastor. Her pastor welcomed her with open arms although she admitted "... I got two beers in my refrigerator and some money in my pocket and I ain't go lie and tell you when I leave here I ain't go get drunk ..." Sharonda's active addiction was not a cause for judgment because he believed she should "... just keep coming. He was like, cause you're clean through the word ... the more word get in you, all that other mess will come out ... I never drank them two beers, I was like get that stuff out my refrigerator." Sharonda did not believe a rehabilitation program for crack cocaine addiction would be appropriate for her. Instead, she believed her addiction was just a phase that she was going through and believed she could overcome her addiction to crack through God's help. Sharonda's rationale for not participating in traditional rehabilitation may sound very similar to a drug addict's denial of a "real" drug problem. However, at the time of my conversations with her, she reported to be clean for more than three years.

The mothers frequently spoke about their relationship with God as a staple in their lives not just for protection but also someone they could reach to for emotional comfort. The mothers' religiosity and spirituality highly influenced their psychological well-being (Reed & Neville, 2014) particularly during times when they desired to be drug free but could not accomplish this alone. Sharonda and Bethena both talk about how their cries out to God for help with their crack addictions. Sharonda says

> Sometimes you just cry out to God and you know he's answering cause … the desires for those certain things are just leaving you. And that's a big part God played in my life. … I can remember one night I mean when I was getting high, I was crying, crying so hard asking God to help me cause I was tired of getting high, you know. And I just wanted to change and I needed to know what, which way to go so I don't come back to this mess. So I'm crying, you know hyperventilating type of crying [LAUGHTER]. I was just crying out to God and um I think when I woke up in the morning he just gave me, I had this peace all over me. And He was like I heard your cry and I will answer. And it was fine, and that's it, He just, He speaks. And He'll tell you, I heard you.

Sharonda believed God heard her cry while she was getting high that day and attending church and her pastor is one way he answered her cry. She refers to her pastor as a "… blessing … Cause he also teaches you if you mess up, just dust yourself off, keep going …" However, she reported that it did not happen overnight, "… I did what I wanted to do. I was like, let me go get high and see if that's what I really want to. That's when I was new in the church …" Sharonda described this process as a way of testing her commitment to stop using crack and being back in church. She said "… And I went and I got high … I was like ugh, it ain't for me. And it isn't, it's just not for me anymore. I think I've out grown it. I think it was just a phase I was goin through …" Experiences within Sharonda's relationships with God, her pastor and church served as the most meaningful component of her drug rehabilitation program and ability to maintain a lifestyle free of crack cocaine.

This idea of crying out to God for comfort and direction is nothing new to Black Christian women. Just as Bethena believed without a doubt that God spoke to her about her use of crack cocaine, she believed that He would show her how. When her youngest daughter was about a year and eleven months, Bethena began to reflect on her life prior to crack cocaine. She "... knew a better life, I knew the good days I had at [name of automobile company]. How I used to live ..." One night Bethena was in her apartment alone with her infant daughter and cried out to God for help.

> I just got tired. I didn't want to live like this. I got tired of people doing you any kind of way when they know you using drugs and misuse you and this and that. This wasn't for me, this wasn't the kind of life for me. I lived better then this here. I talked about people like this here. And I would lay there on the floor ... we didn't have a bed or anything me and her ... we laying on the floor ... I could remember, one, twelve o'clock at night ... I said Lord please I don't know how to get off crack. Bring someone in my life maybe to help me get off the drugs, maybe a man or somebody in my life to help me get off drugs. So I said that prayer a couple a times ...

At that time Bethena and her daughter were not living in their own apartment and soon after this experience she reestablished contact with her previous landlord. Although Bethena had allowed his property to be taken over by drug dealers, he allowed her and her daughter to move back in the house. Bethena also met the father of her younger son who also helped her get off of drugs. During a portion of the interview Bethena speaks passionately with tears in her eyes about how good God is and what he has done for her. Initially, I thought that she was upset because she was very emotional and began to cry as she shared the passage below but as you see in the end she assured me her tears were "happy tears."

> Yes He is, oh yes He is. That's why every Sunday, every Sunday, honey, I gets up and I go to church and I pray to Him like I stay all day. Like I said he just made me President of the Usher Board so I'm obligated to stay all day. I go, I go because I love Jesus, I know what He gonna do for (Bethena). Oh God, I thank Him right now ... just ain't bad cry, just happy tears, honey, I'm OK.

The mothers' relationships with God were central to their entire existence as Black women, mothers and recovering drug addicts. Bethena, Ladonna, Sharonda, Desirea, and Barbara all shared stories of how religious experiences of divine protection contributed to personal safety and recovery. Historically, the resilience of Black families is often a result of strong religious beliefs and practices (Hill, 2003) and these mothers demonstrated the significance of faith in their recovery. Bethena, Barbara, Ladonna, Sharonda, and Desirea's stories really illustrates the transformative power of their religious beliefs and practices in their lives during crank, heroin and powder and crack cocaine addictions. Their narratives provide a unique perspective on drug rehabilitation as their self-defined experiences with drug recovery dispel the myth of the crack ho and junkie that suggests Black mothers make an immoral choice to remain addicted to drugs and just want to get high. Bethena and Sharonda both share how they did not want to use crack but could not and did not know how to stop on their own. But, they cried out to God and believed He answered their pleas for help with their crack addictions.

As mothers addicted to drugs, they often found themselves in dangerous neighborhoods and circumstances where the local police were unable to keep them safe. Yet, these mothers were confident their lives were spared and kept safe because of God's divine intervention. Barbara was the only mother legally mandated to attend a drug rehabilitation program but prior to judge's orders, she encountered God's presence in a dope house warning her to stop. All of the mothers report their path to recovery was initiated by a divine encounter with God as well as their genuine desire to stop using drugs.

As a primary support resource for many, the Black church continues to often be intimately involved with families providing spiritual sustenance as well as material support to mothers and their children (Johnson & Staples, 2005; Robinson, 2006; Reed & Neville, 2014). Sharonda's narratives about her pastor and church clearly illustrate this monumental role in her family's life as a single mother of ten children impacted by crack cocaine. The mothers' stories also illuminate how their religious faith and values strengthened and sustained their psychological wellbeing (Mattis, 2005; Reed & Neville, 2014). Bethena, Barbara, Ladonna, Sharonda and Desirea's confidence in their worthiness of God's favor was impressive. In spite of horrific dangers addiction often placed them in or even in their darkest moments, their solid faith never weakened and they always felt worthy of God's favor. As Christian mothers, they believed all they had to do was call out to Him and He would respond. Bethena, Desirea, Ladonna, Sharonda, and Barbara each presented powerful survival texts of the unique role God played in not just their recovery but their lives in general as mothers. In the upcoming discussion, I will culminate my work with the mothers as I discuss the power of the crack ho image and resisting negative controlled images. I will also share critical thoughts and ideas to consider as I move forward in understanding the full impact of the destruction of crank, powder and crack cocaine, and heroin on Black families and neighborhoods throughout generations.

References

Gregg, G. (2011). I am a Jesus girl: Coping stories of Black American women diagnosed with breast cancer. *Journal of Religion & Health, 50*(4), 1040–1053.

Hill, R. B. (2003). *The strengths of Black families*. Lanham, MD: University Press of America.

Jackson, G., & McHenry, D. (Producers), & Van Peebles, M. (Director). (1991). *New Jack City* [Motion Picture]. United States: Warner Brothers.

Johnson, L., & Staples, R. (2005). *Black families at the crossroads: Challenges and prospects*. San Francisco, CA: Jossey-Bass.

Kupor, D. M., Laurin, K., & Levav, J. (2015). Anticipating divine protection? Reminders of God can increase nonmoral risk taking. *Psychological Science, 26*(4), 374–384.

Lincoln, C. E. (1964). *The Negro church in America*. New York, NY: Schocken Books.

Mattis, J. S. (2005). Religion in African American life. In V. C. McLoyd, N. E. Hill, & K. A. Dodge (Eds.), *African American family life: Ecological and cultural diversity* (pp. 189–210). New York, NY: Guilford Press.

Reed, T. D., & Neville, H. A. (2014). The influence of religiosity and spirituality on psychological well-being among Black women. *Journal of Black Psychology, 40*(4), 384–401.

Robinson, M. H. (2006). The use of spiritual-focused coping among working-class Black women. *Journal of Religion & Spirituality in Social Work, 25*(2), 77–90.

Staples, R., & Johnson, L. B. (1993). *Black families at the crossroads: Challenges and prospects*. San Francisco, CA: Jossey-Bass.

DISCUSSION

What the Mothers Made Me Think About

Barbara, Bethena, Desirea, Sharonda and Ladonna were fortunate enough to rise above powder and crack cocaine, heroin and crank addictions without long-term incarceration or death. Their family resilience kept them together allowing opportunities to rebuild relationships and move beyond the horrors of street drug addictions. The central aim of this book is to present counternarratives from Bethena, Barbara, Desirea, Ladonna and Sharonda that illustrate the myth of the junkie and crack ho' and baby while highlighting family resilience.

The mothers' personal narratives are intended to privilege their perspectives over existing knowledge claims and stereotypes about prenatal and postnatal drug use among Black mothers. Their collective experiences are valued here as their experiential knowledge challenges existing beliefs about the long-term negative outcomes for the so-called crack baby. Their voices dispel the myth the crack ho' and junkie are unable to care for and bond emotionally with her child. The last section of the book will be a culmination of my ideas and critical questions posed as a result of my relationships with Bethena, Barbara, Desirea, Sharonda and Ladonna. These include thoughts about the power of stereotypes, current illustrations of continued criminalization of Black females, society's response to the new heroin epidemic, and Black men's role in the chemical genocide of their own people. I also highlight the most salient lessons learned from my interactions with Bethena, Barbara, Desirea, Sharonda and Ladonna about drug addiction, recovery and parenting.

Power of the Crack Ho'

Bethena, Barbara, Sharonda, Ladonna and Desirea's narratives gave cause for reflections on the power inherent in the crack ho and baby image prevailing years after our country's crack scare. By 1985, typical cocaine and crack users were young White males but television and media print portrayed the typical user as Black. In the onslaught of nightly news programs between 1988 to 1990, 55 percent of females depicted as crack mothers were mostly Black but increased to 84 percent between 1991–1994 (Ortiz & Briggs, 2003). Like that of the lazy Black welfare queen, the term crack ho' has remained a powerful and longstanding stereotype. So much so that after Whitney Houston's death, radio hosts Kobylt and Chiampou (R Shepard 2012) even referred to her as a crack ho during a live radio broadcast. Without sympathy or meaningful condolences, they referred to her based on the crack ho stereotype as being "obnoxious … a mess … bag lady … pain in the ass … crack ho … crazy." People across racial, class, and gender lines with substance abuse problems will most likely engage in behavior unbecoming and troublesome. Behaviors demonstrated during intoxication are not always representative of routine actions and should not be used to summarize their character and identity.

The controlled image crack ho is grounded in racist stereotypes with historical roots originating from the enslavement of African females continuing to shape these White males opinions of Black women. Thus, from KFI AM 640 in Los Angeles, they spoke with authority dehumanizing Whitney Houston over national airways, only days after her death.

> Kobylt: Can you imagine you're Clive Davis and … she hasn't had her head screwed on right for 20 years … at some point you're just sick of it all … so is everybody else in the industry, all her friends … it's everybody who knows her had to deal with this is like Oh Jesus, here comes the crack ho' again what's she gonna do? Oh look at that, she's doing hand stands next to the pool. Very good crack ho' nice try, after awhile everybody's exhausted and then, you find out she's dead. It's like really, it took this long? … I wouldn't be surprised … I would understand if everybody, or most people who knew her, who really had to deal with her, were like, God, who wants to deal with a drug addict? (R Shepard, 2012)

This passage illuminates the longevity of the crack ho' as two White men nationally broadcast such debasing comments reducing a loving mother and daughter with international fame to simply a crack ho. They failed to mention she was a mother, daughter, niece, friend, girlfriend, and ex-wife of people who loved her or acknowledge her accomplishments in the music industry. Kobylt inferred her relationship with Grammy Award winning music producer Clive Davis' was irrelevant. To the contrary, in his eulogy during her nationwide televised funeral, he referred to Ms. Houston as "... one beautiful woman" who "never took anything for granted ... never arrogant ... was always grateful and appreciative ..." He continues:

> Personally, all I can say is that I loved her very much. Whitney was, purely and simply, one of a kind. Yes, she admitted to crises in her life. Yes, she confessed to Oprah about her searing battles. But when I needed her she was there ... for me, an eternally loyal friend ... Yes, I was her industry father and I was and am so proud of it. (Utube Funeral)

Clive Davis' eulogy fall far from being a person who was "... just sick of it all ..." Kobylt also questions "... God who wants to deal with a drug addict? ... Oh Jesus, here comes the crack ho' again ..." as he references Ms. Houston's friends and other entertainers. Yet internationally known movie star Kevin Costner commented "... You weren't just pretty. You were as beautiful as a woman could be ... people didn't just like you, Whitney, they *loved* you." Alica Keyes referred to her "as an angel ... she crept into everybody's heart ... made us feel ... strong ... capable ... loved ..."

During her funeral, Ms. Houston's friends responded to her negative media press as legendary Grammy winner Stevie Wonder said, " ...we loved her so much and that won't stop ..." He adapted words to Whitney's favorite song by him, *Ribbon In The Sky* "... He allowed you to touch our hearts ... with a gift no press or media or nobody can tear apart ... it's that gift from Heaven's Choir of love ..." Entertainment mogul Tyler Perry said "... so say whatever you want, God is for her and she is resting with the angels. Nothing was able to separate her from the love of God. Whitney we love you so much." Images of a crack ho were far from their minds as award winning friends "... in the industry ..." provided counternarratives of Ms. Houston's character, value and worth as a human being.

In 2012, almost 30 years since the origins of the crack ho, its power is being waged against an American music icon as the world mourned her death. Negative controlled image of Black mothers addicted to drugs even looms into the 2015 death of Freddie Gray, a young Black man who died in the custody of police in Baltimore, Maryland. The media in this case, CNN (Richards, 2015) is guilty of minimizing Black motherhood strategically around the same time police officers go to trial for his murder. CNN's news article read "Freddie Gray Son of an Illiterate Heroin Addict" as if his mother's heroin addiction is the cause of her literacy problems. Like the crack ho, a Black mother who is an "illiterate heroin addict" is unworthy of the same virtues of motherhood as a White suburban mother addicted to heroin. This seeks to legitimize Freddie Gray's death, criminalizing him and his mother both undeserving of kindness, compassion and most of all justice for his death. Never mind her son died suspiciously, while in custody of several police officers presumably committing no crime. If there is a silver lining here, unlike the onslaught of 1980's crack ho images, CNN received so much push back they apologized and removed the statement from the article.

Bethena, Barbara, Desirea, Ladonna and Sharonda's resilience and faith allowed them to surmount any residual effects of the crack ho but many pregnant Black women fighting crack addiction had no access to drug rehabilitation (Geiger, 1995; Ortiz & Briggs, 2003; Zerai & Banks, 2002) or the same outcomes. They were also burdened with no employment, inadequate medical care, housing and education (Geiger) and the invasion of crack into their neighborhoods. None of the mothers mentioned specific instances of bartering sex for drugs but did report their recovery was motivated and driven by love and concern for their children. Along with their relationship with God, their children are the primary reason for their abstinence.

Rethinking Policy, Research and Maternal Drug Abuse

Not all Black mothers addicted to crack cocaine and heroin were able to sustain their families with healing relationships like Bethena, Barbara, Desirea, Sharonda and Ladonna. Many families were torn apart as those addicted to crack fell by the waist side with no human regard languishing in our country's prisons. Some were left to cope with untreated trauma from experiences of drug addiction and loss of children and family. As I juxtapose our society's response to the new heroin and opioid epidemic with that of crack, it is almost as if treatment of the crack ho remains forgotten and unchallenged. There is a stark difference in our country's response to the new drug scare of heroin and opioid addictions lurking havoc on White suburban teenagers. The same news programs from the 1980's like 60 Minutes, 48 Hours and even my local news are responding to this "new" problem of heroin with sympathy.

As with Jessica and her newborn Casey in the beginning of the book, these families and communities are met with compassion and care with an urgent call to action from police, politicians and local leaders. Not one news story predicted future costs of caring for heroin and opioid addicts or depicted their prenatally exposed children with unbalanced images of them while actually high on heroin. Most strikingly difference is nobody is calling for mass incarceration to get heroin dealers off the street and no mention of the dangers of the heroin industry. No talk about criminalizing White mothers using heroin deeming them unworthy of motherhood instead they require care and services. This new heroin epidemic is almost portrayed by the media as if the same dangers of the heroin and crack businesses in poor Black neighborhoods do not apply to White suburbanites involved in those businesses.

As I watched in 2015, 48 Hours and 60 Minutes segments about heroin use among White middle class students, I thought to myself "ya'll ain't treat us like that." Black mothers were dehumanized and considered prostitutes with no interviews or filming while not high. Black youth involved in the crack business were considered thugs if a dealer and just irrelevant if a user. This has not been the response for White middle class youth in Ohio in this 60 Minutes (Whitaker, 2015) program. Unlike the young White female recovering heroin addict who had used since she was 15 years old, Black female drug users had no voice when portrayed in the media. The Black news caster, Bill Whitaker says to her in a 60 Minutes segment "Heroin in the Heartland" "… I'm sitting here next to you and you look young, fresh and like the girl next door and you were addicted to heroin (in a tone of being unbelievable)." One of the parents within the group of White middle class parents being interviewed said "Who would have thought *our children* would ever do heroin? in Pickerington?" with an emphasis on *our children*.

The news broadcaster continues to say 23 people die every week by heroin overdose in Ohio and something must be done about it. Where was the outrage when crack and heroin overdoses killed Black children in poor neighborhoods? Between November 2015 and January 2016, 60 Minutes had two episodes and in January 2016, 20/20 dedicated the entire hour to the topic of the new heroin epidemic in American with not one Black person interviewed. The voice of Black families have been completely silenced and removed from this current national discussion of the heroin problem. Freddie Gray's mother did not even receive the same compassion and respect from media as did the White middle class heroin users interviewed for these news programs. Thus, Barbara and Desirea's stories are significant to the discourse of Black Motherhood and heroin but not enough to ensure Black families also benefit from upcoming targeted supports and services.

In 2015, my local television news (CBS 5, WNEM) reported on a town hall meeting to address prescription drug and heroin addiction in a predominantly White city 30 minutes north of my hometown. The panel included local and state law enforcement and leaders as the reporter says they "wanted to tackle the problem" by helping the community. State representative Charles Bronner says "we definitely do have a problem ... it's growing ... what came through is we need treatment, good treatment, proper funding, let's keep them out of jail ... let's make them well because it's an addiction ... it's an illness ..." A White female heroin addict in recovery says "... the addiction is typically enough punishment ... resources to help are much more impactful than jail time." Of the several news programs I have watched about the growing heroin problem, Black people have never been included. We did not see this same outrage and compassion for Bethena, Barbara, Ladonnda, Sharonda and Desirea and other addicts like them in their communities. Instead, the crack cocaine industry resulted in additional neighborhood decay, generational economic devastation and a very lucrative industrial prison business; not to mention that Black people remain silenced as decades of heroin addiction continues to harm their families and neighborhoods.

Michigan's infamous Governor Rick Snyder formed a prescription drug and opioid task force allocating 1.5 million dollars to address the problem plaguing many White Michigan communities. According to Governor Snyder's (n.d.) website, the majority of this money will not go to hiring additional law enforcement or building more prisons. I found it interesting instead of mass incarceration one recommendation is "... limiting criminal penalties for low-level offences for those who seek medical assistance with an overdose." This task force also suggested "increasing training for law enforcement in recognizing and dealing with addiction for those officers who do not deal directly with narcotics regularly." A jarring observation from this state website is learning there is an increase of incidence of Neonatal Abstinence Syndrome resulting in severe withdrawal symptoms in infants born prenatally exposed. With this increase of prenatal exposure to opioids, you did not see White women shown on nightly news dehumanizing them as mothers calling for their incarceration for child abuse, like you did with Black women during the crack scare.

When Governor Snyder allocates 1.5 million dollars to only help families affected by prescription drug and heroin, he continues to abandon those struggling with addictions to crack cocaine and other substances. Public policies targeted for addiction should be culturally responsive and inclusive of all families impacted by addiction regardless of substance, socio economic level and especially those addictions that cross generations. Poor public policies and laws from the crack scare era have harmed generations of Black families. These families deserve the same scrutiny and supportive attention as White middle class families now facing heroin addictions currently presented by the media. I believe all Black families traumatized and wounded psychologically and economically from the crack era should be awarded compensation with services and opportunities to heal. I proclaim this around the same time an online CNN article comes out entitled "Report: Aide says Nixon's War on Drugs Targeted Blacks and Hippies" (LoBianco, 2016),

Although John Ehrlichman's children challenge this report, the interview adds credence to what Black people knew all along. Based on a 22-year-old interview for *Harper's Magazine*, former Nixon domestic policy chief John Ehrlichman indicated that

> The Nixon campaign in 1968 ... and Nixon White House ... had two enemies: the antiwar left and black people ... We knew we couldn't make it illegal to be against war or black, but by getting the public to associate ... hippies with marijuana and blacks with heroin. And then criminalizing both heavily, we could disrupt those communities ... We could arrest their leaders ... raid their homes, break up their meetings, and vilify them night after night on the evening news. Did we know we were lying about the drugs? Of course we did.

Debating the truth of this caption of John Ehrlichman's confession about the intent of the so-called war on drugs related to heroin, which precipitated the crack scare, is futile. That is because even without a confession the historical and current criminalization of Blackness in this country can never be denied. Efforts should be aimed at providing comprehensive services across generations to families with a history of drug abuse, especially crack addictions as a means of establishing and maintaining family resilience. For example, provide wide-ranging services to children or adult children of parents who were incarcerated as a result of unfair crack cocaine laws. This should also extend to families continuing to struggle due to parental absence and crack addiction. These policies should also include access to drug recovery programs that coordinates services to heal families without fear of incarceration and their children being removed from their custody. An example would be Jessica and Casey who were able to benefit from services aimed at healing the addiction disease and not minimizing her worthiness of motherhood by criminalizing her drug use. I also believe that families negatively impacted by all substances (e.g. alcohol & marijuana) should be included in a real effort of helping families heal from addictions and tackle our drug addictions problem.

As pointed out earlier in the book most education research about prenatal drug use is quantitative with noted exceptions (Barone, 1995/96; Tivis, 2013). These studies tend to ignore the media's influence via the crack ho' and her baby on educational practice and philosophies related to maternal drug addictions. Qualitative educational researchers are faced with many challenges as we attempt to establish knowledge claims exposing inequities of Black children impacted by crack and heroin businesses. Qualitative methods allowed me to explore drug addiction, recovery, and parenting with Black mothers and were key to understanding these concepts from her perspectives. Yet, the current political climate, which pushes for evidence-based experimental science through federal legislation, often marginalizes the role of qualitative inquiry (Denzin, 2007). To enhance our knowledge base of prenatal drug use in Black families, continued qualitative work is required when including mothers with crack and heroin addictions with young children. At the same time, this research may be challenging because the Adoption and Safe Family Act of 1997 mandates quick termination of parental rights within the child's first year. Unfortunately, access to and the process of drug treatment and recovery typically takes more than a year. The unreasonable expectation that a year is adequate time to recover from street drugs is unjust. You would not require a time limit for mothers to be cured from diabetes, cancer, high blood pressure or depression to maintain child custody, especially when access to services are scarce and unavailable to many with little or no health insurance. Also as we learned from Desirea and Barbara, these programs do not always meet the needs of their clients.

American Dream and Chemical Genocide

Although nightly news about the dangers of crack cocaine no longer exist, remnants of cocaine and heroin businesses remain evident in many poor Black communities as does many still addicted to those substances. Public policy and planning, economy, and social injustices played a major role in preparing a fertile ground for a prosperous crack business. However, to better understand the world of crack and heroin addiction, we must sometimes look beyond the explanation of the powerful and powerless (Agar & Reisinger,

2002). Here I pose critical questions as I consider possibilities for reclaiming our communities and healing from consequences of crack, cocaine and heroin drug industries. What causes someone in Bethena's economic situation to risk everything and turn to crack addiction? We also must not ignore personal responsibility of The Chambers Brothers, Robert "Midget" Molley, and Frank Lucas and their quest for the American Dream at the expense of their Black community. One might ask how do you explain The Chambers Brothers' and Frank Lucas' responses to their oppressions encountered in the south as they sought out the American Dream up north? Why and how did their quest for the American Dream turn into power and greed aiding in the chemical genocide of their people and destruction of their very own communities?

The Chambers Brothers, Frank Lucas, and Midget Molley have been dethroned although they were all considered to be the richest and most powerful drug kingpins of their time. Some of the Chambers' gang continues to serve jail time, however Billy Joe Chambers, Frank Lucas, and Midget Molley have served their jail time, paid their debt to society and are free to walk the streets safely. Yet, as you walk through any impoverished Black community in Atlantic City and Detroit you can see the remnants of their million-dollar empires still today such as lowered property values, loved ones serving jail time and families torn apart. Also, regardless of economic and social status, it will take many families several generations to recover economically, educationally, and socially from the devastation of crack and heroin addictions.

In March 7, 1965 James Baldwin discusses the absence of the American Negro's participation in the prosperity of the American Dream. He also participated in a debate with William Buckley at Cambridge University in the United Kingdom to address the question: Has The American Dream Been at the Expense of the American Negro? This remains a timely question today as we examine the socio, political and economic context of the crack and heroin industries. I ask myself, where did all of the money from crack and powder cocaine and heroin go once it left the Black community? Who were the true financial and social beneficiaries of the crack and heroin businesses? I believe that we can take it a step further and ask, why is James Baldwin's question still significant to Black America now?

Frank Lucas, The Chambers Brothers, and Midget Molley bear some responsibility as the judge who sentenced Midget Molley said for "spreading death and destruction" (BET *American Gangster*) in their perspective cities. My next question is if local drug addicts know where the dope house is, why can't the police find dope houses and just shut them down? How is it that our country has the resources to defend the borders of other countries from death and destruction? Yet, be unable to keep "death and destruction" from our country's major cities with this so-called war on drugs. At the time of this writing, our country is engaged in war while there are battlefields on many streets in impoverished Black neighborhoods our country's children have to navigate daily. With the exception of individual and community grass roots efforts, there is no major plan on a grand scale in place to rescue or provide support for these children. Instead, local school districts and community support programs are being stripped of required governmental funding to function adequately.

Flawed public policy and planning, an unfair justice system, and ineffective public schools are directly related to Black families (especially poor Black neighborhoods) being so disproportionately devastated by the heron and crack business. The question is why is this allowed to continue without question? Does anybody in power care? Next, poor public policy and planning set the stage for the heroin and crack business to succeed in poor Black inner cities. However, how is that a Black man's quest for the American Dream results in "death and destruction" of his own people and their community? Historically, Kentucky Avenue in Atlantic City and Black neighborhoods in Detroit are significant to the richness of these cities' culture and legacy. Detroit was among the first major cities to have a Black mayor. These communities were Black cultural centers, representing pride and resistance to the racist regimes of those two cities. Pride and knowledge of our heritage flowed freely through those spaces where crack, heroin, and other illegal drugs now have their way. Why is it that those participating in spreading the "death and destruction" in their own communities do not understand the link between the plantation, drug business and the prison?

The Fake War on Drugs

Barbara, Bethena, and Desirea speak candidly about the dangers of crack and heroin businesses and dangerous encounters that took place in Black neighborhoods. I learned firsthand from the mothers about the disparities in the quality of daily living and safety in their poor Black neighborhoods. Why are neighborhoods left to be so dangerous without any real recourse from public safety services? Instead, the community's interactions with police officers are often met with brutality that is if the police even bother to respond to calls for assistance. With all of the black and brown men and women incarcerated for drugs offenses due to the so-called war on drugs, you would think that drugs would be completely eliminated from the streets. This of course considering crack and heroin are not made in these neighborhoods but transported there from outside. It appears as if there is an assumption most Black people in neighborhoods are criminals themselves, thus supporting assumptions of our inhumaneness and propensity toward criminality.

Racist and negative controlled images of the condemnation of blackness (Muhammad, 2010) result in racial stereotypes about Black people and criminal activity. These stereotypes were historically used to justify false depictions of Black men's deviant acts linking to their criminalization. These racist stereotypes and negative images also helped support the manipulation of Black crime statistics, making Black people appear to be more likely to commit criminally acts (Muhammad, 2010). Below, Michelle Alexander (2012) illustrates the power of racial stereotypes used to justify the criminalization of Black males.

> Who is more blameworthy: ... young Black kid who hustles on the street corner, selling weed to help his momma pay rent? Or the college kid who deals drugs out of his dorm room so that he'll have cash to finance his spring break? Who should we fear? The kid in the 'hood who joined a gang and now carries a gun for security, because his neighborhood is frightening and unsafe? Or the suburban high school student who has a drinking problem but keeps getting behind the wheel? Our racially biased system of mass incarceration exploits the fact that all people break the law and makes mistakes at various points in their lives and with varying degrees of justification. Screwing-up failing to live by one's highest ideals and values-is part of what makes us human. (Alexander 2012, p. 217)

Similarly, although Black mothers are aligned with the main image of the crack ho', White mothers also use drugs while they are pregnant. However, the media hype of the crack ho' tells us pregnant drug using Black mothers deserve to go to jail, as we have seen earlier, sometimes for even a life sentence. They do not receive compassion and care with opportunities for recovery.

The crack and heroin business has been allowed to flourish in many Black neighborhoods as their citizens personally unrelated to the industry still dealt with constant threats of fear, terrorism, and violence uncontested by the police? So much money has been made in these businesses housed in poor Black communities. Yet as you drive through these neighborhoods, you see no trace of that money being filtered back into the same community that has suffered the most from those businesses. Mass incarceration has not improved the safety of the streets or inhibited the illegal drug industries from thriving. None of the dangers Barbara and Bethena encountered while purchasing drugs would ever have occurred in my, although not upscale but predominantly White neighborhood. Common knowledge among many Black citizens in my county informs us the only neighborhood White high school has one of the biggest drug problems amongst high schools in the entire county. Yet the neighborhood surrounding that school is not plagued by the same violence and illegal drug activity that occurs in the county's Black communities housing the illegal drug industries. Customers come to poor Black neighborhoods to buy illegal drugs, as the base of the business is housed there. You would never see Black people allowed to purchase illegal drugs openly in my neighborhood to the same degree that it occurs in Black neighborhoods, especially the way it did during the crack era. Nor will the home values be lowered because of crack and heroin businesses. While, these are common sense understandings among many Black people, it is important we continue to expose this and question politicians and policy makers, as to why these atrocities are allowed to happened in our neighborhoods beyond the rhetoric of Black people cause the problems themselves?

What They Taught Me

One major lesson learned from my time spent with each mother is that "she ain' no crack ho', she is hu baby's momma." The mothers in the book were resilient and moved beyond crack, powder cocaine, crank and heroin addiction in Detroit and Atlantic City. As mentioned previously, not all families in these cities were as fortunate and continue to be in the strong holds of these addictions. Thus, my intentions are not to glorify the lifestyles of mothers and dismiss the hardship children endure because of drug abuse but I do want to celebrate the efforts of these resilient mothers as they turned their lives around. Lessons can be learned from their resilience and commitment to making a better life for their families. Understanding the resiliency of these families impacted by illegal street drug addictions provide unique perspectives on establishing and maintaining home/school partnerships and policies.

Bethena, Barbara, Desirea, Ladonna, and Sharonda were not just drug addicts but Black mothers who were multi faceted women attempting to rise above their circumstances and change the course of their families' lives. Understanding the Black parenting styles and home experiences of children impacted by drug abuse provides a means to debunk the myths of the crack ho' and her crack baby. Unless the federal government decides to start a real war on drugs, there will continue to be a "free-flow of drugs into the black community" (McAdoo, 1998, p. 19) and crack cocaine, crank, and heroin will be sold to women in their childbearing ages. Resources will remain scarce and consequently, children will continue to be born prenatally exposed to these substances. These children will attend public schools and have teachers who know very little about their family context beyond negative controlled images. Understanding the knowledge base these children bring to school, helps to facilitate academic experiences that are culturally responsive, builds upon their strengths (González, 2005; Ladson-Billings, 1994; Moll & González, 2004 ;), and validates their home knowledge instead of concentrating on the crack ho' and her crack baby.

I also learned Bethena, Ladonna, Sharonda, Deseria, and Barbara demonstrated acts of parenting that most mothers engage in throughout their children's childhoods. Their children were resilient and based on my knowledge are doing well but that does not mean their mothers' addictions did not forever mark the trajectory of their lives. I also must not forget their stories of parenting, resilience and faith were within the context of crack, powder cocaine, crank, and heroin and that really is not "aight" for children. How do I reconcile my genuine care about each mother and belief that she ain' no crack ho,' she's hu baby's momma and stop calling her that!!!!? While at the same time, as an early childhood and early childhood special education practitioner, researcher and teacher educator, my discipline informs me that their homes are not "good" for positive child outcomes. But I do not want individuals to read this book and make negative judgments about my sista friends and say, "see there, she is a crack ho." I often struggled with these questions as a researcher sharing Bethena, Desirea, Barbara, Ladonna and Sharonda's narratives of their family resilience.

The most salient lesson learned from the mothers was that their drug addictions were symptoms of a much bigger issue. They did not consciously wake up one morning and say, "I think I want to become addicted to crack, crank, powder cocaine, or heroin today." During their active addictions their families were stressed by a mother's chronic illness just as if the she suffered prescription drug and alcohol addictions, heart disease, uncontrolled hypertension, depression other mental illnesses, or terminal cancers. You would not expect for mothers battling these diseases to get well without comprehensive care where professionals across disciplines approached their families with compassion. Why would you expect Black mothers addicted to street drugs to get better all on their own without comprehensive services, care and compassion? Although as we saw with Bethena and Sharonda, many women do kick the crack habit without intervention (Zerai & Banks, 2002), there is a double standard for other mothers who are sick, or White mothers when addicted to heroin. This might be because our country's response to Black mothers addicted to crack was that of anger and rage based on their distain for the negative controlled images of Black motherhood.

Working with Bethena, Barbara, Desirea, Ladonna and Sharonda provided me with a clear picture of the consequences of society's response to crack cocaine. Society's response to the influx of crack resulted in manufactured negative controlled images of a crack ho' and her crack baby. Unlike the other chronic illnesses, Black mothers battling drug addictions endured continued historical patterns of being devalued and unworthy of motherhood and reproductive freedoms. No medical research has substantiated the link between prenatal crack cocaine and permanent negative child outcomes. However, there is a consensus alcohol and cigarette smoking causes permanent birth defects so much so required government labels warning of these dangers must be included on the packaging of these products. Yet, there has been no wide spread trend to criminalize masses of mothers who drink or smoke as pretense for a "war" on these legal unhealthy addictive substances for the sake of the unborn baby.

As long as pregnant Black mothers suffering with drug addictions are to blame, there is no need to offer alternative solutions to their criminalization. The mothers' stories of their gendered experiences, particularly Ladonna, Sharonda, and Deseria's introduction to drugs has the potential to shift the focus from blame to opportunities to enhance Black girls self-esteem. The mothers also taught me that instead of focusing on punishing them, another approach might be to address problems in public school settings that indirectly lead to drug use. Keeping Black girls safe from bullying, gang violence, and sexual trauma during their enrollment at school should be a priority. If not for their storytelling of experiences at school, I would have never thought to link school bullying to initial drug use. Much to my surprise, Ladonna and Desirea also taught me of ample opportunities for sexual assault directly related to their high school experiences and in Desirea's circumstance even resulting in pregnancy. Not to mention, sexual assault occurring outside of school. As young Black girls, these women experience human rights violations and learned early on the consequences of continued historical pattern of sexual assault. It is unfortunate that young Black girls have to deal with such attacks on their spirits and well-being while trying to obtain an education. An interesting inquiry would be to explore more about the influence of bullying and sexual assault on the initial and continued use of drugs in young Black girls and women.

The stereotype of a middle and high school drug addicted drop out was definitely challenged by the mothers' narratives. The mothers taught me that there should be more critical analysis of high school drop-out rates beyond the discourse of poor academic abilities and achievement based on test scores. The idea middle and high school students who are not academically inclined are more likely to become drug addicts and drop out did not apply to Ladonna, Sharonda and Desirea. Ladonna and Sharonda specifically stated they were A and B students and Desirea even attempted to attend classes at the onset of her initial drug use after joining the group of students who bullied her. Barbara highlighted how even when she was expelled from public school and placed in the girl's home, she obtained her education. All of the mothers wished they would have attended college and had hopes their children would obtain some type of post secondary education. Thus, all of the mothers had the potential and at some point in their lives the desire to excel academically beyond high school. Dr. Elaine Richardson's (2013), memoir *PHD (Po H# on Dope) to Ph.D.: How Education Saved My Life* chronicles her life's transformation beyond drug addiction. Similar to some of the mothers here, her mother's strict standards for obedience and expectations of proper behavior could not prevent the strongholds of addiction and street life that consumed their daughters. The functions of spirituality and church attendance were the same for Dr. Richardson and the mothers as they were key to their recovery and abstinence from drug use. Like Dr. Richardson, Bethena, Barbara, Ladonnda, Sharonda, and Desirea's addictions to crack and powder cocaine, heroin and crank did not have to limit their educational aspirations. Sharonda had become discouraged from continuing school to obtain her high school diploma. Although she quit high school the last semester of her senior year, high school requirements had changed requiring her to take more classes and she was not interested. However, during our conversations, Ladonna and Desirea both expressed interest in pursuing additional education in their future.

While the mothers' stories revealed horrors of drug addiction, their stories also tell us about loving mothers who are resilient, kind, and spiritual beings. The mothers' love, hope, and dreams for their children are no different than nondrug using mothers. Bethena, Barbara, Sharonda, Ladonna, and Desirea taught me many things about parenting, drug addictions and recovery. My ideas of drug rehabilitation for crack and heroin were challenged as I believed access to rehabilitation programs was essential to recovery for crack addiction.

However, Sharonda and Bethena who were addicted to crack, through their own agency (Zerai & Banks, 2002) quit using the drug without participating in an institutionalized program. As with all of the mothers, their relationship with God was the basis of recovery. Bethena and Sharonda's recovery process was not unusual because drug treatment was often scarce or unavailable for many women who reduced the use of crack or quit through their own agency. Yet, unlike the myths of the crack ho' and her baby, these truths and fact about mothers addicted to crack never hit the media outlets (Zerai & Banks, 2002).

Desirea and Barbara provide firsthand accounts of the contradictions of drug rehabilitation programs, enhancing my knowledge of the entire addiction recovery process. Ladonna's inpatient rehabilitation and 12-step program for crank and powder cocaine were key to her recovery and still attended weekly meetings weekly during the time of our conversations. Due to the dangerous physical nature of heroin withdrawals, Desirea and Barbara had to participate in inpatient medical supervised rehabilitation. However, when in recovery, they made a conscience effort not to replace their heroin addiction with a methadone addiction. Barbara and Desirea both indicted their rehabilitation programs for often discouraging drug addicts from becoming totally drug-free. Desirea had to go through extreme measures so that she would be released from the methadone program. They also highlighted neighborhood problems and institutional barriers usually interfering with remaining drug-free. Desirea, Barbara, and Ladonna participated in a formal rehabilitation program, yet also credit God's grace and love for their drug recovery and drug free life.

Most of the mothers made conscious efforts to learn from their mothers' negative parenting and did not repeat parenting practices they believed were detrimental to their children's well being. These mothers were trying to change and not pass on negative family legacies in hopes of a better life for their children and grandchildren. The mothers understood that generations of Black mothers before them did not have the knowledge or opportunities to do things differently. Thus, they parented differently in a strong effort to prevent their children from failing academically and turning to a path of addiction. Even in the midst of their addiction, Barbara, Sharonda and Ladonna told us how they stood their ground as parents as a way of raising and preparing their children for the future. Historically, Black families have embraced values of respect and academic orientation (Hill, 2003), which were illustrated in the mothers' stories. They made efforts to protect their children from the same elements of street life they were engaged in themselves. This contradicts the notion families headed by Black mothers simply pass on a legacy of dysfunction across generations.

In spite of the horrid years of drug addiction, these families have moved forward and appear to function just as well as any other family. Although not perfect, the mothers and daughters appear to now share close relationships as evident in the amount of time spent together. They are also very much involved in the lives of their grandchildren. It is sad to think that had these families been an apart of the Adoption and Safe Family Act of 1997, I would have never observed these loving relationships occurring across generations. They were families with hopes of healing mother-daughter relationships and doing for their grandchildren what they were unable to do for their children. But sometimes isn't this in the beauty of being a grandparent anyway, you get to do with your grandchildren what you did not know how to or could not do with your own children. Sharonda, Ladonna, and Bethena have adult children as well as school-aged children. These mothers put forth much effort toward positive relationships with their older children who were young during their years of addiction. As Ladonna pointed out in chapter 7, regardless of the mother's past transgressions, children love and want to be with their mother. The late Tupac Shakur's (1995) music video *Dear Mama* visually and poetically illustrates such a bond as he sings about his love, admiration and appreciation for his mother in spite of her crack addiction. The scenes and lyrics in his music video stunningly delivers a counternarrative of a crack ho." He says:

> ... And even as a crack fiend, mama You always was a black queen, mama I finally understand For a woman it ain't easy trying to raise a man You always was committed A poor single mother on welfare, tell me how ya did it There's no way I can pay you back But the plan is to show you that I understand ...

The lyrics here and in his video are full of descriptions of positive parenting practices in spite of a crack cocaine addiction. As did the mothers in this book, Tupac teaches us how maternal crack addiction does not destroy the mother-child bond or her natural ability to nurture her child. Crack addiction and living in poverty does stress a household but it does not prevent a mother from caring for and loving her child.

The mothers' eagerness to share stories of the past was impressive and they shared things with me about their addiction they never talked about before our conversations. It was an honor for them to share their personal lives with me of struggles and triumphs as they moved through maternal drug addiction and parenting. Some were able to recall exact times and dates of experiences when reflecting on their lives when their children were born as well as special events after their births and childhoods. What struck me most was they spoke about their roles as mothers with so much passion and conviction.

Like any mother, they had dreams and aspirations for their children to have a positive future. Sharonda wants her children's future to include an "education and no drugs and into church. I want them to go to school and know the value of going to school." Bethena, Ladonna, Sharonda, Desirea, and Barbara also spoke of their desires for the next generation of their families having a better life, different than what they experienced as adults. The mothers were also clear about their responsibilities as mothers in making their dreams for their children a reality. These five Black mothers self-defined and spoke truth to their experiences with motherhood and addictions to some of the most powerful street drugs that explicitly defies the junkie and crack ho.' I would like to end this book with a quote from Bethena who I believe captures the sentiments of all of the mothers. She says:

> My two kids mean the world to me. They my other half. As they say, you need 2 kidneys to survive on, OK well you take 1 away from me, you're gonna shut my body down. Cause we like this here. (she held up 3 fingers and twisted them together) … that's why I'm staying on them 2. Yeah, I f——ed up my life, but I be damned if y'all gonna f——up you alls.

References

Adoption and Safe Family Act of 1997. Retrieved from http://www.acf.hhs.gov.
Agar, M., & Reisinger, H. S. (2002). A heroin epidemic at the intersection of histories: The 1960s epidemic among African Americans in Baltimore. *Medical Anthropology, 21*(2), 115–156.
Alexander, M. (2012). *The new Jim Crow: Mass incarceration in the age of colorblindness.* New York, NY: New Press.
Barone, D. (1995/1996). Children prenatally exposed to crack or cocaine: Looking behind the label. *The Reading Teacher, 49*(4), 278–289. CBS 5,WNEM.
Denzin, N. K. (2007). Reflections upon the 2nd international congress on qualitative inquiry. *Qualitative research in organizations and management: An international journal, 1*(2), 130–134.
Geiger, S. M. (1995). African American single mothers: Public perceptions and public policies. In K. M. Vaz (Ed.), *Black women in America* (pp. 244–257). Thousand Oaks, CA: Sage Publishing.
González, N. (2005). Beyond culture: The hybridity of funds of knowledge. In N. González, L. C. Moll, & C. Amanti (Eds.) *Funds of knowledge: Theorizing practices in households, communities, and classrooms* (pp. 29–46). New York, NY: Routledge.
Hill, R. B. (2003). *The strengths of Black families.* Lanham, MD: University Press of America.
Ladson-Billings, G. (1994). *The dreamkeepers: Successful teachers of African American children.* San Francisco, CA: Jossey-Bass.

LoBianco, T. (2016, March 24). Report: Aide says Nixon's war on drugs targeted blacks, hippies. *CNN Politics*. Retrieved from http://www.cnn.com.

McAdoo, H. (1998). African American families: Strengths and realities. In H. I. McCubbin, E. A. Thompson, A. I. Thompson, & J. A. Futrell (Eds.), *Resiliency in African American families* (pp. 17–30). Thousand Oaks, CA: Sage Publications.

Moll, L. C., & González, N. (2004). Engaging life: A funds-of-knowledge approach to multicultural education. In J. A. Banks & C. A. Banks (Eds.), *Handbook of research on multicultural education* (2nd ed., pp. 699–715). San Francisco, CA: Jossey-Bass.

Muhammad, K. G. (2010). *The condemnation of blackness: Race, crime, and the making of modern urban America*. Massachusetts, MA: Harvard University Press.

Ortiz, A. T., & Briggs, L. (2003). Crack, abortion, the culture of poverty, and welfare cheats: The making of the 'Healthy White Baby Crisis.' *Social Text 75*, 39–57.

Richards, K. (2015, December 1). CNN Under fire for calling Freddie Gray "Son of an illiterate heroin addict." *Huffington post media*. Retrieved from http://www.huffingtonpost.com.

Richardson, E. (2013). *PHD to Ph.D.: How education saved my life*. Philadelphia, PA: New City Community Press.

Shepard, R. (2012, February 17). John & Ken Show Hosts suspended for inflammatory comments about Whitney Houston [Web log post]. Retrieved from http://mediamatters.org/blog/2012/02/17/john-amp-ken-show-hosts-suspended-for-inflammat/184639.

Snyder, R. (n.d.) Prescription drug and opioid abuse task force releases findings and recommendations. *Governor Rick Snyder Reinventing Michigan. Getting it right. Getting it done*. Retrieved from http://www.michigan.gov.

Tivis, T. (2013). Self-definitions of daily routines, parent-child interactions, and crack cocaine addictions among African American mothers. In E. M. Zamani-Gallaher & V. C. Polite (Eds.), *African American females: Addressing challenges and nurturing the future* (pp. 303–323). East Lansing, MI: Michigan State University Press.

Shakur, T. (1995). Dear Mama. On *Me against the world* [CD] United States: Atlantic. Retrieved from https://www.youtube.com/watch?v=Mb1ZvUDvLDY.

Unknown. (2008). Robert "Midget" Molley: The king of the boardwalk. (Season 3, Episode 3). In Unknown, *BET American gangster*. United States: A. Smith & Co. Productions.

Whitaker, B. (2015). Heroin in the heartland. In T. Anderson & M. St. John (Producers), *60 Minutes*. United States: CBS Productions.

WNEM TV 5. Local nightly news.

Zerai, A., & Banks, R. (2002). *Dehumanizng discourse, anti-drug law, and policy in America: A "crack mother's" nightmare*. Burlington, VT: Ashgate Publishing.

CONTRIBUTOR BIO

Dr. Laurence J. Parker is Professor at the University of Utah, Department of Educational Leadership & Policy. His research and teaching interests are in the areas of critical race theory and educational leadership at the K–12 and higher education levels. In 2013 he was recipient of one of the Derrick Bell Legacy Awards from the Critical Race Studies in Education Association.

INDEX

2012 Republican Party's Presidential Race 32
48 Hours 140, 190–191
60 Minutes Heroin in the Heartland 190–191

A

Adoption and Safe Family Act of 1997 160, 194, 203
Alcohol use 38, 40, 73, 101, 160, 194, 199–200
American dream 5, 52, 54, 73, 193, 195–196, 204
American dream and chemical genocide 5, 52, 54, 73, 187, 193–196, 204
American Gangster 55, 61–62, 65, 195
Anti-categorical xii
Asset approach 15
Atlantic City, NJ 8, 42, 45, 48, 50, 54, 57, 59–64, 68–70, 73, 76–78, 81–82, 86, 89–93

Atlantic County, NJ 62
At-risk factor 15, 29
Automobile industry 50–53, 75, 87

B

Baldwin, James 195
Bell, Derrick 14, 17
  Also see Interest Convergence Theory
BET *American Gangster Series* 55
Black children 26, 30, 35, 101, 159–160, 191
  removed from home 27, 30
  academic achievement and development 122
  prenatal drug exposed 141–143
  school experiences 141–142, 151
Black church 106, 165, 184
  Also see Christianity
Black Feminist Epistemology 14, 17
Black Feminist Thought, 8, 14, 16–17, 19, 21, 68

Broward County, Florida 6
Buckley, William 195
Bullying 56, 77–78, 84–85, 148–151, 153–155, 157–158, 161, 200

C

Chambers, Billy 51–54
Chambers Brothers 51–52, 62, 195
Chiampou, K. 188
Chicken Bone Beach 62, 92
Christianity 10, 165, 183–184
  See Black Church
CBS 5, WNEM 192
CNN Presents 1, 4–5, 11
Coerced sterilization 28
Controlled images and stereotypes of Black mothers 4, 6–8, 14–15, 19, 25–35, 39, 42, 49, 68, 116, 142, 160, 184, 189, 197, 199–200
Cooper, Anna Julia 17
Counternarratives 7, 21, 67, 116, 136, 158, 189
Counter-storytelling 15, 18
Crack baby 1–2, 4–5, 9, 29–30, 39, 41–42, 76, 100–101, 136, 139–145, 147, 149, 151, 153, 155, 157, 159, 162, 187, 198–200
Crack cocaine xi, 3–4, 10, 13, 16, 21, 29, 34, 37, 40, 45–46, 49–51, 58, 63, 68, 73, 75–76, 84, 87, 95–96, 100, 102–103, 108, 113, 115–116, 132, 139–141, 144, 147, 152, 160, 172–173, 176, 180, 182–185, 187, 190, 192–195, 199–200, 203, 205
Crack cocaine addiction 3, 45, 73, 75–76, 103, 132, 182, 203
Crack ho' v, 2–5, 7–8, 14, 21, 25, 27, 29–31, 33, 35, 37, 39–43, 72, 116, 135–136, 139–140, 157–160, 162–163, 187–190, 194, 197–200, 202–204
Crack industry 5, 46, 50, 53, 91, 96

Crank (methamphetamine) 7, 10, 13, 19, 21, 57, 63, 67, 68, 95, 97, 115–117, 135, 159–160, 179, 184–185, 187, 198, 199, 201–202
Criminalization of Black women 21, 25, 35–37, 39–41, 187, 193, 197, 200
Criminal prosecution of prenatal drug use 37–41, 187, 193, 197, 200
Critical Race Feminism 8, 16–19, 21, 23, 68
Critical Race Methodology 14, 18
Critical Race Theory xi, 14, 18, 21
Cultural deficit 15, 18, 21
Cultural deviant 28–29
Cultural Equivalent Theory 28
Cultural Variant Theory 28–29

D

Dear Mama by Tupac Shakur 203
Deep Whiteness xii
Depo-Provera 27
Detroit, MI 8, 42, 45, 50–54, 62–64, 68, 73–75, 86–89, 102, 149, 152–153, 162, 167, 171, 174, 195–196, 198
Devaluation of Black Motherhood 26, 30
Discourse 7, 11, 14–15, 19, 49, 191, 201
Drug business 6, 8, 45, 49, 57, 60, 162, 196
Drug recovery/rehabilitation 2, 6–7, 10, 34–35, 41, 49, 100–101, 160, 166–170, 177, 179–182, 184, 193, 201–202
Drug scares 47
Drug use trends 47, 49, 62

E

Education 1, 10, 15, 29, 34, 42, 60, 73, 79, 82, 84, 87, 93, 141, 143–145, 148, 150–151, 155–156, 158–160, 162–164, 190, 194, 199–201, 204–205
  drop out 151, 201
  drugs 56–57, 63, 79, 84–85, 143, 161, 198

safety at school 79, 85, 151, 154, 158–159, 161, 200
special education 1, 29, 87, 143–144, 148, 155, 199
Ehrlichman, J. 193
Ethic of accountability 17
Ethic of caring 17, 72

F

Fake War on Drugs 196
Family adaptation 16, 20
Fetal Alcohol Syndrome 40

G

Gibbs, Rennie 38–39
Guardianship and care of grandchildren 80, 95–99, 108, 110, 125–126, 156, 202–204
Gray, Freddie 189–191
Gynecology 26

H

Harlem 48, 55, 60–62, 92
Has The American Dream Been at the Expense of the American Negro? 195
Also see James Baldwin
Heroin,
  addiction xi, xii, 1, 6–7, 40, 45–48, 50, 54–59, 61–63, 68, 85–86, 120, 122, 135, 156–157, 159, 166–170, 191–192
  business 4, 9, 50, 54–59, 61, 98, 191, 197
Home/school partnerships 144, 162, 198

I

Imagined global reality 46
Inter-categorical complexity xii
Intra-categorical complexity xii
Interest Convergence Theory 17
  Also see Derrick Bell 17
Intersectionality xi

J

Johnson, Jennifer 6, 39
Jezebels 15, 25, 31
Jungle Fever 3

K

Kentucky Avenue 60–62, 196
Kinship networks 95–111
Kobylt, J. 188–189

L

Losing Isaiah 3
Lucas, Frank 55–56, 195

M

Mammy 8, 25, 31
Master narrative 4, 8, 15, 21, 30, 47, 49, 67, 149
Matriarch 8, 31, 32
McNight, Regina 38
Media, xii, 1–7, 9, 31, 38–39, 42, 47–48, 55, 87, 89, 100, 127, 140–142, 162, 188–189, 191, 193–194, 197, 202
Methadone clinic 36, 54, 86, 166–170, 177–178
Michigan Court of Appeals 36
Molley, Robert "Midget" 61–62, 195
Moral deficit 15

N

Narrative xii, 4, 6, 9–10, 13–14, 16–17, 21, 36, 47, 96
Neonatal Abstinence Syndrome 192
New Jack City 51, 166, 173
New Jersey's Division of Addiction Services 62
New Jersey's high court 36
New York 8, 42, 45, 48, 50, 54–56, 62–63, 84, 105, 155, 173
Nixon, R. 193

O

Objectivity 70
Opioids 192
Oppression xii, 13, 14, 17–20, 29–30, 35, 39, 41–42, 71, 95, 115, 159, 195
Oxycodone 2, 4–7

P

Pain clinics 4
Parenting 5, 7–9, 31, 59, 67, 70, 97–99, 101, 106, 115–137
Pathological conceptual frameworks 28–30
Prenatal crack exposure 2, 6, 142–143
Prenatal drug exposure 2, 5–6, 19, 21, 29, 40, 45, 141, 143, 160
Prenatal exposure to opioids 192
Post Traumatic Stress Disorder 3
Powder cocaine 7, 9, 19, 48, 67–68, 97–98, 116–117, 159–160, 195, 198–199, 201–202
Prosecution of addiction 25
Prosecution of pregnant women 37
Prostitution (sexual bartering) 3

Q

Qualitative research xii, 29, 30, 162

R

Racial authenticity versus racial sincerity xii
Racism xi–xii, 4, 7, 14–15, 17–18, 20, 39–40, 52, 55, 101, 160
Regan Administration's budget choices 34
Reproductive privacy 37
Reproduction rights (*also fertility rights*) 30
Resilience 3–4, 10, 13, 16, 19–21, 28–29, 36, 41, 95, 103–104, 115, 159–160, 183, 187, 193, 198–199
Rethinking Policy, Research and Maternal Drug Abuse 190–194

S

Silence and silencing 4, 7, 17, 19, 191, 192
Sista-girl conversations 68–72
Slavery 25–28, 30, 32, 35, 95–96, 116, 132, 144, 165, 188
Smack Central 55
Snyder, Rick 205
Sudden Infant Death Sydrome (SIDS) 40
South Florida 4, 6
Systematic oppression 14
Systematic racism 14, 17

T

Tobacco use (nicotine, cigarettes) 40, 170, 200
Trauma 3, 9, 67, 68, 79, 176, 190, 193, 200

W

War on Drugs 1, 10, 34, 36, 40, 47, 96, 161, 193, 196–198
Wayne County, MI 63
Welfare mother 31–32, 34–35
Welfare Queen 8, 31, 33–35, 159–160, 188
Withdrawal symptoms 140, 192

BLACK STUDIES & critical thinking

ROCHELLE BROCK & CYNTHIA DILLARD
Executive Editors

Black Studies and Critical Thinking is an interdisciplinary series which examines the intellectual traditions of and cultural contributions made by people of African descent throughout the world. Whether it is in literature, art, music, science, or academics, these contributions are vast and far-reaching. As we work to stretch the boundaries of knowledge and understanding of issues critical to the Black experience, this series offers a unique opportunity to study the social, economic, and political forces that have shaped the historic experience of Black America, and that continue to determine our future. Black Studies and Critical Thinking is positioned at the forefront of research on the Black experience, and is the source for dynamic, innovative, and creative exploration of the most vital issues facing African Americans. The series invites contributions from all disciplines but is specially suited for cultural studies, anthropology, history, sociology, literature, art, and music.

Subjects of interest include (but are not limited to):

- EDUCATION
- SOCIOLOGY
- HISTORY
- MEDIA/COMMUNICATION
- RELIGION/THEOLOGY
- WOMEN'S STUDIES
- POLICY STUDIES
- ADVERTISING
- AFRICAN AMERICAN STUDIES
- POLITICAL SCIENCE
- LGBT STUDIES

For additional information about this series or for the submission of manuscripts, please contact Dr. Brock (University of North Carolina at Greensboro) at r_brock@uncg.edu or Dr. Dillard (University of Georgia) at cdillard@uga.com.

To order other books in this series, please contact our Customer Service Department:

(800) 770-LANG (within the U.S.)
(212) 647-7706 (outside the U.S.)
(212) 647-7707 FAX

Or browse online by series at www.peterlang.com.